Gender, Sainthood, & Everyday Practice in South Asian Shiʿism

ISLAMIC CIVILIZATION & MUSLIM NETWORKS

Carl W. Ernst & Bruce B. Lawrence, editors

A complete list of titles published in this series appears at the end of the book.

Gender, Sainthood, & Everyday Practice in South Asian Shiʿism

KAREN G. RUFFLE

The University of North Carolina Press *Chapel Hill*

 Set in Quadraat by Tseng Information Systems, Inc.
Manufactured in the United States of America

The paper in this book meets the guidelines for permanence and durability of the Committee on Production Guidelines for Book Longevity of the Council on Library Resources. The University of North Carolina Press has been a member of the Green Press Initiative since 2003.

Library of Congress Cataloging-in-Publication Data
Ruffle, Karen G.
Gender, sainthood, and everyday practice in South Asian Shiʿism / Karen G. Ruffle.
p. cm. — (Islamic civilization and Muslim networks)
Includes bibliographical references and index.
ISBN 978-0-8078-3475-6 (cloth : alk. paper)
ISBN 978-1-4696-1371-0 (pbk. : alk. paper)
1. Shiʿah—India. 2. Shiʿah—Customs and practices. 3. Hyderabad (India)—Religious life and customs. 4. Religious life—Shiʿah. 5. Women in Islam—India. I. Title.
BP192.7.I4R84 2011
297.5′7082095484—dc22

2011000070

Versions of some chapters of this book have been published as "May Fatimah Gather Our Tears: The Mystical and Intercessory Powers of Fatimah Zahra in Indo-Persian, Shiʿi Devotional Literature and Performance," *Comparative Studies of South Asia, Africa, and the Middle East* 30:3 (November 2010): 386–97; "Karbala in the Indo-Persian Imaginaire: The Indianizing of the Wedding of Qāsim and Fāṭima Kubrā," in *Islam in the Indo-Iranian World during the Modern Epoch*, edited by Denis Hermann and Fabrizio Speziale (Berlin: Klaus Schwarz Verlag, 2010), 181–200; and "Who Could Marry at a Time Like This?: Debating the *Mehndi ki Majlis* in Hyderabad," *Comparative Studies of South Asia, Africa, and the Middle East* 29:3 (November 2009): 502–14. Used by permission.

cloth 15 14 13 12 11 5 4 3 2 1
paper 17 16 15 14 13 5 4 3 2 1

THIS BOOK WAS DIGITALLY PRINTED.

For Andreas D'Souza

Contents

Figures & Table

FIGURES

TABLE

Acknowledgments

Several organizations provided generous financial and administrative support for my ethnographic fieldwork and archival research in India, Iran, and Syria. My field research was funded by a Fulbright-Hays Doctoral Dissertation Research Abroad Fellowship and by the American Institute of Iranian Studies (AIIrS). Additional research support was provided by a Center for American Overseas Research Centers (CAORC) Multi-Country Research Fellowship. At CAORC, Mary Ellen Lane was extremely helpful in facilitating my research, and at AIIrS, I thank Erica Ehrenberg and James Clark. I am grateful to the government of India for granting me a research visa and to Girish Kaul and S. K. Bharati at the United States–India Educational Foundation and Purnima Mehta, director general of New Delhi's American Institute of Indian Studies for their assistance. A Doctoral Research Travel Grant from the Center for Global Initiatives (formerly the University Center for International Studies) at the University of North Carolina–Chapel Hill enabled me to travel to Hyderabad, India, in August 2003 to conduct preliminary dissertation research and to establish contacts in the Shiʿi community.

The University of North Carolina at Chapel Hill was an ideal environment in which to pursue my fascination with Shiʿi devotional literature and ritual. Beyond religious studies, my research interests led me in many directions—women's and gender studies, Persian and Urdu language and literature, and ethnography—all of which I was able to pursue and the multidisciplinary imprint of which is evident in this book. UNC's Department of Religious Studies generously supported my training and research, both financially and intellectually. UNC's Center for Global Studies and the North Carolina Consortium for South Asia Studies provided generous financial support, and I benefited from opportunities to present my research. I also thank the Graduate School for its generous support in the form of a Royster Society of Fellows John Motley Morehead Dissertation Year Fellowship.

At the University of North Carolina Press, I am especially grateful to Elaine Maisner for her steadfast support of this book. Elaine has made the editorial process a pleasure, and I have learned much from her. I also thank the editorial staff who have been instrumental in the production of this book: Tema Larter, Paul Betz, Vicky Wells, and Dino Battista. I thank Carl W. Ernst and Bruce B. Lawrence for their support and for their acceptance of this book as part of the Islamic Civilization and Muslim Networks series. The careful reading and insightful critique provided by two anonymous readers was extremely helpful and appreciated. I also thank Lena Rubisova for her work with the illustrations.

In Hyderabad, I received a warm welcome from the Shiʿi community, whose generosity of spirit and time and abundant kindness are truly appreciated. The staff at the Henry Martyn Institute facilitated many aspects of this project, for which I am grateful. I especially thank Andreas D'Souza, the institute's former director. I am indebted to the Oriental Manuscripts Library and Research Institute, the Salar Jung Museum Archives, the Jaʿfari Library, the Osmania University Library, and the State Central Library (formerly the Asafiyya Library). Many people in Hyderabad were extremely generous with their time and support of this project. Dr. Sadiq Naqvi deserves special thanks for serving as the master of my introduction into the Shiʿi community in Hyderabad. Dr. Naqvi was always willing to sit down with me and answer my questions about the history of Hyderabad and about Shiʿi devotional literature and practice. Dr. Riaz Fatima, an expert on Urdu literature, particularly *marṡiya*, opened her home and family to me. The wedding of her son ʿAbbas figures prominently in this book. I am indebted to Dr. M. M. Taqui Khan and his family for introducing me to the *mehndī kī majlis* in Hyderabad. The members of the Khan family are also discussed extensively in this book, and I am grateful for their generosity of spirit. Despite her busy schedule during Muharram, Dr. Zakia Sultana, one of Hyderabad's most prominent women *majlis* orators (*ẕākirah*), always kept me informed of each day's many mourning assemblies. Zakia introduced me to many members of Hyderabad's Shiʿi community, and her patience in explaining the structure and themes of the *majlis* is appreciated. I am grateful to many others, including Mir Shajʿat ʿAli, Alok Bhalla, Zia Shakeb, Muhammad Suleiman Siddiqui, R. Thirumala Rao, Shemeem ʿAskari, Maulana Reza Agha, Sabiha Asghar, Nisar, Salahuddin, Tajuddin, Husain Mir, Hasan ʿAbedi, Naqi ʿAbedi, Salim Rizvi, Ibrahim Hami, Seema, Jahan Ara, the women at Yadgar-e Husaini, Baqir Moosvi, Aijaz ʿAli, Rehmat Hasanali, Raju Hasanali, Sribala, Jaweed Khan, Ismat Mehdi, Aruna Bahuguna, and the faculty of Zahra Academy. I thank Kulsum for her friendship and support.

I am thankful to many people in Iran for their generosity, support, and friendship. At the Dehkhoda Institute, I thank my Persian teachers, and Dr. Mohammad-Reza Jenabzadeh was of much assistance. I thank the British Institute for Persian Studies for providing accommodation and assistance. I received generous access to the collections of the Daʾirat al-Maʿarif Buzurg-e Islami (Greater Islamic Encyclopedia), the Farhangistan, and the National Library, all in Tehran, and the library at Astan-e Qods Razavi in Mashhad. I thank the directors and staff at all these institutions. I am also indebted to many others, including Nasrollah Pourjavady, Nasr Gozashte, Ghasem Kakaie, Fathollah Mojtabaʾi, and those whom I will not name to maintain their privacy. In Mashhad, I am especially grateful for the friendship and assistance of a woman I call Shireen, who facilitated a number of meetings with scholars and librarians at the Astan-e Qods in Mashhad. I am grateful to the Farzanmehr and Balourchi families for their extraordinary kindness and support.

I am grateful to a number of colleagues and friends for their assistance and support of this project. Scott Kugle and Kathryn Lofton read an early draft of the manuscript and made a number of helpful suggestions. I also thank Carl W. Ernst, miriam cooke, Bruce B. Lawrence, Anna Bigelow, Tony K. Stewart, Aya Okawa, Jennifer Dubrow, Josie Hendrickson, Amy Bard, Abdallah Lipton, Youshaa Patel, Maureen O'Brien, Catherine Burris, Stephen Sapp, Michelle Gonzalez Maldonado, Arti Mehta, David Kling, John Fitzgerald, Dexter Callender, Bill Green, Henry Green, David Graf, Ivan Petrella, Irene Oh, Ayesha Irani, Liz Bucar, Afsar Muhammad, Katherine Pratt Ewing, Joyce Burkhalter Flueckiger, Firoozeh Papan-Matin, Sandria Freitag, Denis Hermann, Fabrizio Speziale, Martha Fredriks, Paul Losensky, and Alyssa Gabbay. I am indebted to the University of Miami, especially Michael Halleran, Perri Lee Roberts, and the College of Arts and Sciences, for generous research support that allowed me to complete the revisions to the manuscript. I am especially grateful for the support of my mother, Janet Hood, and my grandparents, Joyce and Francis Haggarty. My husband, Andreas D'Souza, has read countless drafts of this book, traveled with me for field research, and spent many hours discussing sainthood and *mehndī*; his love and support have nourished this project.

Notes on Transliteration

I have translated Persian and Arabic technical terms according to the transliteration system used in the *International Journal of Middle Eastern Studies*. Deccani and Urdu words follow the conventions used to transliterate South Asian languages. In an effort to maintain consistency, all technical vocabulary is transliterated and marked with italics. I have not transliterated names, but they are spelled to reflect Persian or Urdu pronunciation. I have transliterated Persian and Deccani-Urdu technical terms according to how they are pronounced in Iran and South Asia. Thus, the word *marthiya* is transliterated as *marṡiya* to reflect how speakers of Persian and Urdu pronounce the letter ث. *Iẓāfats* are marked by -e or -ye. Aspirates in Deccani-Urdu words are indicated by the addition of -h to the consonant.

For the sake of simplicity and accuracy, I use Shiʿa (plural Shiʿas) as a noun and Shiʿi as an adjective.

ث	ṡ	ظ	ż	ڈ	ḋ
ح	ḥ	ع	ʿ	ڑ	ṛ
ذ	z̲	غ	gh		
ص	ṣ	ق	q		
ض	ẓ	ٹ	ṫ		
ط	ṭ	ں	ṅ		

Introduction

Though I may be asleep, you are in my thoughts,

Though I may be awake, you are in my heart.

—*Husain Vaʿez Kashefi*

The young widow who has broken her bangles and removed her nose ring in grief, and the youthful groom whose hands and feet have been decorated with blood rather than the traditional bridal *mehndī* (henna)—such images are repeatedly invoked in the everyday practices and hagiographical literature of the Shiʿi Muslim community in the South Indian city of Hyderabad. On the seventh day of the Muslim month of Muharram, Indian Shiʿa traditionally observe the tragic battlefield wedding at Karbala, Iraq, in 680 C.E. of eleven-year-old Fatimah Kubra, the daughter of the third Imam, Husain, and her thirteen-year-old cousin, Qasem, son of the second Imam, Hasan. On this day, in the mourning assemblies (*majlis-e ʿazā*) held in Hyderabad's Old City, the battlefield heroics of Qasem and the tragic fate of the young bride/widow Fatimah Kubra are recounted in *marṡiya* (mourning poems) and in the speeches of the orators, known as *ẕākir* (fem., *ẕākirah*). The performed remembrances of these events in the mourning assemblies depict scenes of joy, followed by the rending grief a woman experiences in her abrupt transformation from fortune-bearing wife to inauspicious widow, a particularly traumatizing change in status for women in India, where everyday Muslim culture has adopted the Hindu taboo of widow remarriage. What is most striking about the descriptions of the Karbala wedding and its aftermath is that a distinctively Indian worldview is expressed.

This book is a multidisciplinary ethnographic study of how hagiographical texts and performance commemorating the Battle of Karbala shape both spiritual and everyday life and practice in an Indian Shiʿi community. Devotional texts and ritual performances are integrally entwined, producing the desired effects of grief. More important, these performances also dynamically embody the social, ethical, and religious powers of the hero(in)es of

Karbala, transforming them into imitable exemplars. The hagiographical texts and ritual performance of the mourning assembly are forms of moral communication in which the imagination of Karbala and the family of Imam Husain generates shared sensibilities and an ethical worldview that orders the life of South Asian Shiʿa.

Both poetry and prose commemorating the sacrifice of Imam Husain and his family at the Battle of Karbala hold central places in the spiritual and everyday lives of the Shiʿa in India and throughout the Islamic world. Hagiographies constitute a type of sacred biography extolling a saint's piety and spiritual achievements. This book examines the pivotal function of hagiography as it mediates local social values and defines gendered action through public performance in the *majlis* (mourning assembly). The stories of the saints of Karbala narrated in hagiographical texts and represented in the rituals of the mourning assembly amplify the actions and words of the protagonists of Karbala while rooting them in a culturally relevant social, geographical, and linguistic milieu. In this progression, these idealized figures become saints and heroes, and their lived example as it is remembered in the hagiographical texts and ritual performances guide the listener to cultivate an idealized South Asian Shiʿi self.

Particular events and moments in the life cycle receive special emphasis in the Karbala drama, and they are expressed in dramatic, emotion-inducing vignettes during the *majlis* performance. Mourning assembly poets' and speakers' experiences affect how they imagine Karbala for their audiences. One of the most popular subjects for poets and *majlis* orators is the battlefield wedding of Fatimah Kubra and Qasem. Of the many events that comprise the Shiʿi ritual calendar, this particular scene endures in its popularity among *majlis* orators and everyday Shiʿa because marriage is both an Islamic imperative and one of the most charged life-cycle events in South Asian culture. In South Asian Hindu and Muslim communities, marriage remains nearly universal and usually arranged, and the bride's family customarily provides a sizable dowry. South Asian marriage practices are further complicated by the taboo against widow remarriage, which makes this a life-cycle event that is fraught with risk for both men and women. In the course of my fieldwork, in both structured interviews and casual conversations, women often described their commitment to marriage as being based on the model provided by Fatimah Kubra, who sacrificed her husband to preserve her religion. Here we can see the formative if not coercive nature of Shiʿi hagiography as it mediates everyday life: those who fail to marry turn their backs on an Islamic and South Asian ideal.

Teaching Shiʿism, Socializing the Shiʿa through Hagiography

Hagiography is a vital and dynamic genre of religious literature that extols the spiritual achievements and piety of figures who have been recognized as worthy of veneration by their communities. Hagiographies are accounts of charismatic individuals who embody exceptional qualities that distinguish them from everyday people and who are believed to possess qualities that are a sacred gift from God. The composition of hagiographies, their performed narration, and the construction of spaces memorializing saints thus comprise parts of a profoundly social process. Hagiography reflects how followers have chosen to remember saints and fundamentally functions to increase a community's devotion to the religion through the saints' exceptional lived examples.

The myriad ways in which the heroic feats of the hero(in)es of Karbala are remembered in hagiographical texts, ritualized representations of their lives, and sacred buildings such as *ʿāshūrkhānas* and *imāmbāṛās*, as well as the proliferation of such ritual objects as the metal battle standard (*ʿalam*) that serves as a symbolic representation of the saint, reflect the ways in which Shiʿi communities have performed this social process of integrating the biographical data of the lives of twelve Imams and the family of the Prophet Muhammad (*ahl-e bait*) into culturally meaningful forms that simultaneously express the prescriptive ideals and doctrines of Islam as well as vernacular/local social values.

Although saints such as Qasem; Fatimah Kubra; Imam Husain's sister, Zainab; and his half-brother, ʿAbbas, may be venerated throughout the Islamic world, their hagiographies are not the same everywhere. Hagiography reflects local cultural values, variations in religious practice, political ideology, language, and gender norms. Yitzhak Nakash has observed the Arab tribal character of ʿAbbas in Iraqi Shiʿi hagiography.[1] ʿAbbas is venerated as an extraordinarily brave and valiant warrior whose courage on the battlefield reflects his ardent devotion to his half-brother, Imam Husain, and his faith in Islam. In keeping with the hypermasculinity of Iraqi tribalism and the historically lesser influence of Sufism and mysticism (*ʿirfān*), the physical prowess and spiritual vigor of the Imams and other members of the *ahl-e bait* are emphasized.[2] In Hyderabad, conversely, the hagiographical tradition portrays a much more nurturing ʿAbbas. ʿAbbas the standard-bearer (*ʿalamdār*) is depicted as the protector of children and as a brave, loyal warrior fighting for his family and faith. Hyderabadi hagiographers emphasize ʿAbbas's valiant attempt to fill a water skin in the Euphrates River to quench the thirst of Imam Husain's four-year-old daughter, Sakinah:

> Sakinah recited a lament over the corpse of ʿAbbas, "Rise up, my uncle! Rise up, my uncle!"
> "Now the severity of thirst has inflamed my heart. Rise up, my uncle!"

Suffering from the torments of thirst, Sakinah cries out to ʿAbbas to bring water. As this short, rhythmic poem (*nauḥa*) continues, Sakinah invokes the thirst of her other suffering siblings, especially that of her six-month-old brother, ʿAli Asghar:

> "This is the third day that we have not been able to get even a drop of water—Asghar is also thirsty.
> You are sleeping, now no one will remove our pain—Rise up, my uncle!"[3]

The tragedy lies in the fact that ʿAbbas has already sacrificed his life to bring water for the suffering children, yet Sakinah does not yet understand that her uncle is dead. Hyderabadi hagiographical depictions of ʿAbbas contain little of the tribal valor that is central to his Iraqi Arab persona; rather, he is transformed into the idealized Hyderabadi, deeply committed to nurturing the children of the household. While the kernel of ʿAbbas's historical persona is present in the Deccani-Urdu depictions, he is as much a creation and reflection of the local community and its social mores and culture as is the hypermasculine, martial ʿAbbas outlined in Nakash's study of the Iraqi Shiʿi cult of saints.

Depictions of ʿAbbas as a caring uncle and Fatimah Kubra as the idealized bride and world-renouncing widow serve as reflections of vernacular cultural and social norms; in addition, Shiʿi hagiography plays a vital role in teaching important religious lessons. Hagiography is a dynamic genre of religious literature that makes accessible to everyday Shiʿa the prescriptive Shiʿi traditions of theology and law. Hagiography is the integrating genre that connects the "high" intellectual traditions of law, philosophy, and theology—which are otherwise inaccessible and too otherworldly for lay Shiʿa—with popular ritual and devotional practice, thus assimilating the prescriptive rules of religion into everyday practice and life through the engaging example of *ḥusaini* ethics (the spirit of sacrifice and faith exemplified by Imam Husain and his family at the Battle of Karbala) and imitable sainthood of Imam Husain and his family. The activities of the mourning assembly include a fusion of the high traditions of theology and philosophy based on the esoteric concepts of Imamate and transcendent sainthood and the popular rituals that vitalize Shiʿi spirituality in the form of *ḥusaini* ethics (referred to in Urdu as *ḥusainiyyat*) and imitable sainthood. The concepts of socially engaged *ḥusaini* ethics and imitable sainthood exemplified by Imam Husain and his family and the divinely granted transcendent sainthood of the Imamate are assimilated in Shiʿi hagiography. Shiʿi theology and law are translated and made manifest through the hagiographic process of the mourning assembly, in which poems and stories about the hero(in)es of the *ahl-e bait* transform them into "real" men and women resembling everyday Shiʿa, albeit of a distinctly higher order of being. The Shiʿa venerate and transform the members of Imam Husain's family into socially, culturally, and morally relevant figures through whom one can cultivate an idealized self.

The cultivation of an idealized self, an important aspect of hagiography's didactic function, is not limited only to men in the Shiʿi tradition. Hagiography, both as text and performance, constructs a sacralized space for women, who tend to be excluded from the intellectual traditions of law, theology, and philosophy. Women have a central place in the Shiʿi hagiographical tradition, which in large part is based on the voices and emotions of the women of Imam Husain's family who survived the Battle of Karbala and were entrusted with keeping the *ḥusaini* ethic alive. *Majlis* orators focus on the Karbala hero(in)es' bravery, piety, and commitment to sacrifice themselves for family and faith, and composers of mourning poetry engage the voices and emotions of the women of the *ahl-e bait* to great effect, thereby conveying religious and social messages to the local Shiʿi community. The women of the *ahl-e bait* are charismatic embodiments of *ḥusaini* ethics, teaching both men and women how to cultivate an idealized self based on the saints' imitable, worldly model.

Gender, Sainthood, and Everyday Practice examines the relationship between text and religious performance in the Hyderabadi remembrance of Qasem and Fatimah Kubra's battlefield wedding and its aftermath. The stories told about Qasem and Fatimah Kubra as well as the ritual performances that reproduce aspects of their wedding provide a socioethical model for men and women to cultivate. A Hyderabadi Shiʿi woman learns from Fatimah Kubra's example how to be an idealized wife who questions her husband when necessary, who is obedient and honors her in-laws, and who is ever-faithful and removed from the affairs of the world as a widow. In the course of attending the hundreds of mourning assemblies and celebrations (*jashn*) that punctuate the Hyderabadi Shiʿi ritual calendar, the incessant repetition of stories about these charismatic saints become internalized and seamlessly integrated into the practice of everyday life.

The Ten Saddest Days

Over the past fourteen hundred years, historians and hagiographers have established a standardized chronology of the events leading up to, during, and after the Battle of Karbala. At the local, vernacular level, variations in the ritual calendar have developed over time, reflecting cultural, linguistic, and gender particularities. In this section, I briefly outline the historical events leading up to the Battle of Karbala, noting variations in the Hyderabadi Shiʿi ritual calendar. The first five or six days of Muharram are relatively quiet in the Old City. Mourning assemblies take place, and the Shiʿa begin to wear black clothing; tents for serving water (*sabīl*) to Muharram participants are erected along the streets. Ritual activity and emotional fervor increase dramatically on 6 Muharram and are in full pitch by the next day, when Imam Husain's entourage was denied access to the waters of the Euphrates River by the ʿUmayyad *khalīfah* Yazid's army.

On 22 Rajab 60 A.H. (28 April 680 C.E.), the ʿUmayyad *khalīfah*, Muʿawiyya, died; his son, Yazid, assumed political leadership. As a means of consolidating political power, Yazid continued his father's practice of demanding from his governors and other members of the court (*darbar*) an oath of allegiance (*bayʿah*). When Yazid assumed the title of second *khalīfah* of the ʿUmayyad dynasty, Husain had been the Imam of the partisans of ʿAli (*shīʿat ʿAlī*) since 670 C.E., when his elder brother, Hasan, was poisoned. Ascending the throne, Yazid demanded an oath of loyalty from Imam Husain, who refused to submit. As pressure mounted for Imam Husain to pledge his loyalty to Yazid, the Shiʿa of Kufah invited their leader and his supporters and family members to seek refuge in their city. In a series of letters, the people of Kufah encouraged Imam Husain to stage a revolt against Yazid and reclaim the title of *khalīfah* of the Muslim community. To determine the Kufans' sincerity, Imam Husain provisionally accepted their invitation and dispatched his cousin, Muslim ibn ʿAqil, with instructions to report back on whether

Husain and his entourage were truly welcome and whether the Kufans were truly willing to risk their lives by rebelling against Yazid. Muslim wrote a letter to Imam Husain affirming the Kufans' loyalty to him and suggesting that he leave Mecca as soon as possible. In the interim, ʿUbaidallah ibn Ziyad, the governor of Kufah and a Yazid loyalist, discovered the Shiʿi Kufans' incipient treachery and threatened the community into submission. On 11 September 680 C.E. (9 Dhu'l-hijja 60 A.H.), having already written and dispatched a letter affirming Kufah's safety and the loyalty of its citizens, Muslim was assassinated by forces loyal to Yazid and Ibn Ziyad. Imam Husain performed *ḥajj* and the *ʿumrat al-tammatu* (pilgrimage completed concurrently with the *ḥajj*), gathered his followers together, and deflected the discouragement of many of his Meccan allies, who argued that he would not be safe in Kufah.

Encouraged by Muslim ibn ʿAqil's report, Imam Husain set out from Mecca on 1 Muharram with an entourage of seventy-two men and many women and children. Imam Husain did not receive the news that his cousin had been killed at Ibn Ziyad's command and therefore had no idea that Kufah was no longer safe for him and his followers. The caravan traveled through the Arabian desert in the direction of Kufah (106 miles south of Baghdad), where Husain's father, the first Imam (and fourth of the *Rāshidūn* [Rightly Guided] *khalīfahs*), ʿAli, had based his capital. On 2 Muharram, the caravan continued its trek northeast toward Kufah, arriving in the Iraqi desert at Karbala the following day. In Hyderabad, the Shiʿa have assigned 2 Muharram to commemorate Imam Husain's departure from Mecca to Kufah, and this is the subject of the poems and speeches performed in the mourning assemblies.

As the caravan made its way from Mecca, Imam Husain learned from a number of sources that all was not well in Kufah. At al-Zubalah in Iraq, Imam Husain was informed that Ibn Ziyad had arrested and beheaded Muslim as well as Hani ibn ʿUrwa, who had given Muslim shelter and protection in Kufah. Imam Husain informed his followers of the tragedy and gave them the opportunity to leave. Most of the Shiʿa remained loyal to Imam Husain and continued their journey to Kufah. At Karbala, Hurr ibn Yazid al-Riyahi, a commander in Yazid's army, intercepted the members of Imam Husain's caravan and prevented them from continuing on their journey. Imam Husain explained that the people of Kufah had invited him, to which Hurr replied that Ibn Ziyad had prohibited Husain from entering the city. The two groups marched together until Hurr received further instructions to halt the caravan at an open place in the desert that was devoid of food or water. The Shiʿa of

Hyderabad observe the military blockade, led by General ʿUmar ibn Saʿd and including more than four thousand troops, against Imam Husain on 3 Muharram.

On 4–6 Muharram, Yazid's military commanders and Imam Husain negotiated to reach an agreement. Yazid remained adamant that Imam Husain must declare his absolute loyalty, which he repeatedly refused to give. Tensions between the two groups increased with each passing day, for neither side was willing to compromise. Each night, negotiations took place, and Imam Husain finally convinced Ibn Saʿd to agree to a compromise. A letter was drafted to Ibn Ziyad outlining the details of the agreement, which all those involved hoped would avert bloodshed and violence against the grandson of the prophet. Shimr ibn Dhu'l-Jawshan, a former loyalist to ʿAli, was appointed to deliver the letter of agreement to Ibn Ziyad. Muslim historians consider Shimr to be a fomenter of sedition whose insinuations and misleading words caused Ibn Ziyad to refuse to accept the agreement forged by Ibn Saʿd and Imam Husain. At Shimr's provocation, Ibn Ziyad ordered Ibn Saʿd to either attack Imam Husain or relinquish control of the army to Shimr. Ibn Ziyad instructed Ibn Saʿd that if Imam Husain fell in battle, his body was to be trampled into the dust, because he was "a rebel, a seditious person, a brigand, an oppressor."[4] Violence against the grandson of the Prophet Muhammad was inevitable.

In Hyderabad, 4–6 Muharram continues to be a period of emotional anticipation and preparation for the upcoming remembrance of the increased suffering of Imam Husain and his entourage on 7 Muharram. On 4 Muharram, Hyderabadi Shiʿa commemorate Hurr's defection to Imam Husain's side. The next day, they mourn the martyrdom of the young sons of Husain's sister Zainab, ʿAun and Muhammad. The martyrdom of Imam Husain's seventeen-year-old son, ʿAli Akbar, is commemorated in South Asian Shiʿi communities on 6 Muharram. With each passing day, the emotional atmosphere in the Shiʿi neighborhoods of Purani Haveli, Darulshifa, Yaqutpura, and Dabirpura becomes increasingly charged as the number of mourning assemblies multiplies. There is a sense of anticipation for the events that are commemorated on 7 Muharram: the wedding and martyrdom of Qasem and the encampment's inability to get water from the nearby Euphrates River because Ibn Saʿd had stationed five hundred troops along its banks.

In 680, Muharram fell during the month of October, when temperatures in the Iraqi desert remain very hot. In an attempt to quench the thirst of the children in the caravan, especially that of young Sakinah, Imam Husain's half-brother, ʿAbbas ibn ʿAli ibn Abi Talib (popularly known as Abu Fazl in Hyderabadi devotional literature), evaded the troops along the river and managed to fill several water skins. On 8 Muharram, the Shiʿa of Hyderabad commemorate the martyrdom of ʿAbbas, the "protector of children," whose gruesome death as he was filling his skins at the Euphrates River is recounted in mourning assemblies throughout the Old City, although according to historical accounts, he fought alongside his half-brother in the penultimate Battle of Karbala on the 10 Muharram, known as *ʿāshūrā*. In the countless mourning assemblies held from early morning until late at night, ʿAbbas's martyrdom is graphically recounted in narratives and poems of suffering (*maṣāʾib*):

> The children are waiting for ʿAbbas to come,
> Sakinah said, "Uncle will bring water.
> Uncle will quench our thirst,"
> But the sentinel of the women's quarters has not returned to the children.
> Today we mourn Umm al-Banain's beloved.[5]

On 9 Muharram, Ibn Saʿd received orders from Ibn Ziyad to prepare to attack Imam Husain. In the evening, after it became obvious to both sides that there would be no peaceful settlement to this struggle for power, Imam Husain gathered together his family and supporters and encouraged them to escape into the safety of the night. Virtually all of his followers remained, and the next morning, Imam Husain prepared himself for battle and rode before his followers and delivered a moving sermon: "O God, you are my only Trust in every calamity; you are my only hope in every hardship; you are the only promise in the anxiety in every hardship; you are the only promise in the anxiety and distress in which hearts become weak. . . . O God, I submit myself to You. . . . You alone are the custodian of every blessing and the Master of every excellence and the last resort for every desire."[6] Following Imam Husain's impassioned testament to his faith in God, the two sides exchanged insults, and intermittent skirmishes took place throughout the morning. At noon, Imam Husain led his followers in the recitation of the prayer of fear (*ṣalāt al-khawf*) performed during warfare (*Sūrat al-Nisāʾ* [Chapter of the Women], 4:102). Then the battle became more deadly.

First to sacrifice their lives were Imam Husain's supporters; then his sons and other blood relations attained martyrdom (*shahādat*) on the battlefield.

After the martyrdom of a number of members of Imam Husain's extended family, his seventeen-year-old son was killed, followed by his nephew, Qasem, "the bridegroom of Karbala," who was subsequently trampled by horses. Imam Husain became increasingly outnumbered after his half-brother, ʿAbbas, was cut to pieces. Returning to the encampment (*khaimeh-gāh*), Imam Husain comforted his infant son, ʿAli Asghar, whose neck was pierced by an arrow while the parched infant was resting in his father's arms. In the late afternoon, Shimr and his associates approached Imam Husain for the battle's final skirmish. Imam Husain was surrounded and was attacked on all sides; he was decapitated, and horses trampled his body into the dust. The women's tents were burned and looted. In the following days, the women were imprisoned and dragged from Karbala to Kufah and eventually on to Yazid's court (*darbar*) in Damascus.

Hyderabadi Shiʿi commemorations of Karbala reach a fever pitch on 9 Muharram, as devotees enter into transhistorical time and the streets of the Old City are transformed into the dusty plains of Karbala. Women and men walk about barefoot, in dusty black clothing, and with aggrieved looks on their faces as they immerse themselves in Imam Husain's world. The martyrdom of six-month-old ʿAli Asghar is remembered, and many of the *ʿāshūrkhānas* in the Old City display empty cradles (*jhulā*), stimulating tremendous feelings of grief in the hearts of mothers and fathers. Just as marriage is socially and religiously compulsory in Hyderabadi society, a premium is placed on large families, and children are greatly desired in Telangana culture. The tenth day, *ʿāshūrā*, is the climax of Muharram ritual in the Old City. At several shrines there, men gather in the morning to perform bloody *mātam*, a type of self-flagellation that is performed with a variety of implements, including hands, razors, flails, and finally knives with which the top of the head is struck. Later in the morning, Shiʿas, Sunnis, and Hindus line the streets of the Old City to observe and participate in the *bībī kā ʿalam* procession, which involves a metal standard in which is embedded a wood fragment of the funeral bier of the Prophet's daughter, Fatimah al-Zahra. Men's Muharram associations (*mātamī gurūhān*) march through Old City neighborhoods with the *bībī kā ʿalam* and perform *mātam*. This public display of grief physically connects the Hyderabadi Shiʿi community to the hero(in)es of Karbala.

Although Muharram is the ritually structured time for the collective remembrance of Karbala for the global Shiʿi community, in Hyderabad as elsewhere, the sacrifices of the *ahl-e bait* are an integral aspect of everyday lived experience and religious practice.

Everyday Shiʿism

The incessant narration and ritual performance of hagiographical stories and poetry about Imam Husain's family that takes place year after year in Hyderabadi mourning assemblies and celebrations transforms Karbala's saints into real people who are both of great spiritual attainment and deeply rooted in family and society. Saints such as Fatimah Kubra and Qasem are brought to life in the mourning assembly through dramatic orations, recitation of poetry, and the display of ritual objects, and their sacrifice at Karbala is absorbed into the everyday lives of the Shiʿa, who remember in vivid and culturally relevant detail how each member of Imam Husain's family was married; was an ideal wife, husband, or daughter; and even engaged in such quotidian activities as prayer and performing domestic labor with a sense of piety and social commitment.

Hagiography engages with the daily, lived experience and religious practice of everyday people. The everyday bricolage of family, work, and religion constructs individual and communal imaginal landscapes in which identities and ways of being in the world are established. For the Shiʿa, the spiritual-religious world of the Imams and the *ḥusaini* ethics of sacrifice and loyalty to faith and family embodied by the hero(in)es of Karbala are the integral fibers in the identity tapestries woven by individuals and communities. I begin chapter 2 with an account of my conversation with Sabiha Asghar, a gracious and self-confident woman who is the principal of a private English-medium school in the Old City as well as the daughter of the city's most senior Shiʿi religious scholar. When I first met Asghar in her office in February 2005, I was stunned by what seemed to be her incontrovertibly paradoxical self-identification as a professional, self-determined woman who also strongly believed, citing the example of Qasem and Fatimah Kubra, that it is a religious responsibility to marry and that it is better for the wife to die before her husband. From my North American feminist perspective, I was confounded by Asghar's attitude about marriage and widow(er)hood.

With the perspective gained by time and scholarly reflection, I concluded that Asghar's multiply situated self and beliefs reflect a seamless integration of the prescriptive rules of Islam and the socioreligious model of the *ahl-e bait* with South Asian cultural and gender norms, all of which shape the practice of everyday Shiʿism. "Everyday" refers to the individual and collective realities of lived Shiʿism, distilling the practices and life-cycle events of the religious community through culturally specific gender, social, and linguistic norms that often fall outside of the prescriptive control of the scholarly religious elites. Anwar Alam notes in his study of everyday Islam in South Asia and Europe that the majority of Muslims "acknowledge the general concepts dictated by Scholarly Islam, but they choose to live according to more particularistic notions of Islam, which conform to the patterns of their daily experience."[7] Asghar accepts the prescription set forth by God in the Qur'an that all men and women should marry, and she considers the sacrificial wedding of Fatimah Kubra to Qasem to provide an idealized ethical model. Yet the Indic, Hinduism-inflected taboo on widow remarriage that Asghar has absorbed contradicts the Islamic imperative for widows and widowers to remarry.

Asghar's everyday Shiʿism is shaped by the rules set forth by the intellectual (textual and patriarchal) traditions of law and theology and is brought to life through a centuries-long process through which South Asian Shiʿism have become enculturated and vernacularized through a continuous process of assimilation and negotiation in its local, non-Muslim environment. The Shiʿa employ a variety of strategies to integrate Islamic prescriptive traditions and laws through culturally meaningful forms of everyday practice. For Asghar and the Shiʿa of Hyderabad, the narratives recounting the life and death of the hero(in)es of Karbala are fully integrated into the practice of daily life.

In this book, I use the term "everyday" in three specific ways. First, I do not intend to conflate "everyday" with the more conventionally used category of "popular" religion. "Everyday" refers to the lived experience of individuals and communities. Second, "everyday" reflects the nonelite, nonscholarly practice of Shiʿism that shapes the religious worlds of most men's and women's daily lives. Many individuals navigate both the everyday and scholarly/intellectual spheres with ease; however, this approach does not reflect the lived experience of most people. I also do not gender the everyday as the realm of feminine practice, as both men and women equally share in the practice of integrating religious norms and socioethical ideals (as articulated in textual sources) into daily practice. Third, the everyday is the site of accommodation and integration of the Shiʿi Islamic cosmopolitan with non-Muslim South Asian cultural, linguistic, and gender norms.

I place special emphasis on the imperative to understand the central role of everyday Shiʿism and how the Shiʿa integrate religion into their vernacular daily life practices. This book endeavors to de-Orientalize Islam and to recognize the vitality of the Muslim world beyond modern scholarly and political tendencies to reduce the tradition to its Arab origins.[8] Islam's origins in the Arabian Peninsula need not be its destiny; rather, we must look for the signposts that orient Muslim identity through two common denominators: first, the memory of a shared history embodied in the life of the Prophet Muhammad; second, a universal submission to God's will (*islām*).

Fieldwork in Sacred Spaces and Everyday Places

With the ever-shifting start times for religious events, I had arrived early at Yadgar Husaini, a female-run *ʿāshūrkhāna* located in the Purani Haveli neighborhood in the Old City,[9] for a *majlis* during the frenetic final days of the two-month mourning period (*ayyām-e ʿazā*). Seated on broad white sheets spread on the floor in the oppressive April heat, I felt annoyed by the two women seated some distance away who kept staring at me and whispering to each other. Sarah approached me and introduced herself, and when I identified myself, she immediately responded that she knew all about me and my interest in Qasem and Fatimah Kubra's battlefield wedding and its meaning for Hyderabadi Shiʿa. "I feel very close to Qasem," she declared, waiting for me to ask why. "I am twenty-seven and not married," Sarah lamented.

Sarah jumped from topic to topic in our brief conversation. The child of a Sunni-Shiʿa love marriage, Sarah now felt that she could not bridge the sectarian divide to find a husband. Devotion to various members of the *ahl-e bait*, including Qasem and the Prophet Muhammad's daughter, Fatimah al-Zahra, constituted a form of palliative care for Sarah as she tried to reconcile her spinsterhood with the deep religious, social, and familial pressure to marry that South Asian men and women face. Sarah described many of the miracles that she had witnessed that proved the power of the *ahl-e bait*, but she had not yet received what she believed to be the greatest gift: marriage to an Indian Shiʿa who was a respectable few years older than her and would give her the love for which she yearned. Moreover, Sarah hoped for a kind husband who would understand that she was "an extremely sensitive person." Until she could transform her status from spinster to wife, Sarah existed in a paradoxical state of frenzied suspension, willing to try any ritual or supplicatory act that would prove that the Shiʿi saints had heard her petition and had interceded on her behalf.

Each month, Sarah visited many of the *ʿāshūrkhānas* in Hyderabad's Old City, especially Bibi ka Alava, dedicated to Fatimah al-Zahra. This year, Sarah engaged in a more powerful ritual act of supplication by attending a performance of bloody self-flagellation, watching men cut themselves with razor blades or flails in time with the rhythmic recitation of *nauḥa* mourning poems. At performances of bloody *mātam*, it is common to see a group of women standing in one corner of the shrine and periodically reaching out to take daubs of blood from the men's bodies. Unmarried women smear this blood on their right palms, imitating the ritualized daubing of henna on the hands by young men and women at the 7 Muharram *mehndī* mourning assemblies dedicated to Qasem and Fatimah Kubra. For women desperate to marry, the blood of the *mātamdārs*, charged with the charismatic power of Qasem's blood, is far more potent than henna.

Even though Sarah usually could not stand the sight of men performing bloody *mātam*, she had faith that Qasem's blood was transubstantiated into the blood of the everyday Shiʿi men who perform this ritual, effecting the saint's merciful intercession and a marriage alliance for her. "Sarah," I asked, "Did the blood work?" She evaded my question and reiterated, "I am very depressed." Sarah's emotional state was shaped by her failed previous relationships with men; her parents' intersectarian marriage, which she viewed as limiting her marriage options; and the countless women she saw whose marriages seemed so easily arranged. Sarah had heard countless stories about the exemplary wifehood and motherhood of Fatimah al-Zahra, Fatimah Kubra, and the other women of the *ahl-e bait*, and she yearned to emulate their embodiment of marital loyalty, love, and sacrificial spirit.

Sarah's story is one of painful nonfulfillment, of feeling marginalized by family and her spinster status, yet running throughout her "troubles talk"[10] is a profound faith in the intercessory powers of the *ahl-e bait* and a desire to cultivate a selfhood based on their embodiment of an Indian Shiʿi socio-ethical ideal. Sarah's story makes me feel deeply uncomfortable, yet I find the incessant narration of her troubles that is intertwined with her faith compellingly illustrative of how the imitable sainthood of the *ahl-e bait* provides a coping mechanism that enables the Shiʿa to navigate the pressures to conform to Hyderabadi social ideals of marriage, family, and piety. Sarah's act of daubing blood on her hands in a more ritually potent attempt to gain Qasem's intercessory assistance in finding a husband is one of many such stories I heard in both Iran and India. I frequently heard tales of dreams in which an Imam appeared and explained why a young couple in Mashhad, Iran, was unable to conceive children. Another man in Mashhad who had been struggling with career issues had a dream in which he was visited by the eighth Imam, Reza, who told the man that he would be offered a job at

Astan-e Qods, the massive shrine complex where the Imam is buried and the site of a university, research institute, and library.

Stories such as these are vital to understanding the meaning and function of religion. The messiness and awkwardness of Sarah's story and her faith in Fatimah al-Zahra, Qasem, and other Shi'i saints are as important and necessary for us to interpret as the sacred texts and intellectual traditions such as law and theology that are privileged by scholars of religion. Robert Orsi eloquently argues for the necessity of including these stories of individual encounters with the sacred: "There are aspects of people's lives and experiences within religious worlds that must be included in our vision and attended to beyond what is officially sanctioned. This is a call, then, for attention to religious messiness, to multiplicities, to seeing spaces as always, inevitably, and profoundly intersected by things brought into them from outside, things that bear their own histories, complexities, meanings different from those offered within the religious space."[11]

Hagiography—the stories of Imam Husain's family and their embodiment of the *ḥusaini* ethic of faith and sacrifice—must be understood through the ways in which people interact with the text, especially in its ritual performance. Fieldwork forces one to understand that saints are not merely dead people who attained a high degree of spiritual knowledge or were especially pious; rather, they are dynamic, "living" beings whose lives—as told in the poems and narratives of the mourning assembly—provide compelling models for how to be good Muslims and Indians. The act of reading a hagiographical text in an archive or office will not show how its narration of the saint's piety, bravery, and sacrifice is a form of moral communication that directly engages devotees and obliges them to cultivate an idealized self that is based on the exemplars' imitable model, especially that of the women of the *ahl-e bait*. A whole world of experience and meaning exists outside the text. The moment a person hears the words of a hagiographical text, the saint enters the subjective realm of the listener's personal history.

This book engages texts, historical data, and information gathered on the ground in ethnographic fieldwork conducted in Iran and Hyderabad, India, from 2004 to 2006. Hagiography typically is examined solely as a literary/biographical genre of religious literature in its textual (and perhaps architectural) form. By engaging in ethnographic fieldwork, observing the behavior and actions of people in the religious context of the *majlis* and in the course of everyday life, one can identify the ways in which hagiography is brought to life—embodied—through the examples of imitable sainthood established by Imam Husain and more specifically his female relatives. This ethnographic approach highlights the prominent role of females and the feminine in Shiʿi sainthood, devotional literature, and ritual. Women's voices as orators in the mourning assembly and in the central role of the women of the *ahl-e bait* in constructing Shiʿi memory of the Battle of Karbala provides a compelling religious and social model for both men and women.

Ethnographic fieldwork among religious scholars, orators, and everyday male and female practitioners amplified my position as an outsider to the Shiʿi tradition. I am a female North American, non-Muslim, academic scholar of religious studies, and much of my identity thus firmly places me on the hermeneutic and confessional margins. I felt my outsider status more profoundly at some times than at others. The rare mullah who refused to converse with me because of my gender and the elder in the Hyderabadi Shiʿi community who did not want to tell me about rituals such as burning an effigy of the second *khalīfah*, ʿUmar, to mark the end of the lengthy mourning period signaled my role as religious and cultural outsider. Despite these occasional moments, Hyderabadi Shiʿa exhibited a remarkable degree of openness and willingness to share their ritual activities, devotional literature, and personal histories with me.

I begin each chapter with an experience from my fieldwork. These are accounts of conversations or ritual and life-cycle events in which I participated with Shiʿi men and women, moments when a particular aspect of the structure of imitable sainthood and the *ḥusaini* ethic of sacrifice and faith became clear, moments that illustrate how hagiography is integrated into the everyday lives of devotees, or moments when I came to understand why women have such an important role in Shiʿi theology and devotion. I began fieldwork in Hyderabad in 2003 with a brief trip to introduce myself to leaders of the Shiʿi community. As a graduate student preparing for comprehensive exams, my credentials as a scholar were not significant. In 2004, I spent four months in Iran and Syria conducting research on a text that figures prominently in this book, *Rowẓat al-shohadā*, an important early-sixteenth-century Persian hagiographical Karbala narrative written by Mullah Husain Vaʿez Kashefi. Returning to Hyderabad just before the start of Muharram in January 2005, I quickly discovered that my time in Iran had paid unexpected dividends. Word of my work there spread quickly within the Hyderabadi Shiʿi community, according me a degree of legitimacy and scholarly authority.

This authority did, on occasion, land me in awkward situations in which members of the community asked and even expected me to speak authoritatively on the historical authenticity and the permissibility of observing the *mehndī* (henna) mourning assembly. On several occasions, certain members of the Hyderabadi Shiʿi community exhorted me to write a "proof text" that would put the debate to rest. I was often drawn into the role of arbiter of the authenticity of Qasem and Fatimah Kubra's battlefield wedding, a position that I declined and make no claim to possess. Such encounters exemplify the boundary crossings (transgressions) that are inevitable in ethnographic fieldwork among religious communities. After nearly two years of fieldwork, I found it impossible not to be drawn into the devotion and personal histories of the community I was studying.

In describing the beliefs, practices, theological categories, and lifeworlds of Hyderabad's Shiʿa, I do not seek to speak for this community or constructively to define the religion. I intend to bring everyday Shiʿi practice into contact with the prescriptive, elite traditions of theology and law through hagiography, which teaches people the doctrines and rules of religion through the imitable model of Imam Husain's family. Descriptions of my interactions with Shiʿi men and women and my participation in and observation of various ritual events highlight the awkward "position of religious studies as a modern academic discipline, caught somewhere between religious practice and imagination, on the one hand, and critical analysis on the other."[12]

Saints, Exemplars, and Other Critical Terms

I intentionally vary the terminology in this study, using the terms "saint" and "exemplar" to convey two different dimensions of the exceptional qualities embodied by Imam Husain and his family. I use terms that already exist and have been delineated by Shiʿi theologians and others, and I place these terms into pairs that express their homologous relation to one another theologically, devotionally, and socially. Thus, the pairings of Imamate–transcendent sainthood (*imāmah-walāyah*) and *ḥusaini* ethics–imitable sainthood (*ḥusainiyyat-wilāyah*) are constituted from preexisting categories in the theological and hagiographical Shiʿi tradition. Shiʿi theology and law are translated and made manifest through the rituals of the mourning assembly, where poetry and stories about the hero(in)es of the *ahl-e bait* are brought vividly to life and transformed into "real" people—imitable saints and socioethical exemplars—aspects of whose model devotees can aspire to cultivate.

In chapter 1, I outline a theory of sainthood in Shiʿism that focuses on the religioethical example established by Imam Husain and his family, to which I refer in its paired form, *ḥusainiyyat-wilāyah* (*ḥusaini* ethics–imitable sainthood). Shiʿi hagiographers and religious scholars have variously used both of these terms to describe two different yet complementary dimensions of these holy people. I draw the term *ḥusainiyyat* (hereafter glossed as *ḥusaini* ethics) from the writings of numerous Shiʿa and others, including Pakistani intellectual Muhammad Iqbal, whose theory of *khudī* is based on the cultivation of a "higher self" symbolized by Imam Husain.[13] In much of the Karbala hagiographical literature, *ḥusainiyyat* is set up as the binary opposite of *yazīdiyyat*, referring to the ʿUmayyad *khalīfah*, Yazid, who symbolizes tyranny and greed in Shiʿi ethics. Saghar Khayyami describes *ḥusaini* ethics as grounded in the value "that the wants of others should be given preference to one's own wants" and as preaching "justice, truth, fraternity, peace and social welfare."[14] The ethic of sacrifice and commitment to social welfare and justice is defined by the doctrine of *ḥusaini* ethics. For the *ḥusaini* ethic to be an effective socioethical model for Muslims, it must be embodied by exemplars, who establish a "paradigm that sets the shape for a series of imitative phenomena that follow in its wake."[15] These exemplars of the *ḥusaini* ethic compel the cultivation of an idealized self through the incessant reiteration of hagiographical stories about faith and sacrifices that are fully absorbed and seamlessly integrated into everyday practice. While the *ahl-e bait*'s embodiment of *ḥusaini* ethics instantiates a powerful socioethical model for the Shiʿa, the socially recognized sanctity of these figures provides the foundation of their imitable sainthood (*wilāyah*).

The Shiʿa consider the family members of Imam Husain to be saints—otherwise, there would not exist the profusion of ritual events commemorating their lives and deaths, and the plethora of sacred spaces and objects would not constitute an important, even central, aspect of Shiʿi spirituality. The distinguishing quality of Shiʿi *wilāyah* is the charisma that is established through blood relationship to the Prophet Muhammad through his daughter, Fatimah al-Zahra. Mulla Sadra (Sadr al-Din Shirazi, d. 1045/1636), one of the great Iranian philosophers of the Safavid period, asserts that the term *awliyā* (pl. of *walī* [friends of God]) includes both Muhammad's genealogical descendants and his spiritual heirs.[16] Of particular interest in our definition of Shiʿi *wilāyah* is that it stands in distinct contrast to the esoteric, initiatic knowledge and transcendent sainthood (*walāyah*) possessed by the Imams. The *walāyah* is transcendent, for it is an incomparable quality that cannot be imitated by any other Shiʿa. Maria Dakake observes that "the term *walāyah* is frequently discussed in relation to *risālah* and *nubuwwah* (messengerhood and prophecy), with *risālah* and *nubuwwah* referring to the particular commission of the Prophet to publicly proclaim the exoteric revelation, and *walāyah* referring to the specific vocation of . . . the Shiʿite Imams . . . to transmit and explain its inner meaning."[17] *Wilāyah*, conversely, is a social phenomenon that makes saints into religious role models who provide spiritual and religious guidance and inspiration for everyday Shiʿa. Shiʿi saints such as Zainab, Salman Pak, Qasem, ʿAbbas, and Fatimah Kubra embody the moral and ethical qualities of *ḥusainiyyat* and radiate a high degree of spiritual and religious mastery that is based on the charismatic blood that literally or fictively (for example, Salman Pak, whose sainthood via fictive kinship will be analyzed in more detail in chapter 1) runs through their veins. Everyday Shiʿa can aspire to live a life that conforms to the ideals of religion and can cultivate an ethicomoral world that is made understandable and meaningful through the living model of Imam Husain and his family. *Ḥusainiyyat-wilāyah* is profoundly mimetic, and the vitality of hagiographical literature, sacred spaces, and ritual objects that connect everyday Shiʿa to these exemplary ethical and religious figures attests to the centrality of imitable sainthood in Shiʿism.

There is a deep tradition of imitable sainthood embodied by the charismatic members of Imam Husain's family and many other blood relatives of the twelve Imams, whose tombs are important sites of Shiʿi pilgrimage and the stories of whose lives are a source of inspiration and serve as a model for imitation. The phenomenon of imitable sainthood stands in distinct contrast to the transcendent sainthood that is divinely bestowed on the Imams, through which God has inspired them to serve as guides to humanity. The terms *wilāyah* and *walāyah* are very clearly distinguished in Shiʿi theological literature, a finding I have corroborated in conversations with religious scholars in India, Iran, and Pakistan. Shiʿi sainthood does not exist in the sense of veneration of spiritual masters (*pīr*, *shaykh*), mystics, and teachers of the Sufi mystical tradition. Shiʿi Sufi orders were systematically suppressed by the Iranian Shiʿi Safavid dynasty in the sixteenth and seventeenth centuries, and the hero(in)es of the *ahl-e bait* and the Imams were actively promoted as models of spiritual attainment and as social-moral exemplars.

Like the epic hero of the Indo-Muslim tradition, Imam Husain is not a saint in the sense of being an imitable saint. He is an Imam and therefore primarily possesses transcendent sanctity (although *ḥusaini* ethics is infused with his spirit and values). Imam Husain in particular (and to a lesser extent his son, the fourth Imam, Zain al-ʿAbidin) is a static figure in Karbala hagiographical literature. As I note in chapter 3, Imam Husain often plays a peripheral role in the emotional activity of the Karbala narratives. In his role as Imam, Husain is transcendent because he is chosen by God to be the guide for humanity. Henry Corbin describes Imam Husain's transcendent sanctity (*walāyah*) as the "'theophanic form' in which God manifests Himself—this 'Face of God' is the Imam."[18] As a theophanic form, the Imam's *walāyah* is characterized by transcendence.

Structure of the Book

Chapter 1 offers a structural analysis of Shiʿi sainthood. I propose a stipulative definition of Shiʿi sainthood based on the identification of a second category of sanctity that structures everyday lived religious life for the Shiʿa. Because Shiʿi identity centers on the ritualized remembrance of the martyrdom of Imam Husain and his family at the Battle of Karbala and on the devotional literature and performance of the *majlis*, these hero(in)es are transformed into religious and social role models that teach people how to be in the world. Using a framework of complementary pairing, this chapter examines the typologies of sainthood in Shiʿism, tracing the contours of a model of imitable sainthood based on the pair *ḥusaini* ethics–imitable sainthood (*ḥusainiyyat-wilāyah*).

Chapter 2 elaborates on the theoretical framework for this imitable model of Shiʿi sainthood as it is manifested in the form of female sainthood. The women of the *ahl-e bait*, whose descent is traced through the house of Fatimah al-Zahra, are in some instances transcendent and imitable (Fatimah and her daughter, Zainab). In other cases, these women are models of an imitable sanctity that is both spiritual and socioethical (Fatimah Kubra, Umm Kulsum, Sakinah). Yet all are venerated throughout the Shiʿi world for their potent femininity, devotion to God and family, and involvement in the affairs of the world. The women of the *ahl-e bait* are God's strong women, and their survival at the Battle of Karbala and their mission to keep the memory of Imam Husain alive make them powerfully imitable social, ethical, and spiritual role models for Shiʿi women and men.

Chapter 3 traces the role of the feminine voices and emotions of the women of the *ahl-e bait* in the Indic Karbala epic tradition. Using the example of Sita from the *Rāmāyaṇa* epic, this chapter highlights the ways in which writers employ strategies of narrative engagement with the audience and the ways in which female characters are dynamically constructed in Indic epic traditions. This chapter presents *Dah majlis* (The Ten Assemblies), Mir ʿAlam's late-eighteenth-century Deccani-Urdu translation of *Rowẓat al-shohadā* (The Garden of the Martyrs), as an example of how the Karbala epic tradition became Indianized. The emphatic use of feminine voices and emotions is based on the fact that the women of the *ahl-e bait* survived the Battle of Karbala and lived to tell their story.

In chapter 4, I take the paradigmatic example of Fatimah Kubra, the bride/widow of Karbala, to examine the ways in which the hero(in)es of Karbala teach proper gender roles to men and women through hagiographical transformations into locally meaningful typologies (e.g., good wife, self-sacrificing widow). Fatimah Kubra teaches both men and women how to be good members of family and society by being self-sacrificing and doing one's duty even if it means enduring hardship. An analysis of the preparations and performance of the 7 Muharram *mehndī* mourning assembly and Hyderabadi marriage ceremonies shows that Fatimah Kubra's gendered performance as ideal bride and renouncing widow fulfills a crucial hagiographic and thus social function. The imitable nature of her performance teaches Hyderabadi men and women their proper gender roles, which are life-cycle specific, culturally relevant, and compulsory because of her sacralized embodiment of *ḥusaini* ethics–imitable sainthood.

In chapter 5, I examine the current debates in India and Iran about the authoritativeness of *Rowẓat al-shohadā*, which is an important part of the tension between forces that desire to homogenize Shiʿi devotional practices (assuming Iran as center of cosmopolitan Shiʿism) and those that resist abandoning local ritual traditions (affirming vernacular Hyderabad, India). The act of translating *Rowẓat al-shohadā*, which forms the foundation for both textual and ritual devotional tradition in India, from Persian to Urdu made the text linguistically understandable to the average Indian of the Deccan, who may not have been fluent in the original language of composition. More specifically, the translation of *Rowẓat al-shohadā* transformed the ecology of Karbala and its hero(in)es to reflect an Indic worldview. Like the term "vernacular," the word "Indic" is multivalent and ambiguous, often leading to obfuscation rather than specificity. In the style of Marshall G. S. Hodgson, who coined the term "Islamicate" to refer "not directly to the religion, Islam, itself, but to the social and cultural complex historically associated with Islam and the Muslims, both among Muslims themselves and even when found among non-Muslims," I extend the religiocultural connotations of "Indic" to include all groups that have contributed to the construction of some sort of essential South Asian identity, worldview, and ethos, groups that include but are not limited to Hindus, Muslims, Buddhists, Iranians, and Europeans.[19] In the case of the enculturation of Shiʿi devotional literature and ritual in the Deccan, the foundation of the tradition is Iranian; however, its expression is Indian.

In the Deccan, *Rowẓat al-shohadā* was vernacularized, constructing a memory of Karbala refracted through an Indic lens. In chapter 5, I take the 7 Muharram *mehndī* mourning assembly as an example of this vernacularizing impulse in Hyderabad. In the cultural context of South Asia, the elaborate rules of marriage and the enduring power of the taboo on widow remarriage make the battlefield wedding of Fatimah Kubra to Qasem resonate on deeply personal and societal levels. Vernacularizing the story of Qasem and Fatimah Kubra and transforming them into idealized Hyderabadi Shiʿas orients faith and allegiance to the *ḥusaini* ethics of the *ahl-e bait*, because people can imagine and feel Karbala in their Indic worlds.

chapter one

Saints Are "Real" People

IMITABLE SAINTHOOD IN SHIʿISM

Live like ʿAli,
Die like Husain.

Each month, the Shiʿi students' association at Osmania University sponsors a mourning assembly (*majlis-e ʿazā*) to commemorate the martyrdom of Imam Husain, his family members, and his supporters at the Battle of Karbala in 680 C.E. Each month a different *majlis* orator (*ẕākir*) is invited to deliver the discourse; in early June 2005, Dr. M. M. Taqui Khan spoke. A retired professor of chemistry at the university and a popular majlis orator, Khan sat in the mourning assembly and listened to the invocatory poems (*salām* and *marśiya*) commemorating the wedding and martyrdom of Qasem before deciding that it was more appropriate to speak on this topic rather than the one he had prepared. Discoursing on Qasem's martyrdom is a familiar subject for Khan. For decades, his family has hosted one of Hyderabad's most popular 7 Muharram mourning assemblies dedicated to Qasem.

Qasem and Fatimah Kubra's battlefield wedding is observed with special vigor in South Asia. Although the events of 7 Muharram are some of the most popular in the Karbala cycle, not all Shiʿa recognize the historical veracity of Qasem's battlefield wedding (see chapter 5). Throughout the Old City, where the majority of Hyderabad's approximately two hundred thousand Shiʿa live, numerous mourning assemblies, both small and large, take place, representing Qasem and Fatimah Kubra's wedding and sacrifice for faith and family in a special *mehndī* ritual. This event is one of the most popular in the Hyderabadi Shiʿi ritual cycle, in which vernacular social ideals, particularly the emphasis on the central role of marriage and the family, are fully integrated into the cosmopolitan drama of Karbala. For the Shiʿa of Hyderabad, this battlefield wedding invokes feelings of grief both for the martyrdom of the thirteen-year-old bridegroom/warrior and for the plight of his bride, who, according to hagiographical tradition, became a widow after one night of unconsummated marriage. At the same time, the mourning assembly involves a deep sense of play, for in spite of this event's tragic pathos, the frenzied struggle of male and female devotees to obtain a smear of henna as a means of making a good marriage alliance reflects the community's life-affirming optimism—an affirmation of the power of the *ḥusaini* ethic embodied by imitable saints such as Fatimah Kubra and Qasem. The Shiʿa of Hyderabad believe that the family of Imam Husain suffered and that modern Shiʿa must remember the events of Karbala to celebrate the joyful moments of life: marriage, pregnancy, and the birth of children.

Khan believed that his decision to change the topic of his discourse was fortuitous, perhaps proof of Qasem's powerful and positive role in the chemist's personal spiritual life. Spontaneously changing the subject of his discourse was not a problem for Khan: a good *ẕākir* is expected to be an astute reader of his audience and must be able to draw from an expansive repertoire of topics to connect with his listeners. People typically go from one mourning assembly to the next during the days of mourning (*ayyām-e ʿazā*), which stretch over two months and eight days, from 1 Muharram until 8 Rabiʿ al-Awwal, and expect to hear something different at each *majlis*.

Delivering the hagiographical account of the sufferings (*maṣāʾib*) of Qasem and Fatimah Kubra presented Khan with an opportunity to present a somewhat different perspective on their sacrifice. Rather than focus his discourse on Qasem's battlefield heroics and martyrdom, Khan spoke almost exclusively about Fatimah Kubra's embodiment of the *ḥusaini* ethic based on her willingness to sacrifice herself and her husband for the preservation of Islam. During the preceding couple of months, I had been meeting with Khan at his house in the Yaqutpura neighborhood of Hyderabad's Old City, where we spent much time discussing points of Shiʿi theology, issues of gender in Islamic tradition, and Fatimah Kubra and Qasem. Our conversations were usually wide-ranging and intellectually stimulating; on many occasions, our discussions of Fatimah Kubra and Qasem became an inquiry into what Khan clearly saw as a feminist impulse within the Shiʿi tradition.

In his discourse for the Shiʿi students' association, Khan drew the *majlis* participants into Fatimah Kubra's world, commenting on her embodiment of the *ḥusaini* ethic of sacrifice and faith. In our conversations, Khan repeatedly emphasized that Fatimah Kubra's active participation in the sacrifice of Karbala provides important lessons for Hyderabadi Shiʿa, reflecting both vernacular social values and religious ideals of faith and commitment to justice (*ʿadālah*). Khan crafted a hagiographical persona for Fatimah Kubra, portraying her as a strong-willed warrior of the faith who loved her husband enough to sacrifice their lives for the cause of justice, and this image deeply affected the *majlis* participants. As he recounted the details of what he considered a most successful discourse, producing the desired emotional effects of grief and spiritual introspection, he marveled at how many young men approached him after the mourning assembly to express their feelings of gratitude. Even more of an accomplishment, in Khan's estimation, was that many of these men expressed a sense of astonishment at what they perceived to be a new and attention-grabbing version of the Qasem narrative that emphasized Fatimah Kubra's role. The young men who wept for Fatimah Kubra felt an emotional and spiritual connection that was forged through Khan's hagiographical discourse. It is not difficult to perceive why Khan instinctively spoke about Fatimah Kubra in the *majlis* on that June day. Khan is the loving father of six daughters, and he always thinks of them when he recounts the stories of Sakinah and Fatimah Kubra, who were young girls at the Battle of Karbala. Imam Husain's daughters are like Khan's daughters.

I begin this chapter with this ethnographic anecdote because Khan's experience delivering his discourse on Fatimah Kubra and the attendant emotional response of the *majlis* participants demonstrates that the theological and hagiographical construction of sainthood in the Shiʿi tradition is complex and provides significant space for the inclusion of female saints whose femininity is positively acknowledged and embraced. Khan's focus on Fatimah Kubra was not exceptional, nor was this a special one-time-only topic; the following chapters illustrate how the women of the *ahl-e bait* are constructed in the hagiographical texts and ritual performance of the mourning assembly. The hero(in)es of Karbala are reified into certain distinguishable types, yet the characterization and symbolic function of these hero(in)es are remarkably fluid and are subject to adaptation to fit new vernacular contexts.

The men and women of Imam Husain's family are revered as consummate socioethical exemplars and imitable saints whose spiritual attainments are anything but otherworldly. This chapter identifies the structures of Shiʿi sainthood, paying close attention to how the hero(in)es of the *ahl-e bait* have been constructed in hagiographical writing and theology to embody an imitable sainthood (*wilāyah*) that is fully fused with a *ḥusaini* ethics of faith and sacrifice (*ḥusainiyyat*). Within the discipline of religious studies, a considerable body of scholarship defines sainthood in Sufism as well as in Roman

Catholicism. Although this scholarship is significant for its contributions to our understanding of what it means to be a saint, these frameworks have certain limitations in that they require the presentation of a stipulative definition of Shiʿi sainthood that will help us more fully to understand Khan's hagiographical discourse on Fatimah Kubra.

Toward a Stipulative Definition of Shiʿi Sainthood

In contemporary Islamic studies scholarship, the English word "saint" is sometimes used uncritically, obscuring the myriad forms of sainthood that exist. In terms of historical origin, the term refers to one who is holy, and we often analyze sainthood through a Christocentric lens, although Muslim thinkers and religious practitioners have developed a sophisticated taxonomy for categorizing the varieties of sainthood in Islam. In both Christianity and Islam, at the most basic level, saints become saints because they have manifested miracles, exhibited exemplary faith in God, and quite often suffered for their faith. While this is a sufficient starting point, this general definition of the qualities of sainthood must be expanded to posit a stipulative definition of imitable Shiʿi sainthood that is manifested through the complementary pairing *ḥusaini* ethics–*wilāyah*. This stipulative definition of imitable Shiʿi sainthood is predicated on four criteria: (1) examining hagiographical text and ritual performance in relationship to one another to develop a full understanding of how a community constructs a saint through memorializing practices; (2) identifying the positive and central role of females and the feminine in the articulation of a model of imitable Shiʿi sainthood; (3) establishing a taxonomy and working vocabulary of sainthood that is derived from categories and concepts preexistent in Shiʿi theological and hagiographical literature; and (4) outlining the criteria for Shiʿi imitable sainthood by identifying typological qualities and characteristics that make the *ahl-e bait* both exceptional and imitable. These typologies are meant not to be exhaustive of how Shiʿi sainthood is constituted but rather to illustrate the qualities that mark an individual as a socioethical exemplar and imitable saint.

In formulating our stipulative definition of Shiʿi sainthood, textual traditions and the lived, performed dimension of religious life require equal attention. One challenge to formulating a working definition of Shiʿi sainthood resides within the Orientalist legacy that continues to influence the scope and orientation of Islamic studies research.[1] According to Edward

Said, Orientalist scholars have resolutely maintained a "textual attitude" that privileges the written word as the source and basis of reality.[2] Solely engaging texts to establish a basis of knowledge about a civilization or religion manufactures realities that distort and may ultimately disappoint, especially when the lived, practical dimension is introduced. Scholars who tend to define religion textually give credence neither to the dynamic interactions that take place between text and ritual performance nor to the role of vernacular interpretations and reformulations of the text.

Khan's *majlis* discourse draws on a rich tradition of Shiʿi hagiographical martyrdom narratives known in Persian and Urdu as *maqtal* (martyrdom narrative) and *shahādat-nāmeh* (martyrdom chronicle). Like those of many of the *majlis* orators who speak in Hyderabad's countless mourning assemblies throughout the year, Khan's discourse (*khuṭbah*) was derived from Mullah Husain Vaʿez Kashefi's early-sixteenth-century Persian-language *Rowẓat al-shohadā* (The Garden of the Martyrs). While *Rowẓat al-shohadā*'s Iranian narrative imprint is discernible, the text's vernacularization in the context of the Hyderabadi mourning assembly transforms the hero(in)es of Karbala into a Deccani-Indian idiom. For the Shiʿa of Hyderabad, *Rowẓat al-shohadā*, in its Deccani-Urdu iteration, preserves the stories of the hero(in)es of Karbala; however, the ritual performance of the mourning assembly brings them to life as idealized yet imitable Indian Shiʿi Muslim men and women whose model is to be cultivated by *majlis* participants.

The second dimension of this stipulative definition of Shiʿi sainthood is based on the necessary inclusion of both male and female holy people who are equal to one another in their religious functions. Several issues contribute to this lacuna in the study of sainthood in Islam. First, the tendency to privilege textual traditions virtually eliminates the presence of female sanctity in Islam. This textual predilection is exacerbated by the limitations imposed on male-female nonkin relationships by the segregation system known as *purdah*. Biographies of female Muslim saints have often been excluded from the textual tradition because of sexual segregation and the concomitant feelings of ambivalence about placing a woman in the public sphere by revering her in either text or practice.

In the introduction to her translation of the eleventh-century Persian Sufi Abu ʿAbd al-Rahman al-Sulami's *Memorial of Female Sufi Devotees*, Rkia Cornell reveals the darker side of why Muslim female saints have been relegated to the margins of Islam: Islam is a patriarchal religion in which its masculine arbiters of power maintain their dominant status through the subordination of women. In Cornell's estimation, al-Sulami believed in the spiritual equality of women, although their biographies must necessarily differ from those of male saints.[3] Al-Sulami brackets the perceived inferiority of the female Sufi saint by focusing on her disciplined practice of "making oneself a slave" (*taʿabbud*), the type of quality that he believes enables such exceptional women to attain the heights of spiritual knowledge (*maʿrifah*) and union (*fanā*) with God.[4] At first glance, al-Sulami's willingness to include women within the realm of Muslim sainthood appears admirable, although his approach differs little from the approach taken by biographers of Roman Catholic female saints, who must overcome the inferiority of their sex through a process of hagiographical transvestism to become like men striving toward Christ.[5] Both male and female Catholic ascetics enact a symbolic marriage to Jesus Christ, thereby separating these spiritual aspirants from the requirements of society. Unlike Catholic and Sufi models of female sainthood, in the Shiʿi conception of sainthood, the feminine and female are necessary and central.

The third facet of the formulation of our stipulative definition of Shiʿi sainthood focuses on the ambiguity within Islamic studies scholarship about the meaning and function of the technical vocabulary (*walāyah* and *wilāyah*) employed in reference to saints. The preponderance of scholarly analysis of the notion of Islamic sanctity focuses on Sufism, neglecting the centrality of *wilāyah* and *walāyah* in Shiʿi theology and devotional practices. Shiʿi conceptions of *wilāyah* and *walāyah* place the roles of guardianship and friendship into a complementary relationship in which the exoteric, socio-ethical, public function of *wilāyah* is the corollary to the esoteric, initiatic, juridical function of *walāyah*. In her study of the charismatic authority of the Imams in the early Shiʿi community, Maria Massi Dakake identifies *walāyah* as the "specific vocation" of the Imams, who bear a divinely bestowed responsibility to "transmit and explain" the hidden meaning of the Qurʾan and the cosmos.[6] *Wilāyah* is sainthood that is socially determined and circumscribed. Embodiment of the moral and ethical qualities of the *ḥusaini* ethic (*ḥusainiyyat*), coupled with exceptional spiritual and religious mastery, makes the sainthood (*wilāyah*) of Imam Husain's family a profound model for imitation by everyday Shiʿa.

The final feature of our speculative definition of Shiʿi sainthood focuses on typologies of imitable sainthood. In her study of medieval European Roman Catholic female sainthood, Catherine Mooney observes that "saints are not only presented as models to others for imitation, but also are often themselves described typologically."[7] Comparative analysis of Roman Catholic and Sufi typologies of sainthood brings into relief the contours of the types of saints most prominent in Shiʿism. The masculine metanarrative of theological and hagiographical textual traditions does not dominate in Shiʿi theories of sainthood; rather, the essential criterion for qualifying as a saint in the Shiʿi tradition is a direct blood relationship to the Prophet Muhammad through his daughter, Fatimah al-Zahra. In conceptualizing these typological categories and in identifying the features of Shiʿi imitable sainthood as it is articulated in Shiʿi thought and devotional practice, a hermeneutic framework of complementary pairing is useful.[8]

In our stipulative definition of Shiʿi sainthood, complementary pairing makes it possible to distinguish two correlated, mutually dependent aspects of sanctity. Despite the poststructuralist turn in academic thought, certain aspects of binary theory retain much value. The human tendency to think in binary terms is aptly illustrated in the case of Shiʿi sainthood but betrays clear deficiencies with regard to the analysis of gender, which transcends the obvious binary limits of masculine-feminine. By adjusting structuralist binary theory to transform binary opposites into complementary pairs, two sets or pairings of qualities that define transcendent and imitable Shiʿi sainthood may be defined. The Imamate (*imāmah*) and its complementary pair *walāyah* (sainthood bestowed by God without choice and not imitable), the most studied dimension of Shiʿi sanctity because of its masculine and textual foundation, enables one to identify its complementary pair of *ḥusaini* ethics (the spirit of sacrifice and faith embodied by Imam Husain and his family) and its necessary component, *wilāyah* (sainthood that is socially recognized and a model for imitation). Whereas the first pair is abstract and theologically oriented, the second pair is culturally specific, and its meaning constantly shifts according to time and place and is socially grounded, compelling everyday Shiʿa to imitate the socioethical and religious model of Imam Husain and his family. How these pairs function as forms of Shiʿi sainthood will be examined in greater detail later in this chapter.

Although the word "saint" has a long tradition of Christocentric meanings and significations, its meaning in the Shiʿi tradition refers either to the transcendent sainthood of the Imams or the imitable socioethical, religious model of the *ahl-e bait*. Only a select few—the twelve Imams, the Prophet Muhammad, and his daughter, Fatimah al-Zahra—possess the inimitable quality of *walāyah*. A second class of saints (and the focus of this study) is a group of people known as the *ahl-e bait*—that is, the family members of the

Prophet Muhammad and his direct blood descendants through his daughter, Fatimah, and her husband, the first Imam, ʿAli ibn Abi Talib. Based on their blood relationship to Imam Husain and the socioethical model of sacrifice and faith (*ḥusaini* ethics) that they embodied at the Battle of Karbala, the exemplary religious model offered by these individuals is socially recognized as a form of imitable sainthood through which an individual can cultivate an idealized self. Because consanguinity is an integral aspect of Shiʿi sainthood, the female members of the *ahl-e bait* are venerated for their femininity and spiritual attainments. These female saints are models of religious accomplishment and the *ḥusaini* ethic and provide sources of inspiration for both women and men.

In Shiʿi hagiographical literature, the imitable yet transcendent model of the Prophet Muhammad is mirrored to a certain extent by his grandson, Imam Husain. Muslim devotional literature refers to Muhammad as the "perfected man" (*insān al-kāmil*), the reflection of God's vision of the ideal human being. Although a prophet, a messenger, and a man who communicated with God, Muhammad was also an ordinary man of exemplary morality whose ethical virtue was admired by many. The lived tradition of the Prophet Muhammad, which records his sayings, judgments, and deeds, is known as the Sunnah, and in the Prophet's perfected model of humanity, everyday Muslims imitate his exemplary human qualities in their religious and daily practice.

Like the Prophet Muhammad, Imam Husain and Fatimah al-Zahra do not fit precisely within the binary model of Shiʿi sainthood. As an Imam, Husain is a transcendent figure, selected by God to possess esoteric knowledge and to guide humanity, yet Karbala hagiographical literature has occasional ruptures that bring his exemplary socioethical qualities to the forefront. Not only an Imam, Husain is also an imitable saint who embodies the *ḥusaini* ethic. Likewise, Fatimah al-Zahra is endowed with a special *walāyat-e fāṭimiyyah* that marks her transcendence. The Shiʿa also venerate Fatimah for her embodiment of the ethic of faith and sacrifice. For the most part, the members of the *ahl-e bait* possess either Imamate–transcendent sainthood or *ḥusaini* ethics–imitable sainthood; only a few are simultaneously imitable and transcendent.

Comparative analyses of normative typologies of sainthood in Roman Catholic tradition and Sufism highlight the complex and mutually informing traditions of text and ritual practice in the construction of Shiʿi sainthood. The example of the martyr is one of the most important typologies in

Christian sainthood, finding its analog in Shiʿism with the model of Imam Husain and his family. The Shiʿi martyr typology is based on the doctrine of the *ḥusaini* ethic of social engagement and commitment to justice. The second typology of sainthood popular in Sufi traditions is that of the warrior (*ghāzī*), whose military exploits and spiritual piety are a source of veneration. In the context of Shiʿi sainthood, the warrior saint (*mujāhid*) is a distinctive type whose persona is exemplified in the model of Imam Husain and his family. The third typology of sainthood, the female saint, is more difficult to analyze. More sustained scholarship has been produced on the topic of female sainthood in Christian traditions, and although research on gendered aspects of Sufi sainthood is still slowly expanding, much of this work reflects a deep patriarchal ambivalence about the nature and possible fullness of femininity for female saints. Such patriarchal metanarratives are undermined in Shiʿi sainthood and hagiographical traditions because the women of the Prophet Muhammad's family, especially Fatimah al-Zahra and her daughter, Zainab, are central figures in conveying and exemplifying the socioethical and religious message of Shiʿism. These women are revered not only for their religious mastery and embodiment of *ḥusaini* ethics but also for their womanliness. Highlighting the distinctive features of these typologies of sainthood enables us to discern the qualities of and requirements for being a socioethical exemplar and imitable saint (*ḥusainiyyat-wilāyah*) in Shiʿi hagiography and ritual practice.

Typology: The Roman Catholic Martyr Saint

In Christianity, the word "saint" is derived from the Greek *hagios* (holy).[9] The notion of saints and the institution of sainthood did not develop during the lifetime of Jesus Christ. At the beginning of the fourth century C.E., during a period of intense persecution of Christian communities in Byzantine lands, a number of stories began circulating about exemplary men and women who sacrificed their lives for their faith in Jesus. The phenomenon of *martyrium* (witnessing)—that is, a desire to relinquish life as a statement of faith in Jesus Christ—established the foundation one of the earliest and most emotionally captivating types of Christian sainthood, martyrdom.[10] We can compare the Greek *martyrium* to the Arabic word *shahādat*, which also refers to witnessing faith in God by sacrificing life.

The witnessing martyr who is willing to die a gruesome death became memorialized in stories (*passio*) narrating the individual's sufferings as a means of demonstrating absolute faith in God. In his study of the rise of the cult of the saints in late antiquity and early medieval Europe, Peter Brown argues that saints are not only heroes but more importantly "friends of God" whose intercession may be sought through the saint's *praesentia*, or "living" presence in the grave.[11] The martyrs are the elected friends of God, "to whom the gift of perseverance had been given and had been seen to be given."[12] Visiting saints' graves enables devotees vicariously to experience a bit of heaven on earth; in addition, they can petition the martyrs to become their patrons, interceding on their behalf with God. The martyr's intercessory power (*shafāʿat*) is manifested in Shiʿi sainthood through the proliferation of shrines and sacred spaces (*imāmzādeh*, *ʿāshūrkhāna*, *imāmbāṛā*) and ritual objects (particularly the *ʿalam*, a metal battle standard symbolizing various members of the *ahl-e bait*) from which emanate potent grace and sanctified power (*baraka*). Later in this chapter, the typology of the Shiʿi martyr saint, whose sanctity is derived from charismatic blood relationship to the Prophet Muhammad, is examined.

The martyr type is an active and socially engaged figure. The martyr differs from the ascetic, otherworldly type of saint because transgressive acts of faith and opposition to authority require social involvement. This idea certainly does not mean that many of these martyr saints were not ascetics, but their act of opposition against what they perceived to be the greed or faithlessness of their oppressors forces a degree of social engagement that renunciation of the world does not allow. The witnessing martyr type is predicated on engagement with the world or at least the public rejection of the authority to which the martyr is opposed. With the example of the active martyr saint, it is clear that even in Christianity, the singular term "saint" is inadequate for indicating the individual's source of sanctity; qualifying words must be appended to specify the source or reason for sainthood.

The cult of saints emerged for several reasons, and the martyr saint was a compelling and unifying symbol for Christians to reflect upon and venerate. The first factor in the development of the cult of saints was "the lurching forward of an increasing proportion of late-antique society toward radically new forms of reverence shown to new objects in new places, orchestrated by new leaders, and . . . new bonds of human dependence, new intimate hopes for protection and justice in a changing world."[13] Second, with the establishment of monastic communities by the fourth century, people came to see monks as idealized otherworldly figures whose renunciation of social life indicated a greater closeness to God based on the desire to replicate the life of Jesus as remembered or imagined.[14] Rapid social change, the consolidation of Christian legitimacy, shifting axes of political power, and the development of monastic movements generated among the laity a profound need to seek the succor and protection of these saints.

The development of the cult of the saints depended on the establishment of idealized social relations and religious models for imitation by a society that had become fractured in the course of urbanization and social change. Furthermore, "the cult of the saints . . . was a form of piety exquisitely adapted to enable late antique men to articulate and render manageable urgent, muffled debates on the nature of power in their own world and to examine in the searching light of ideal relationships with ideal figures, the relation between power, mercy and justice as practiced around them."[15] The saint's life, piety, suffering, faith, and ability after death to intercede on behalf of everyday Christians reflect the ways in which the saints help people establish structure and religioethical order in their lives.[16] Reading the saint's biography (*vita*), visiting the saint's grave, and celebrating the saint's feast day are means of entering the saint's presence and ultimately of connecting to God from here on earth.

The saint's life is exemplary in its supreme success in imitating the life of Jesus Christ (*imitatio Christi*), the consummate martyr of the Christian tradition. In imitating the religious model and ethic of sacrifice embodied by the saint, the devotee enters into an act of mimetic doubling: living the life of the saint living a life in *imitatio Christi*. Not only is imitation interiorized through meditative practices and remembrance of the saint's life, but the saint's cultivation of *imitatio Christi* is externalized through socially defining bodily practices—what Pierre Bourdieu calls *habitus*.[17] Imitating saints imitating the life of Christ leads to the internalization of church values by training the body to enact belief, to perform ideology. Thus, *habitus* as the "embodied set of dispositions, learned and internalized through bodily practices" contributes to the notion of the "living" saint whose holiness changes with the ideology of the church and the needs of society.[18] Jesus Christ is the most vivid example of the martyr saint, and the bodily practices that are ritually remembered and practiced in such events as the Passion during the Easter Holy Week demonstrate the enduring model and meaningfulness of the martyr saint in Christian tradition.

Typology: The Sufi Warrior Saint

Some of the most revered saints in Sufi traditions are warriors (*ghāzī* or *mujāhid*). Warrior saints are typically depicted in hagiographical literature as deeply pious men who are also great, skilled warriors who fight on behalf of religion and/or dominion. In some hagiographies, such as that of the "two Yusufs" of Golconda, the warrior saint is further depicted as a socioethical exemplar whose model is to be imitated by others.

In *Realm of the Saint*, Vincent Cornell identifies seven typological categories of sainthood in Moroccan Sufism. For example, the *ghawth* (synonymous with *quṭb* [pole]) embodies what Cornell calls "generative authority," which is the "most feminine type of sainthood."[19] The *ghawth* provides succor and nurturance to his devotees. Cornell's typological framework provides a useful model for understanding the myriad manifestations and institutions of sainthood within a specifically Moroccan context. Cornell takes the tension between the *sharīʿah*-minded tendencies of the urban religious elite and the tribal culture of Morocco's rural outposts into careful consideration as he examines how sainthood is manifested and signified both at the institutional level and within the realm of everyday practice. Cornell's concern with the everyday and its relationship to institutionalized categories of sainthood is exemplified in his question, "Unless one tests Sufi models of sainthood against the data at hand, how can one be sure that such models, created as they were by an educated mystical elite, have much bearing on the 'popular' interpretation of Moroccan sainthood?"[20]

The most important type of saint in Moroccan Sufism is the *ṣāliḥ*, the "ethical authority," who embodies social virtue (*ṣalāḥ*). The *ṣāliḥ* is the most idealized type of saint, the consummate exemplar of social virtue, setting a clear example of how to be a good Muslim in the world. Because the parameters of social virtue are "clearly known from Qur'an, *ḥadīth*, and treatises on Sufi practice," the *ṣāliḥ* serves as a leitmotif of Moroccan Sufi sainthood.[21] *Ṣalāḥ* is a socioethical responsibility, a vital aspect of imitable sainthood, outlined in scriptural texts, and embodied in the lived practice of the Prophet Muhammad as well as the saint of social virtue. The typology of the *ṣāliḥ* attests to the social function of an imitable model of sainthood, because "a *walī Allah's* public image must conform to consensually validated standards before his or her holiness is acknowledged."[22] One might perform the most amazing miracles, but without social recognition of the exemplary socioethical and religious virtue that is the source of inspiration for everyday Muslims, such wonder making is merely magic.

Just as typologies of sainthood reflect the shifting ideologies of religious institutions and the ever-changing needs of the religious community, in the context of Sufism the "changing socio-political situation every time calls for an urgently necessary type of saint: a stern warrior for faith or a pacifier-philanthropist; a conservative missionary or a *mu'aḥḥid* [*sic*] indifferent to religious differences, a virtuous ascetic or a *qalandar*, indulging in all sorts of vices; an enlightened preceptor of the elite or an illiterate leader of the lower classes."[23] Saints recognized and venerated for their exemplary social virtue represent distinctly different Muslim social and political modalities from contexts where heroism and piety are integrated to create warrior saints.

In South Asia, where the hero is a popular leitmotif in religious, political, and social life, the warrior (*ghāzī*) has universal appeal for Hindus, Muslims, and Sikhs.[24] This section examines two typologies of South Asian Sufi warrior saints that exemplify two different subcategories and functions.

Hyderabad is home to the Yusufain *dargāh* (the shrine of the two Yusufs). Stories abound regarding the piety and bravery of two spiritual brothers (*pīr bhā'ī*), Yusuf and Sharif, who were soldiers in the Mughal emperor Aurangzeb's army during the siege of Golconda in 1687 C.E. Neither of these men was Indian: Yusuf was from Cairo, and Sharif hailed from Kanan, Iraq. The two men met while on *ḥajj* in Mecca, where they found their spiritual teacher, Shaykh Kalim Allah Shahjahanabadi, a Chishti Sufi master born in Delhi in 1650 who had come to Arabia to further develop his religious and mystical knowledge. Yusuf and Sharif followed their teacher to Delhi, and some years later, he encouraged them to join Aurangzeb's army and go to the Deccan.[25]

In his attempt to unseat Abu'l-Hasan (r. 1672–87), the last Shi'i Qutb Shahi king of Hyderabad, Aurangzeb laid siege to the great fort of Golconda for eight months. In *Muntakhāb al-lubāb* (also known as *The History of Khafi Khan*), Khafi Khan, the historian of Aurangzeb's reign, writes that "the period of the siege was prolonged. Owing to the large stock of gun-powder and material for the artillery, which the fort contained, cannon-balls, musket-balls, rockets and gunpowder-flasks were shot continuously day and night (on the besiegers) from the gates, walls, towers and ramparts of the fort. . . . No day passed without a number of the besiegers being wounded or killed, but the emperor's men showed great courage in the enterprise."[26]

According to historical and hagiographical narratives, one night during the monsoon season, a terrible storm blew up, and all but one of the tents in Aurangzeb's encampment were destroyed. Throughout the violent storm, the flames of two candles steadfastly burned, a remarkable sight that drew Aurangzeb to the lone surviving tent. Sitting there were Yusuf and Sharif, reading the Qur'an by candlelight. It was a miracle that these men and their tent were untouched by the storm, and Aurangzeb recognized Yusuf and Sharif as saints. Aurangzeb beseeched them to pray that he would defeat Golconda, and the two warriors told Aurangzeb to visit a particular merchant whose shop was located near the Golconda fort's main gate, later known as the Victory Gate (*fāteḥ darwāzah*) following Aurangzeb's victory.[27] As Yusuf and Sharif had predicted, this merchant informed Aurangzeb of the fort's weakness, allowing his army to conquer the Qutb Shahi dynasty without violence. Aurangzeb was victorious because of Yusuf and Sharif's intercessory miracle work (*karāmat*).

Today, the Yusufain *dargāh*, located behind the Nampally railway station in downtown Hyderabad, is popular with people of all faiths. People throng the shrine on Thursday nights to listen to *qawwālī* (mystical Sufi songs), and countless others ask the two saints to intercede on their behalf. Engaged in service to both God and ruler, Yusuf and Sharif enabled Aurangzeb to infiltrate Golconda's walls. The two saints' piety, embodiment of ethical authority (*ṣalāḥ*), faith, and charisma were qualities most likely learned from their Chishti spiritual guide (*murshid*), Shaykh Kalim Allah Shahjahanabadi. Yusuf and Sharif are most un-Chishti in their willingness to serve political authority. Unlike the Naqshbandi order (*silsilah*), the Chishtis have long eschewed involvement in political matters and have tended to avoid the patronage of political figures. It is rather unusual that Kalim Allah Shahjahanabadi, in his role as a Chishti *pīr*, encouraged Yusuf and Sharif to join Aurangzeb's military campaign in the Deccan, although their presence at Golconda was necessary for the manifestation of their *karāmat*.

The second type of Sufi warrior saint finds its analog in the exemplary socioethical and religious model of Imam Husain's nephew, Qasem, whom South Asian Shiʿa venerate as the bridegroom of Karbala. For more than eight hundred years, Hindus and Muslims in North India have venerated Ghazi Miyan (also known as Salar Masʿud) as a bridegroom/warrior.[28] Ghazi Miyan's tomb is located in Bahraich, near the Hindu holy city of Ayodhya, in Uttar Pradesh.[29] He was a warrior (*ghāzī*) and a bridegroom (*naushāh* [literally "new king"]), who according to some hagiographical traditions was killed in battle at the age of nineteen on 15 June 1034 while trying to build a mosque over the remains of a sun temple in Bahraich.[30]

Ghazi Miyan is a complex and ambiguous figure because he is portrayed in the hagiographical texts in astonishingly different ways. Shaykh ʿAbdur Rahman Chishti's seventeenth-century *Mirʾāt-e maṣʿūdī* (The Mirror of Maṣʿūd) hails Ghazi Miyan as a brave warrior. ʿAbdur Rahman's text is largely synthetic, compiling the many hagiographical accounts of Ghazi Miyan that were in circulation in North India for at least five centuries. Much of the *Mirror of Maṣʿūd* is based on Mullah Muhammad Ghaznavi's history (*Tārīkh-e mullāh muḥammad ghaznāvī*), which is no longer extant.[31] In *Mirʾāt-e maṣʿūdī*, ʿAbdur Rahman reports that Ghazi Miyan was the nephew of Sultan Mahmud of Ghazna (r. 998–1030) and that Ghazi Miyan encouraged his uncle to destroy the temple at Somnath in 1026 C.E.[32] In such chronicles as *Mirʾāt-e maṣʿūdī*, Ghazi Miyan is the stereotypical warrior conquering "infidels" in the name of Islam. Romila Thapar observes that Ghazi Miyan's "early exploits are enveloped in fantasy. . . . [T]he stories of his exploits as a warrior may well have surfaced at the time when Ghazi Miyan was acquiring popularity as a protector of the lowly. The biography may have been an attempt to give the *pīr* appropriate Islamic credentials."[33] In addition, other hagiographies represent Ghazi Miyan as a friend of the Hindu and a tragic bridegroom.

Ghazi Miyan is called the warrior bridegroom because of the many stories in circulation about his marriage to Zahra Bibi. Ghazi Miyan "and his bride managed only to conclude the marriage-contract, but actually the marriage was not consummated: the bridegroom was killed before the nuptial night, and Zahra Bibi remained a virgin."[34] This story remarkably echoes the story of Qasem and Fatimah Kubra's wedding. The parallels between Qasem and Ghazi Miyan and their brides/widows illustrates the ways in which saints become vernacularized, not only reflecting universal religious ideals but also embodying local cultural values. The hagiographies of both Qasem–Fatimah Kubra and Ghazi Miyan–Zahra Bibi powerfully reinforce the Islamic imperative and the Indic premium placed on marriage, yet both narratives also reflect vernacular taboos on widow remarriage.

Ghazi Miyan's Hindu credentials are further solidified by the attendance of Yashoda (the mother of the god Krishna) at Ghazi Miyan's wedding. Yashoda came to beseech Ghazi Miyan to save the cows belonging to the Ahirs (an agrarian caste) and their cowherds from being slaughtered by an evil king. According to Hinducentric hagiographical narratives, Ghazi Miyan went out into battle to save these cows and was martyred.[35] Each year on his death anniversary (ʿurs), Ghazi Miyan's battlefield wedding is ritually reenacted by his devotees in Bahraich, an event that draws both Muslims and Hindus, who play wedding and martial music and exchange the bridegroom's clothing for a suit of armor. The same transformations and inversions are enacted in hagiographical texts and ritual performances dedicated to Qasem.[36]

I emphasize these two typological examples of the warrior saint to demonstrate that the role of saint (*walī Allah*) is indeed complex and that saints often possess a multitude of qualities that make them exemplary. Most important, with each of these typological categories—martyr, warrior saint, and warrior/bridegroom saint—the socioethical exemplar and imitable saint is vernacularized to reflect the environment and worldview of particular, localized communities. Furthermore, these typological categories exhibit a high degree of fluidity. Ghazi Miyan is much more than a monodimensional warrior martyr—he is a hero for Hindus and the underclass, and his tragic wedding reflects vernacular Indic anxieties about marriage and widowhood. In fact, many of the Sufi figures who are revered as saints arguably do not necessarily appear at first glance to be especially pious, great teachers, or miracle makers. What, then, makes these individuals saints?

The Role of Wilāyah *and* Walāyah *in Theorizing Muslim Sainthood*

Developing out of early Shiʿi theories of Imamate and transcendent, God-given sanctity (*walāyah*), much of the earliest Sufi conception of sainthood is indebted to the esoteric verses of the Qur'an and *ḥadīth* traditions in which the Prophet Muhammad appointed his cousin and son-in-law, ʿAli, as his guardian and friend (*maulā*). The scriptural foundations of sainthood and the theoretical conceptions of *walāyah* and *wilāyah* in the writings of al-Tirmidhi and Ibn al-ʿArabi provide a useful hermeneutic framework. To understand the pragmatics of *ḥusaini* ethics–imitable sainthood (*ḥusainiyyat-wilāyah*) and how it structurally orders the everyday practice of the Shiʿa, we must first understand idealized forms of sainthood in Shiʿi thought.

Walī and its forms are derived from the Arabic triliteral root *w-l-y*, which conveys the sense of being "near, close, friend, patron, and legal protector."[37] The root has two distinct meanings, one of closeness and friendship, and the other conveying the sense of patronage and guardianship; these two meanings correlate to the immanence of *wilāyah* and the transcendence of *walāyah*, respectively. Neither of these two categories means "saint" in the strict sense of the word, although close analysis of the Qur'an and *ḥadīth* illustrates the broad semantic range of this root and its derivations. *Walī* and its various forms appear more than 227 times in the Qur'an. One of God's ninety-nine names is *al-Walī*, and this quality reflects God's relationship of guardianship and friendship with humanity, thus conveying both categorical senses of the word: "Allah is the *Walī* of those who believe; He causes them to come out of darkness into the light" (*Sūrat al-Baqarah* [Chapter of the Cow], 2:257).[38]

God is not only the friend of the believers (*mu'min*) but also the guardian who protects Muslims and brings them into the light of knowing him. The saint (*walī Allah*) is therefore secure in his or her close relationship with God. Such security is assured by God's promise that saints will feel no fear on the Day of Judgment: "Verily, the Friends of God have nothing to fear, nor are they sad" (*Sūrat al-Yunus* [Chapter of Yunus], 10:62). Just as human friendship is reciprocal, so, too, is the *walī's* relationship with God.

Both Shi'i and Sunni commentators agree that some Qur'anic verses refer to 'Ali's sainthood: "Your friends are God, His Messenger, and the Believers. . . . As to those who turn in friendship to God, His Messenger, and the Believers, it is the party of God that must certainly triumph" (*Sūrat al-Mā'ida* [Chapter of the Table Spread], 5:55–56). In Shi'i theology, *walāyah*, the inimitable quality with which God endowed 'Ali and all of the twelve Imams, is the esoteric corollary to Muhammad's exoteric prophecy and messengership. Imamate and *walāyah* interpenetrate one another, as the Qur'an and *ḥadīth* explain. One scriptural reference to God's creation of an inner and outer meaning of leadership, sanctity, and revelation can be found in the *Sūrat al-Najm* (Chapter of the Star), in which God approaches the Prophet Muhammad in the heavens within a "distance of but two bow's lengths" (53:9). Muhammad describes to 'Ali what he saw during his journey to heaven, especially the signs of their complementary roles as divinely selected guides to humanity: God tells Muhammad, "I wrote thy Name and his Name on my Throne before creating the creatures because of my love of you both. Whoever loves you and takes you as friends numbers among those drawn nigh to Me. Whoever rejects your *walāyah* and separates himself from you numbers among the impious transgressors against Me."[39] Whoever rejects the guardianship and spiritual authority of 'Ali also rejects the Prophet Muhammad and ultimately God. God has selected specific individuals to possess the esoteric quality of transcendent sainthood (*walāyah*), and the individual bears responsibility for accepting the leadership of the Imams, who are the guides to humanity and the possessors of hidden, initiatic knowledge of the Qur'an.

The Qur'an and *ḥadīth* are the foundational sources for the basic conception of Muslim sainthood, although Sufi scholars have produced some of the most sophisticated theories of *walāyah* and *wilāyah*. The theoretical development of the doctrine of sainthood is most clearly elaborated in Andalusian Sufi scholar Muhyi al-Din Ibn al-ʿArabi's *Fuṣūṣ al-ḥikām* (The Bezels of Wisdom), although he was not the first scholar to elaborate such a theory. In the ninth century, preceding Ibn al-ʿArabi, al-Hakim al-Tirmidhi, a Persian Sufi, developed the first theoretical articulation of the concept of *walāyah*.[40] Al-Tirmidhi was born into a family of religious scholars—his father was a *ḥadīth* specialist—and was trained as a legal scholar (*faqīh*). In his autobiography, al-Tirmidhi recounts that he began studying the religious sciences at age eight and continued his study until he was twenty-seven, when he set off for Mecca to further his spiritual development.[41] Returning home, al-Tirmidhi endeavored to memorize the Qur'an, and from this experience he began reading widely, although apparently without a teacher to guide him. Consequently, al-Tirmidhi recalls in his autobiography that he was "now bewildered (*mutaḥayyir*) and I did not know what was required of me—except that I did begin to undertake fasting and ritual prayer" intensively.[42] Drawing ever more into meditative seclusion (*khalwah*), al-Tirmidhi began to have a series of dreams in which he saw God and the Prophet Muhammad and received knowledge of the meaning of *walāyah*. Both al-Tirmidhi and his wife received these divinely inspired dreams.[43] In fact, more than half of al-Tirmidhi's brief autobiography contains reports about his wife's dreams in which the two encounter the Prophet Muhammad or God. That al-Tirmidhi's wife was the conduit for so many instructive dreams about sainthood is significant, for it provides us with an insight into the central role of women and the feminine in the theory and praxis of sainthood.

Whereas the dreams of al-Tirmidhi's wife influenced his theoretical conception of sainthood, his scholarship clearly shaped the thought and writings of Ibn al-ʿArabi. In his *Sīrat al-awliyā* (Lives of the Friends of God), al-Tirmidhi expostulates a theory of transcendent sainthood (*walāyah*) in relation to the institutions of prophecy (*nubūwwah*) and messengership (*risālah*). One day, a student asked al-Tirmidhi to describe the supreme individual who is the Seal of the Saints (*khātim al-awliyā*). In a lengthy discourse, al-Tirmidhi explained that God has made prophecy a public calling, whereas the Seal of the Saints is special because his knowledge is hidden from the rest of humanity:

> Know that God has chosen prophets and Friends from among His servants, and He has given preference to certain prophets over others. There is he whom God has favored with friendship (*khulla*) [Abraham] and he whom God has favored with direct speech (*kalām*) [Moses]. One He has allowed to praise Him and that refers to the Psalms [of David]. Another He has allowed to raise the dead [Jesus] and to another He has given life of the heart so that he does not commit a sin and does not even think of sin [Muhammad]. And in this manner he has favored certain Friends of God above others. Upon Muhammad he has bestowed special honors such as He has not given anyone else amongst mankind. There are things from this special status, which are hidden from men at large, except God's chosen few, and there are things, which everyone else necessarily knows.[44]

God has bestowed special favors (friendship, speech, the ability to raise the dead) on special prophets and has endowed saints with divinely inspired esoteric knowledge. The Prophet Muhammad is a special figure in this divine hierarchy because he is the Seal of Prophecy (*khatm al-nubūwwah*): "God gathered the whole of prophethood together in Muhammad. He made his heart into a vessel for perfected prophethood and put a seal on it. . . . God did not conceal that proof [the seal] in the interior of the Messenger's heart but actually caused it to be apparent."[45]

If Muhammad is the Seal of Prophecy, al-Tirmidhi postulates that there must also exist a Seal of Sainthood—that is, a final guide to humanity who possesses divinely inspired esoteric knowledge that complements the public mission of prophecy. Al-Tirmidhi's theory of the Seal of Sainthood (*khātim al-awliyā*) places distinct emphasis on the superior intercessory power of the saint, who

> possesses completely the seal of Friendship with God. . . . [H]e will be their intercessor as *imām* of the Friends of God. He is their chief, being first among them as Muhammad is first among the prophets. The Station of Intercession (*maqām al-shafā'ah*) will be set up for him and he will praise his Lord with such praise and commend Him with such commendations that the Friends of God will recognize his superiority over them with re-

gard to knowledge of God. . . . The Friend of God was what God thought of first in the primal beginning, and he was the first in His thinking (*dhikr*) and the first in His knowledge (*ʿilm*).[46]

Just as God designated Muhammad as the Seal of Prophecy, the extraordinary qualities possessed by the Seal of Sainthood (*khātim al-awliyā*) must be made manifest to humanity. Unlike prophecy and messengership, which are historical and social institutions albeit divine creations, *walāyah* is preeternal and will extend until the Day of Judgment. Not only did God create the saint in preeternity, but the saint will exist after the Resurrection.

According to the Prophet Muhammad, the saints are "those who when they are seen cause people to think of God."[47] The difference between the saints, on one hand, and prophets and messengers, on the other, is that the former receive and understand supernatural speech from God, whereas the latter simply receive God's word. The divine word is given to prophets and messengers in the form of revelation (*waḥy*), whereas God's supernatural speech is conveyed to the saint in ways that generate love (*maḥabba*) and peace of mind via closeness to God.[48] Being a recipient of and understanding God's supernatural speech (*muḥaddath*) is one of the most important qualities with which the Shiʿi Imam is endowed, an aspect of the Shiʿi notion of inimitable sainthood (*walāyah*) that is discussed in greater detail later in this chapter.

Although we know that Muhammad is the Seal of the Prophets (*khātim al-nabiyyīn*), al-Tirmidhi never identifies the Seal of the Saints. Ibn al-ʿArabi, however, names the Seal of the Saints in *The Bezels of Wisdom*, his twelfth-century treatise on sainthood and prophecy. Ibn al-ʿArabi's theories of sainthood and prophecy are more complex than those of al-Tirmidhi, although his influence on Ibn al-ʿArabi is palpable. As is the case for al-Tirmidhi, dreams play a significant role in the formulation of Ibn al-ʿArabi's theory of sainthood. In the preface to *The Bezels of Wisdom*, Ibn al-ʿArabi reveals that in 1230, the Prophet Muhammad appeared in his dream holding the book that Ibn al-ʿArabi was about to write, a powerful legitimizing symbol of his theory of sainthood.[49]

The Bezels of Wisdom is divided into twenty-seven chapters in which Ibn al-ʿArabi outlines his theory of *walāyah* and its qualities. The first bezel is the "wisdom of divinity in the word of Adam," and the final bezel is "the wisdom of singularity in the word of Muhammad." Although Adam is the first prophet and Muhammad is the last, the other prophets are listed not in chronological order but rather typologically. Ibn al-ʿArabi demonstrates that prophecy (*nubūwwah*) and messengership (*risālah*), while integral offices for delivering God's revelation to humanity, are finite in function, subordinate, and encompassed within *walāyah*.

In Ibn al-ʿArabi's theory of *walāyah*, the station of the Seal of the Saints is the pinnacle of human sainthood. In chapter 14, "The Wisdom of Destiny in the Word of Ezra [ʿUzayr]," Ibn al-ʿArabi posits that "*walāya* is the sphere which encompasses all the other spheres, and for this reason has no end in time."[50] Drawing on al-Tirmidhi's notion of the historical limits of prophecy and messengership, both of which have come to an end on earth, *walāyah* exists beyond eternity. Despite this fact, according to Ibn al-ʿArabi, there is a Seal of Muhammadan Sainthood, who, like the Seal of the Prophets (Muhammad), existed "when Adam was between the water and the clay."[51] Therefore, the existence of the Seal of the Saints is preeternal, "while other saints became saints only when they had acquired all the necessary divine qualities."[52] Whereas Ibn al-ʿArabi likens the Prophet Muhammad to the final clay brick needed to make a wall sturdy, the Seal of the Saints is like two bricks that are far more precious than the brick of the Seal of Prophecy:

> The Seal of the Saints perceived that two bricks were missing. The bricks of the wall were of silver and gold. Since he saw himself as filling the gap, it is the Seal of Saints who is the two bricks and who completes the wall. The reason for his seeing two bricks is that, outwardly, he follows the Law of the Seal of Apostles [Muhammad the messenger], represented by the silver brick. This is his outer aspect and the rules that he adheres to in it. Inwardly, however, he receives directly from God what he appears [outwardly] to follow, because he perceives the divine Command as it is [in its essence], represented by the golden brick.[53]

Ibn al-ʿArabi's allegory elucidates several important points regarding the relationship between and hierarchical ordering of transcendent sainthood and prophecy. First, a clear tension exists between the status of the Seal of the Prophets and the Seal of the Saints. The roles of prophet and messenger are like the earthen brick—utilitarian, necessary, and worldly. One cannot build an entire house from bricks made of precious metals. The refraction of its divine effulgence (*nūr*) is distracting, far too precious, and beyond the scope of the average person's understanding. Certain types of saints are like those precious bricks: few and far between, without imitation, and distinctly otherworldly. The role of the prophet is to deliver God's revelation, and that of the messenger is to implement God's law. To protect and establish theological order, these positions are as functional, this-worldly, and necessary as the earthen brick for building houses.

The Seal of the Saints, conversely, perceives himself not as just a single brick that completes the divine structure but rather as two bricks, one of silver and one of gold. The Seal of the Saints is who he is because he perceives his ontological and theological duality. The silver brick represents the exoteric (*ẓāhir*) *wilāyah* that is "limited and circumscribed, confined within a particular locality or jurisdiction,"[54] as a form of socially recognized and sanctioned imitable sainthood. His exemplary ethical authority (*ṣalāḥ*, or, in the Shiʿi context, *ḥusaini* ethics), symbolized by the silver brick, is recognized and emulated by others: he is a model of being in the world.

The more precious and subtle golden brick represents the esoteric (*bāṭin*) and inimitable aspect of the seal's sainthood (*walāyah*). The seal receives God's supernatural speech (*ḥadīth*), and because the seal possesses supreme initiatic knowledge, God's divine communication is perceived and understood. Perception of the self, God, and law (having knowledge of the hidden meaning of the Qur'an and possessing other books) is the foundation of *walāyah* and the Imamate in Shiʿi tradition. Ibn al-ʿArabi's golden brick radiates the quality of perception, which is saints' ability to recognize and understand that God has chosen them for this special form of friendship and knowledge. In the unfolding of saints' self-knowledge of the fundamental reality of God's unity of being (*waḥdat al-wujūd*), the transcendent, inimitable quality of sainthood is made manifest.

In an act of implicit intertextuality, Ibn al-ʿArabi's vision of the brick dwelling mirrors the account of the Prophet laying the keystone of the Kaʿba. In *The Life of the Messenger of God* (*Sīrat rasūl allah*), Ibn Ishaq tells of the Quraysh tribe's plan to rebuild the Kaʿba in 605 C.E., five years before the Prophet's first revelation. While the Kaʿba was being rebuilt, the different tribes began to debate which one would have the honor of laying the keystone. While the tribesmen bickered, Muhammad arrived, and he was asked to arbitrate the dispute. Muhammad said, "'Give me a cloak,' and when it was brought to him he took the black stone and put it inside it and said that each tribe should take hold of an end of the cloak and they should lift it together. They did this so that when they got it into position he placed it with his own hand, and then building went on above it."[55] This act both foreshadows his prophetic career and reveals his esoteric friendship with God, which had not yet even been made manifest to the future Seal of Prophecy.

More than the eschatological role of the Seal of the Saints, Ibn al-ʿArabi prizes the status of both the saint and the Seal of Sainthood for their mastery of knowledge and annihilation of the self (*nafs*) in God. The saint's identity as the supreme knower (*ʿārif*) makes these figures extraordinary and worthy of an exalted cosmic status. Ibn al-ʿArabi's Seal of Muhammadan Sainthood is an Arab and a Hashemite and most important has "sealed the sainthood which comes from the Muhammadan heritage."[56] Although consanguinity is not a necessity for the Sufi Seal of the Saints, in the context of both imitable and transcendent sainthood in the Shiʿi tradition, blood relationship to the Prophet Muhammad is an absolute requirement.

Theoretical Conceptions of Sainthood in Shiʿism

A close reading of Shiʿi theological and hagiographical literature and close observation of ritual performance in the mourning assembly permits the identification of four features of practical, imitable sainthood (*ḥusainiyyat-wilāyah*). These four indexical features draw on categories and qualities of sainthood preexisting in the Shiʿi theological and devotional tradition and highlight the *ḥusaini* ethic embodied by Imam Husain and his family, which the Shiʿa must cultivate and imitate to realize an idealized selfhood.

At the foundational, structural level, a Shiʿi theory of sainthood is situated within a cosmology of structural complementary pairs, creating a dynamic dimension of sanctity in which inimitable, transcendent sainthood and the Imamate (*imāmah-walāyah*) is balanced by a socioethical, imitable (*ḥusainiyyat-wilāyah*) model of sainthood. These forms of sainthood mirror one another. Second, the exaltation of the martyr is a typology that is amplified in Shiʿi devotionalism, and Imam Husain is the paradigm for this martyrdom trope. Being revered as a martyr in Shiʿism does not necessarily confer saintly status. The third indexical feature of Shiʿi sainthood is based on blood relationship to the Prophet Muhammad. Whether a transcendent saint chosen by God to be an Imam and to serve as a guide to humanity or an imitable saint whose religious and socioethical model is publicly recognized (*wilāyah*) and cultivated by everyday Shiʿa, blood relationship to the *ahl-e bait* is the primary qualification. The fourth indexical feature of imitable sainthood–*ḥusaini* ethics, the sanctity accorded to women and the centrality of the feminine in Shiʿi sainthood, is examined in chapter 2.

Complementary Pairing: Imāmah-Walāyah *and* Ḥusainiyyat-Wilāyah

Imamate-transcendent sainthood and *ḥusaini* ethics–imitable sainthood reflect two complementary aspects of Shiʿi sanctity. The first is abstract and theological and is based on the pairing of the Imamate and transcendent sainthood; the second, which is practical and devotional, centers on the exemplary socioethical and imitable model of Imam Husain's family. These two expressions are characterized by a complex interrelationship. Islamic studies has tended to focus on the high textual traditions of the Qur'an, philosophy, and law, causing the Imamate–transcendent sainthood pairing to obscure the more popular practical, ethical expression of sanctity (*ḥusainiyyat-wilāyah*), yet these theological and practical expressions of sainthood are mutually dependent. Shiʿi devotion to the *ahl-e bait* and particularly to Imam Husain and his family cannot be explained by the doctrine of the Imamate. The hagiographical accounts of the embodiment of *ḥusaini* ethics and imitable sainthood by Imam Husain's family subtly teach everyday Shiʿa the tenets of religious doctrine and law. The *ahl-e bait* do not possess special knowledge of the hidden meaning of the Qur'an, but through their exemplary socioethical and religious model, they bring it to life.

A theory of complementary pairing leads to the idea that for the universe to function properly, all things must have a complement that provides contrast and balance. As Vincent Cornell notes, *walāyah* and *wilāyah* must exist as complements to one another, just as in Taoism, femininity (yin) can only exist alongside masculinity (yang).[57] Masculinity without femininity results in severe disruption of the universe and ultimately leads to its self-destruction.

The principle of this cosmologic balance is perhaps most clearly articulated within Ismaʿili Shiʿism. Ismaʿili cosmology is based on "the divine imperative *kun*, consisting of the letters *kāf* and *nūn*, through duplication formed the two original principles *kūnī kadar*. *Kūnī* was the female and *kadar* was the male principle."[58] From God's command, "Be!" (*Sūrat al-Maryam* [Chapter of Mary], 19:35), both male and female principles mutually and simultaneously came into being on earth. In the first revelation to the Prophet Muhammad, God proclaimed that he had "created humanity out of a clot" of blood (*Sūrat al-ʿAlaq* [Chapter of the Clot], 96:2). The Qur'anic vision of humanity's creation in no way resembles biblical narratives of the masculine creation found in the second chapter of Genesis. From the very first Qur'anic revelation, masculine-feminine symmetry is stressed. Without male-female balance—animal, human, and vegetal—the universe cannot perpetuate itself. Likewise, sainthood in Twelver Shiʿism requires both masculine and feminine spiritual and ethical exemplars.

Islamic theology abounds with examples of complementary pairs, all of which reveal God's preeternal ordering of the universe. Although to know God is supposed to be truly ineffable, the ninety-nine names that God reveals in the Qur'an allow human beings to gain insight into aspects of his essence (*ṣifat*). For some, the designation of attributes by which to describe the ineffable God is in tension with the notion of unity of being (*waḥdat al-wujūd*). How can God be truly unique if distinctly human qualities are ascribed to "him"? Drawing on the Taoist yin-yang principles, Sachiko Murata compares the two qualities of God's being, *al-Jalāl* (the Majestic) and *al-Jamāl* (the Beautiful), as complementary gendered categories.[59] Najm al-Din Kubra (d. 1221), the eponymous founder of the Kubrawiyyah Sufi order, created a gendered taxonomy of God's ninety-nine names in which "the attributes of beauty (*al-ṣifāt al-jamāliyya*) relate to attributes of majesty (*al-ṣifāt al-jalāliyya*) as women relate to men."[60] Although God has been imagined in the popular and theological imagination as male, the divine is composed of equally masculine and feminine qualities: God has forty-nine names (*al-asmā al-ḥusna*) that denote his feminine qualities, including *al-laṭīf* (the kind), *al-wahhāb* (the constant giver), and *al-ṣabūr* (the patient). Examples of his forty-nine masculine qualities include *al-qawī* (the most strong), *al-ḥaṣīb* (the reckoner), and *al-muntaqīm* (the avenger).

God's beautiful and majestic attributes reflect his totality of being, which is mirrored in that which is hidden (*bāṭin*) and that which is manifest (*żāhir*) to humanity. We can gender code God's majestic qualities as masculine and manifest, for he has made his revelation to humanity, and its divine command is to be obeyed. Through the male messengers (*rasūl*) and prophets (*nabī*), God has sent down books of law and clear (*żāhir*) revelation. Complementing the exoteric divine command is the hidden truth (*al-ḥaqq*) of God and his creation, which can be coded as generative and feminine. According to Shiʿi theology, the Imam has a special closeness to God and the ability to perceive and understand the hidden aspects of God's revelation. Although all of the Imams are male, God's beautiful (*jamālī*) qualities can be coded feminine and are perhaps best exemplified in the imitable sainthood of the Prophet Muhammad's daughter, Fatimah al-Zahra.

Prophet-messenger and Imam form a related complementary pair with *żāhir* and *bāṭin*, respectively. In a famous *ḥadīth*, the Prophet Muhammad declared, "I am the City of Wisdom and ʿAli is its threshold."[61] Muhammad is the prophet and messenger who received the Qurʾan as God's clear revelation to the Arabs—that is, he is the giver of the exoteric book and law. Mirroring Muhammad's manifest mission, ʿAli is the Imam endowed with the ability to interpret (*taʾwīl*) the hidden meaning of the scripture. In *Sūrat al-Raʿd* (The Chapter of Thunder), God explains the difference between Muhammad's role as messenger and prophet for the Arabs and ʿAli's ability to interpret the hidden meaning of the Qurʾan (*taʾwīl*): "The Unbelievers say: 'You are not a messenger.' Say: 'God is an adequate witness between you and me and the one who has knowledge of the book'" (13:43). In Shiʿi exegetical traditions (*tafsīr*), ʿAli has the "knowledge of the book." This verse can be further interpreted in concordance with the *ḥadīth* in which Muhammad declared himself the "city of wisdom" and ʿAli its threshold and the guide for humanity. In a popular Shiʿi *ḥadīth*, the Prophet Muhammad declared, "For whomever I am *maulā*, ʿAli is his *maulā*, too." Interpreted from the Shiʿi perspective, the meaning of *maulā* refers to ʿAli's designation by God through Muhammad to be the patron or executor of the divine truth (*al-ḥaqq*). *Maulā* also implies that whoever considers the Prophet Muhammad a friend must also take ʿAli in friendship, as Prophet and Imam complement one another.

The Imamate exists in a direct hierarchical relationship to Muhammad as the Seal of Prophecy (*khātim al-nubūwwah*), and both the Imamate and the Seal of Prophecy existed in the form of divine light (*nūr*) before Creation. According to a tradition attributed to the sixth Imam, Jaʿfar al-Sadiq,

> Two thousand years before creation, Muhammad and ʿAli were one light before God . . . light formed from one main trunk from which sprang a shining ray. . . . And God said: "Here is a light [drawn] from my Light; its trunk is prophecy and its branch is the Imamate; prophecy belongs to Muhammad, my servant and messenger, and the Imamate belongs to ʿAli, my Proof and my Friend. Without them I would have created none of my creation. . . ." This is why ʿAli always said: "I proceed from Muhammad [or from Ahmad] as one clarity proceeds from another."[62]

The Prophet Muhammad is the teacher (*nāṭiq*) of God's exoteric revelation, and ʿAli is the executor (*waṣīy*) authorized to carry out the Prophet's teachings. ʿAli was the first Imam, the threshold of God's revelation, the *ṣāmit* (silent one) initiated into the esoteric meaning of the Qurʾan. The Imams can communicate with all of the more than 122,000 prophets sent by God, and all revelatory scripture "was revealed to us before it was revealed to the people and we commented upon it before it was commented upon by others."[63] Imam Ja'far al-Sadiq's statement, "We are the ones who are deeply-rooted in knowledge and we know its explanation," firmly establishes the connection between the Imamate and transcendent sainthood.

The ability to discern and decipher God's supernatural speech is one of the distinctive qualities of the Shi'i Imams. The Imams maintain a direct connection through the Prophet to God, therefore granting them the ability to perceive the esoteric meaning of the Qur'an in addition to a deeper cosmic understanding of God and the order of the universe. As one endowed with superlative perceptive abilities, the Imam is the *muḥaddath* who can hear but not see the revelatory Angel Gabriel. The Imams do not need to see the angel because they are already initiated and have obtained the deepest spiritual knowledge (*ma'rifah*) of the divine.[64]

Walāyah represents the esoteric (*bāṭin*) realm and has a metaphysical connotation. *Walāyah* is a gift bestowed on selected individuals by God through divine designation (*naṣṣ*). One does not choose to possess *walāyah*, nor can one designate oneself the executor of the Prophet Muhammad's received revelation and law. Only God chooses the Imam, and only a very few have the ability to interpret the hidden meaning of the Qur'an and to receive and understand God's supernatural speech.

God made his choice, and it behooves humans to give their loyalty to the Imams, for they are the proof (*ḥujjat*) of God's totality of being. Muhammad ibn 'Ali ibn al-Husain ibn-e Babawayh al-Qummi, popularly known as Shaykh al-Saduq, a tenth-century Shi'i theologian, writes in *The Beliefs of the Imamis* (*I'tiqādāt al-imāmiyyah*), "Their command is the command of Allah, their prohibition is the prohibition of Allah, and disobedience to them is disobedience to Allah."[65] Muhammad declared to the nascent Muslim community (*ummah*), "He who denies 'Ali his Imamate after me, verily denies my apostleship (*nubuwwa*). And he who denies my apostleship has denied Allah his divinity."[66] For the Shi'a, a true Muslim accepts 'Ali's Imamate and is loyal to the *ḥusaini* ethic.

Dedication to the *ahl-e bait* and the exercise of spiritual power and ethical authority (*wilāyah*) comprises the second of the complementary pairings that order Shi'i theology and devotional life. *Wilāyah* is socially recognized sainthood that provides a model of religiospiritual and socioethical imitability for the saint's devotees. For virtually all Twelver Shi'as, Imam Husain's martyrdom at the Battle of Karbala constructs the foundation of the Shi'i model of imitable sainthood. In the mourning assemblies, the ritualized remembrance of the battle centers on the embodiment of the *ḥusaini* ethic of faith and sacrifice by Imam Husain's family. Shiʿi ritual and devotional life focuses on venerating Imam Husain and his family through the doctrine of *ḥusaini* ethics, which provides a socioethical blueprint that articulates the ideals of Islam through the exemplary sacrifices of the hero(in)es of Karbala. The cultural specificity of *ḥusaini* ethics–imitable sainthood that is articulated in Shiʿi hagiography allows vernacular values, variation in religious practice, political ideology, language, and gender roles to be expressed through this legitimating sacralized modality.

Shiʿi Muslims recognize that their idealized selfhood derives from the model man, exemplified by Imam Husain, and his model family, which sacrificed and suffered with him at Karbala. Imam Husain's family is portrayed, performed, and stereotyped in the mourning assembly as the embodiments of the idealized Muslim. Through *ḥusaini* ethics, a public image of the Karbala hero(in)es is constructed. They are "living" beings who provide compelling models for how to be good Shiʿa.

The members of Husain's family are recognized as the ultimate exemplars of submission to God's will. Lallan Nazmi eloquently describes the kind of role model Imam Husain provides for the Shiʿa: "His lessons on self control, courage, justice, cooperation and world unity are the guidelines for us. He displayed the value of self-respect and honour and established to act well in our life to gain honour and prestige. If we tread his path, the welfare of society and community and the world at large is guaranteed. Imam Husain displayed noble qualities of heart and mind. He offered water to his dying foes but never used it as a weapon of victory. His noble qualities brought more than a dozen (fourteen) of his deadly foes from the Yazidian forces to his ranks."[67] Although he does not use the word, Nazmi defines *ḥusaini* ethics. Imam Husain and his family are ethical exemplars because even as he suffered, a commitment to the well-being of others took precedence over his family's thirst. Pakistani philosopher-poet Muhammad Iqbal similarly defines *ḥusaini* ethics as the Islam that "preaches justice, truth, fraternity, peace and social welfare."[68] *Ḥusaini* ethics is based on a commitment to justice (*ʿadālah*), the foundational tenet of Shiʿi theology. Imam Husain and his family are models of courage. They traveled to Kufah despite knowing the inevitability of their suffering and death.

Hyderabadi Shiʿa frequently debate whether Imam Husain knew before setting off for Kufah that he would be martyred at Karbala and why he did not seek divine intervention. Dr. Sadiq Naqvi, a retired professor of Persian history and literature at Osmania University and a popular *majlis* orator (*ẕākir*), explained that "the Imam's knowledge [*ʿilm*] is not complete without having knowledge of all that has happened from before Creation until the Day of the Resurrection [*yawm al-ḥashr*]. Therefore, if any Imam doesn't know that something is about to happen, then he is no different from any other human being." While Naqvi used the term *ʿilm* to refer to the special esoteric (*bāṭin*) knowledge possessed by the Imams, Husain differs from his family members because of his embodiment of *imāmah-walāyah*. In his discourse on Imam Husain's knowledge of his martyrdom, Naqvi provided several reasons why Imam Husain could not ask for God's intervention. First, prophets and Imams do not seek God's intercession. God's divinely imposed challenges must be accepted as tests of strength, faith, and resolve. Second, "when an Imam or prophet (*nabī*) asks for help, every creature in the world must reply." Finally, speaking from a more hagiographical perspective, Naqvi said that when the *jinn* asked Husain whether he wanted God's intervention, Husain's infant son, ʿAli Asghar, fell out of his cradle prepared to fight. Even this six-month-old baby embodied the *ḥusaini* ethic.[69]

Complementary to the doctrine of *ḥusaini* ethics, imitable sainthood functions as a manifest spiritual closeness to God. A late-thirteenth-century Iranian Sufi, ʿAla al-Dawla al-Simnani (d. 1336), argues that *wilāyah* is distinct from *walāyah*, which represents prophecy and by extension the Imamate.[70] Simnani's theory of the divinity (*ulūhiyyat*) and its emanations (*fayd*) connects *wilāyah* to the earth and to humankind.[71] *Wilāyah* is the exoteric manifestation of one's spiritual perfection and gnosis and is imitable. Imam Husain is endowed with both *walāyah* and *wilāyah*, although the following chapters demonstrate the points of rupture in his imitability and transcendence (see table 1).

Through the doctrine of *ḥusaini* ethics, everyday Shiʿa can cultivate the spiritual and moral perfection of Husain's family into an idealized selfhood. Shiʿi devotional life depends on *ḥusainiyyat-wilāyah*. At first glance, the model set forth by the prophets and Imams seems to be the source of imitation and the guide for proper religiosity, but otherworldly, transcendent sainthood does not constitute the imitable model; rather, that model is embodied by Imam Husain's family through the *ḥusaini* ethic. These pairs complement and are integral to one another. Imam Husain's family members are real people because they are not Imams, although they possess the necessary consanguinity to mark them as special saints. In Shiʿi collective memory, Imam Husain's family members are simultaneously portrayed as very human

Table 1. Complementary Pairing of *Imāmah-Walāyah* and *Ḥusainiyyat-Wilāyah*

Imāmah-Walāyah	Ḥusainiyyat-Wilāyah
God chosen, involuntary (not dependent on social recognition)	God-chosen, situational, socially ordered
Theological dimension	Socioethical dimension
Abstract, theological	Imitable, practical, social-ethical
Esoteric (*bāṭin*)	Exoteric (*żāhir*)
Consanguinity through Fatimah Zahra (matrilineal aspect). Status based on *naṣṣ* (divine designation)	Consanguinity through the Prophet Muhammad (patrilineal aspect)

people and as paragons of ethical and religious being in the world. In terms of the ideal types that each member of Imam Husain's family exemplifies (bride, widow, warrior, sacrificing baby, loyal sister), these hero(in)es are constructed to embody vernacular values that are culturally relevant to the Shiʿa of Hyderabad. Hyderabadi Shiʿa can identify with these people, and their personalities and experiences remind the Shiʿa of themselves and their families. They love, they feel anger, and they suffer as human beings, albeit of an extraordinary kind. The stories of the hero(in)es of Karbala shape people's everyday lives. The Shiʿa of Hyderabad have integrated into their everyday practice Jaʿfar al-Sadiq's injunction to live as though "every day is *ʿāshūrā* and every place is Karbala."

Witnessing and Faith in God: Martyrdom in Shiʿi Sainthood

Less than fifty years after the death of the Prophet Muhammad in 632 C.E., the Battle of Karbala created a vividly dramatic and horrifying story that in many regards has exhausted the need for an extensive corpus of martyr saints in the Shiʿi tradition. Virtually all of the martyrs venerated by the Shiʿa are either members of Imam Husain's family or Imams. The *ḥusaini* ethic of Imam Husain and his family is "the emotional mainspring of the Shiʿah religious experience" and does not require any further expansion of the saintly canon.[72]

Martyrdom is an important typological manifestation of the socioethical dimension of imitable sainthood. One's willingness to sacrifice life as proof of one's submission to and faith in God is exemplified by the hero(in)es of

Karbala. The impossibility of Husain's military victory over Yazid's tyranny (*żulm*) and the fear that Islam was rapidly degrading is amplified in the hagiographical narratives, which dramatically claim that the size of Yazid's army ranged from two thousand horsemen and foot soldiers to upward of one hundred thousand warriors. Husain could never win such a battle, but he nonetheless struggled to shock the early Muslim community into recognizing how quickly the ideals of the Prophet Muhammad had been abandoned in the pursuit of wealth and power (*ṭāghūt*). For the Shiʿa, the Battle of Karbala draws this perceived degradation of religion into dramatic relief. Hagiographical narratives emphasize that Imam Husain and his family had to sacrifice their lives to preserve Islam and those who survived the battle. Martyrdom (*shahādat*) does not, however, automatically confer sainthood in Shiʿi theological and hagiographical traditions. Over the past fourteen hundred years, countless Shiʿa have attained martyrdom, earning the epithet *shahīd*, but this does not mean that they are recognized as friends of God. The doctrine of *ḥusaini* ethics has established an extraordinary standard for recognition as a martyr saint.

For the Love of the Family: Ḥusaini Ethics, Consanguinity, and Sainthood

Textual evidence of Shiʿi theological and hagiographical traditions indicates that consanguinity is the most important requirement in the manifestation and recognition of imitable sainthood in Shiʿism. Direct blood relationship to the Prophet Muhammad through his daughter, Fatimah al-Zahra, is the foundation of sanctity in both Shiʿi theology and devotional practice. Who actually belongs to the *ahl-e bait* is a matter of debate. Most Sunni scholars and theologians include all of the Prophet's wives and some other family members. Some Shiʿa, however, look to the *ḥadīth* of the People of the Cloak (*ahl-e kisāʾ*) as the criterion for inclusion in the *ahl-e bait*, which is limited to the *panjetan-e pāk* (the Five Holy Ones): the Prophet Muhammad, Fatimah al-Zahra, ʿAli, Hasan, and Husain. Other Shiʿa identify the *ahl-e bait* as the Fourteen Infallibles (*chārdah maʿṣūmīn*): the Prophet Muhammad, Fatimah, and the twelve Imams. Yet others are more inclusive with regard to the *ahl-e bait*. When asked, Shiʿa typically identify many of the extended family members (siblings, children) of the Imams as members of the *ahl-e bait*. The literature and performances that invoke the memory of Karbala are dedicated to all of the members of the Prophet's family descended through his daughter, Fatimah, and her husband, ʿAli, because the daughters, wives, sons, and other relatives of Imam Husain embody the ethical and spiritual authority of *ḥusaini* ethics–imitable sainthood.

The Shiʿa believe that one must feel *wilā*, the fidelity of love (*maḥabbat*) and closeness (*qarāba*) for Prophet's family.[73] The bonds of love and affection connect a family, and the doctrine of *ḥusaini* ethics compels the Shiʿa to imitate the socioethical and spiritual model of this exemplary family. Hyderabadi poet Jenab Shah Nawaz's *nauḥa* (short, rhyming Karbala poem) declares love for Imam Husain's family:

> We are the people of Haidar and will abide in every age
> In every era, Husain, we will celebrate your grief
> It isn't easy to cease in remembering Husain, o "Nawaz."[74]

In the first line of the poem, "Shah Nawaz," a professional reciter and composer of Karbala poems (*nauḥa-khwān*), declares his identity as *ḥaidarī* ("the people of Haidar," an epithet for ʿAli, referring to the Shiʿa); he declares his love for Imam Husain in subsequent lines, in which he confirms that all Shiʿa share in the sacrifice and suffering of Karbala. Nawaz cannot forget Imam Husain and promises that the Shiʿa will always remember Karbala as an affirmation of their love for him and his family. Nawaz yearns to participate in the *ḥusaini* ethic, and his poem calls on Hyderabadi Shiʿa to seek justice and to nurture their faith in Islam.

The necessity and virtue of love for the *ahl-e bait* is a requisite topic in Urdu Shiʿi hagiographies. Many of these works engage a variety of authoritative sources such as the Qurʾan and its scholarly interpretation (*tafsīr*), *ḥadīth*, history, and hagiography. While many of the sources employed by these hagiographers were originally written in the cosmopolitan Islamicate languages of Arabic and Persian, much care is taken to make these texts accessible to everyday Hyderabadi Shiʿa. Through translations, everyday Shiʿa can participate in the power and authority vested in the Arabic text while reading and understanding the Urdu translation. In such hagiographical works, the sacred proof texts connect devotees to the distant places of Karbala, Mecca, and Medina, while rendering the texts into vernacular languages and idioms reinforces the emotional bond and fidelity that people feel for the Prophet Muhammad and his family.

The *ahl-e bait* serves as a form of shorthand for the Prophet Muhammad, his daughter, all of the Imams, and by extension all of their progeny (fig. 1). *Ḥusaini* ethics is a central theme in hagiographical Karbala narratives that is constantly repeated and thus embedded in Shiʿi collective memory and

Figure 1. Lithograph of the Panjetan-e Pāk *(the Holy Five): the Prophet Muhammad, Imam Hasan, Imam ʿAli, Imam Husain, and Fatimah al-Zahra. The Angel Gabriel is in the background. Photograph taken at the Khilwat* ʿāshūrkhāna *near Charminar in Hyderabad's Old City. Khilwat belonged to the Nizams and has been closed to the public for several decades. Located near the Charminar bus stand, the seven Khilwat* ʿāshūrkhānas *are a haven in the midst of the chaos of the Old City's main shopping and transportation area.*

is dramatically brought to life through the ritualized embodiment of the suffering of the members of Husain's family. Their socioethical authority provides a model for how to live the best life possible within the limits of religion and vernacular social norms. This profusion of hagiographical literature indicates the extreme importance of a shared lineage through the Prophet Muhammad and Fatimah al-Zahra.

The Shiʿa consider Imam Husain's family members to be saints, or the profusion of ritual events commemorating their lives and deaths would not exist and the plethora of sacred spaces and objects would not constitute an important, even central aspect of Shiʿi sainthood and spirituality. All of the major Shiʿi shrines worldwide are dedicated to the hero(in)es of Karbala, the Imams, and their relatives. The Shiʿa make pilgrimages to the tombs not only of the Imams but also of Imam Husain's daughter, Sakinah (Damascus, Syria), and the sister and brother of the eighth Imam, Reza (Fatimah Maʿsumeh in Qom, the second holiest shrine in Iran, and Shah Abul ʿAzim in Reyy). The distinguishing quality of Shiʿi imitable sainthood is the charisma that is established by blood descent from the Prophet Muhammad. Max Weber defines charisma as "a certain quality of an individual personality by virtue of which he is set apart from ordinary men and treated as endowed with supernatural, superhuman, or at least specifically exceptional qualities."[75] The embodiment of the *ḥusaini* ethic by Imam Husain's family and their absolute faith in Islam and exemplary fulfillment of the obligations of religion are exceptional qualities. This type of charisma is contagious in that direct lineal descent from the Prophet Muhammad, Fatimah, and ʿAli imbues Shiʿi imitable saints with idealized qualities that place them above the norm. Blood matters.

In fact, blood matters so much that whatever exemplary spiritual or socio-ethical qualities they may possess, those who are not directly related to the Prophet are simply excluded from the exceptional family of Shiʿi sainthood unless a fictive blood relationship is established. Direct blood relationship is an absolute requirement for the transcendent sainthood of the Imams and requires no further discussion. To illustrate the premium placed on consanguinity in Shiʿi sainthood, I offer the example of Salman Farsi's induction into the *ahl-e bait* through the establishment of a fictive blood relationship to the Prophet Muhammad and ʿAli. The second example draws on the requirement of blood relationship to the *ahl-e bait* in the Shiʿi martyr saint typology and the death at the Battle of Karbala of a young bridegroom, Wahab.

One of the Prophet's closest companions was a slave, Salman al-Farsi (the Persian), who purchased his freedom after converting to Islam. He is revered as the first Persian to convert to Islam, and according to hagiographical traditions, Salman foretold of Iran's mass conversion to Islam. Salman is famous in early Islamic history for his strategic plan to dig a trench (*khandaq*) around Medina in one of the many battles the Muslim community fought and won against the Meccans in the 620s. Following the Battle of the Trench (627 C.E.), Muhammad established a fictive blood relationship with Salman by declaring, "Salman is one of us, we, who are the people of the House."[76] With regard to Salman's membership in the *ahl-e bait*, ʿAli also attests to Salman's special charismatic status: "Salman is a member of our family, where can one find someone like Salman who is like the Wise Luqman?"[77] Such repetitive statements erased the lack of true blood descent between Salman and the Prophet's *ahl-e bait* so that he became one of them and assumed the qualities of imitable sainthood. Beginning in the tenth century, a cult of sainthood developed around Salman's tomb, which became an important site of pilgrimage in Mada'in, Iraq; Shiʿi pilgrims to Karbala include this holy place on their spiritual itineraries.

In the example of Wahab's martyrdom, the emphasis placed on blood relationship is brought into vivid relief in Kashefi's *Rowẓat al-shohadā*, which contains a martyrdom narrative that remarkably parallels the hagiographical account of the bridegroom/warrior Qasem.[78] The small band of Shiʿa loyal to Imam Husain included an Iranian youth, Wahab ibn ʿAbdallah al-Kalbi, who was accompanied by his new wife and mother and was martyred on the battlefield; his wife was the only woman martyred at the Battle of Karbala.[79] I first learned of Wahab and his martyrdom from Kashefi's Karbala narrative, but Kashefi's treatment of this bridegroom/warrior is distinctly unhagiographical. Why is Wahab's martyrdom obscured? Why do the majority of *majlis* orators not make Wahab the subject of their discourses, especially since his story so strikingly resembles Qasem's?

Wahab is inconsequential because he lacks the necessary blood relationship to Imam Husain. Despite being a martyr, Wahab lacks blood descent from the Prophet Muhammad and unlike Qasem does not embody the *ḥusaini* ethic: Wahab does not fully understand that Imam Husain and his family are fighting to save Islam. Wahab is an outsider from Biʿr Jud in Iran without even Arab blood coursing through his veins. A comparison to Ghazi Miyan, whose sainthood is not predicated on a charismatic blood relationship to the Prophet Muhammad, makes even more obvious Wahab's lack of the necessary qualities of Shiʿi sainthood. Muslims recognize Ghazi Miyan, a Sunni, as a warrior for his faith who sacrificed his life for God and venerate him as a saint.

Kashefi's account of Wahab's martyrdom demonstrates the rules determining who can be an imitable saint in the Shiʿi tradition. If they have ever heard of Wahab, most Shiʿa will acknowledge his status as a martyr, but they do not venerate him and call him a saint. Wahab's lack of the Prophet's charismatic blood coursing through his veins causes him to have doubts about the true meaning of his sacrifice at the Battle of Karbala. Wahab's doubts about the battle and the deal making that takes place among himself, his mother, and new bride dramatically prove that he does not embody the *ḥusaini* ethic. Much of the narrative centers on Wahab's entreaties to his wife, who is initially chagrined that her new husband is willing to sacrifice himself for the Imam's cause and thus reap the rewards of paradise. Wahab's story is remarkably similar to Qasem's, but Kashefi treats the latter with the utmost respect and writes of his martyrdom with pathos and sensitivity, whereas the account of the former is more dispassionate and emphasizes the human pettiness of fear and self-interest. Without the *ḥusaini* ethic and the charismatic blood of the Prophet's family, Wahab can be nothing more than a martyr.

A true martyr does not seek out martyrdom. There is little concern for the eschatological results of martyrdom. The single goal for a true martyr at Karbala is to protect the faith and the family of Imam Husain. After granting her young sons, ʿAun and Muhammad, permission to go into battle and face certain death, Imam Husain's sister, Zainab, is moved by the boys' heartfelt gratitude for her pragmatism and commitment to justice and faith. Thanking his mother, ʿAun says, "Mother, we both feel so elated to know that we have your permission to fight in defense of our uncle and his family. . . . We shall offer such a fight tomorrow that, whenever you will remember us and mourn for us, your grief will be mingled with pride that we lived up to the reputation of our family."[80] More important to these boys than the drama of battlefield heroics is their moral commitment to protecting their family and faith. Shiʿi hagiographical narratives emphatically assert that none of the mothers at Karbala wanted their young sons to enter into battle and die, but how could they not fulfill the *ḥusaini* ethic that is inextricably linked to their imitable sainthood? To preserve the lineage of Fatimah al-Zahra and the vision of a true Islam, the sons must die, and the mothers must survive the Battle of Karbala and keep its memory alive. Rather than looking forward to the rewards of paradise, the martyrs and female survivors of Imam Husain's family seek to preserve the holiness of their family and Muhammad's original message of Islam. The women of the *ahl-e bait* are crucial in the propagation of *ḥusaini* ethics–imitable sainthood. Chapter 2 incorporates the role of women and the feminine into our stipulative definition of Shiʿi sainthood.

chapter two

God's Strong Women

FEMALE & FEMININE IN SHIʿI SAINTHOOD

Those who left
Committed a Husaynic act;
Those who remained
Must perform a Zaynabic act;
Otherwise, they are Yazidic.
—ʿAli Shariʿati

I met Sabiha Asghar in February 2005, during the days leading up to Muharram. Asghar is the principal of the Solar School, an English-medium institution located in Hyderabad's Old City. She is also the daughter of Sayyid Maulana Reza Agha, Hyderabad's most senior Shiʿi religious scholar and a popular *majlis* orator (*ẕākir*). I met with Asghar on several occasions to learn more about the meaning of the *mehndī* mourning assembly and other votive rituals dedicated to Qasem and Fatimah Kubra as well as to ascertain people's understanding of Fatimah Kubra's role and meaning in the embodiment of *ḥusaini* ethics–imitable sainthood. In particular, I wondered how Hyderabadi Shiʿa look to figures such as Fatimah Kubra as socioethical exemplars and models of piety and faith.

Asghar sits behind her desk in a large, open room. Her hair is neatly covered, and she has a youthful, inquisitive, and businesslike air. Her large desk is the focal point, and the room is readily accessible through several doorways that are covered only by curtains. The atmosphere is informal, and a steady stream of mothers enters the office, seeking admission for their children and perhaps a reduction in the already low school fees. In between visits from the petitioning mothers and their children, Asghar and I spoke at length about the upcoming *mehndī* mourning assembly on 7 Muharram. By her reckoning, more than one hundred *mehndī* mourning assemblies take place at large and small *ʿāshūrkhānas* throughout the city. Many Hyderabadis believe that 7 Muharram is a particularly auspicious day to make a votive request (*mannat*) to the many metal battle standards (*ʿalam*) dedicated to Qasem. Asghar explained that not all requests are related to matrimony; however, most of the offerings presented to the Qasem *ʿalams* are wedding clothing and jewelry: *sāṛīs*, bangles, *shalwār-qamīẓ*, and perfumes (*ʿiṭr*).[1] Devotees certainly seek Qasem and Fatimah Kubra's intercession and grace (*baraka*) in financial, health, and other personal matters, but supernatural assistance in arranging good marriage alliances is the primary concern for most Hyderabadi Shiʿa on 7 Muharram. The Shiʿa believe that their wishes and desires will be fulfilled for two reasons. Marriage is an especially auspicious event, and the refusal to grant any request that is made in good faith is a sign of poor hospitality. More important, Fatimah Kubra and Qasem are saints, idealized Muslims imbued with the Prophet Muhammad's charismatic blood, and they (and their family members) are empowered to serve as intermediaries with God. The material dimension of these offerings to the Qasem *ʿalam* possesses potent symbolic power that connects the everyday life of the Shiʿa of Hyderabad with the socioethical and religious model embodied through the *ḥusaini* ethics–imitable sainthood of Imam Husain and his family. Fatimah Kubra's embodiment of *ḥusaini* ethics–imitable sainthood in her role as the bride/widow of Karbala serves as a powerful role model for the male and female devotees of Hyderabad. Through such votive acts as smearing henna paste on their right palms and making offerings of the brilliant red cloth (*bībī Kubrā kī sohā*) worn by brides on their wedding day, Hyderabadi Shiʿa ascribe vernacular feminine ideals of wifehood and widowhood onto Fatimah Kubra's body and venerate and seek guidance in her absolute faith and submission to God.

I interviewed Asghar several times over a period of three months and learned much about her spiritual and personal life. Asghar makes little distinction between the personal and the spiritual: her everyday practice fully integrates the socioethical and religious lessons that she has heard all her life in the mourning assembly. During our first meeting, I asked Asghar about what it means to be a wife and a widow in the Shiʿi culture of Hyderabad. Asghar's mother inculcated in her daughter an idealized vernacular, Hyderabadi femininity authenticated by the example of the women of the *ahl-e bait*. While Asghar's mother encouraged her daughter to be socially engaged, like Zainab; to get an education; and to have a job, she also taught Asghar to cultivate Fatimah Kubra's vernacular ethic of wifely sacrifice for her husband. Asghar accepts the Qur'anic imperative that all men and women must marry and believes that Qasem and Fatimah Kubra's sacrificial wedding establishes a compelling socioethical example, powerful lessons learned in both the domestic space of the home and the sacred realm of the mourning assembly.

As Asghar was growing up, her mother taught her to cultivate the Islamic and vernacular feminine ideals of piety, loyalty to husband and family, and service to the community. One of the most important and most often repeated lessons emphasized the ethic of wifely sacrifice. Asghar's mother frequently declared that as long as a woman's husband is alive, her life is bright and meaningful. When a man dies, life loses its luster for his widow. Asghar has fully internalized her mother's maxim, which reflects a belief held by many Hyderabadis: "The wife who dies before her husband is very lucky."[2] I found it difficult to interpret this powerful statement as something other than patriarchal socioreligious subordination of women through the erasure of a woman's autonomous self into her husband, but Asghar does not believe that such aphorisms can be reduced to proof of patriarchal domination. Rather, she explained that women should make such prayers and that these types of formulaic declarations compel Shiʿi women and men to remember Fatimah Kubra's willingness to marry Qasem on the battlefield and her understanding of the necessity of sacrificing her bridegroom's life for the preservation of faith and family. I was startled to hear Asghar's beliefs about women aspiring to be like the widow Fatimah Kubra. After my first meeting with Asghar, I struggled to understand why women cultivate an ethic of wifely sacrifice as an act of faith and embodiment of vernacular gender ideals.

In my next two meetings with Asghar, I returned to the question of how Fatimah Kubra is an exceptional person in terms of both her faith and the exemplary *ḥusaini* ethic of sacrifice. I wanted to understand how Asghar's personal experiences and religious practice intersect with her integration of the *ḥusaini* ethics–imitable sainthood of the *ahl-e bait* into her everyday life as a wife and professional. How do the example of the women of the *ahl-e bait*, portrayed by their hagiographers not only as socially engaged women fighting for social justice and Islam but also as mothers, sisters, wives, and daughters, create space for Hyderabadi Shiʿi women to fully participate in the family and to engage in religious and professional activities? The religious and socioethical model of the women of the *ahl-e bait* provides a powerful legitimating model for Shiʿi women to contribute to society through religious, educational, social service, and legal professions. At the same time, the women of the *ahl-e bait* fully participated in family life and roles, and their model compels Shiʿi women to be good wives, daughters, mothers, and sisters.

Like Fatimah Kubra, Asghar is married to her first cousin. The many pre-wedding rituals in which Asghar participated included the recitation of special hagiographical poems of mourning extolling Fatimah Kubra and Qasem's *ḥusaini* ethic of sacrifice and love for each other, for their families, and for God. During one of the ritual events, a *marśiya* (narrative hagiographical poem) dedicated to Qasem and Fatimah Kubra was recited, deeply affecting Asghar. Although she may have felt nervous about beginning this new married phase of her life, Asghar prayed for Fatimah Kubra and Qasem's intercession with God to ensure that she would have a happy marriage to a good husband. Remembering Fatimah Kubra and Qasem also provided strength and courage, for Asghar was only getting married, not facing war and the slaughter of her family. Asghar believes that this exceptional couple has interceded, helping her to have a happy, fulfilling marriage: "It is by the grace of God that this marriage has taken place. I pray that I will be happy with my husband always."[3] Asghar feels blessed by the spiritual power and protection of Qasem and Fatimah Kubra, and her daily practice of mirroring their model of faith and the *ḥusaini* ethic makes her feel grateful for what she has, and she is prepared and willing to confront future challenges.

In South Asia, marriage has traditionally been arranged and socially compulsory, and it is a life-cycle ritual that is fraught with tension. Islamic law gives women the right to refuse potential marriage partners, and women ideally must consent to marry the men their families select. In reality, however, many women lack the right of refusal, although such is not necessarily the case in the Hyderabadi Shiʿi community. There, most of the women and men that I met had arranged marriages but had actively acquiesced to the selection of their spouses. According to Asghar, "Nowadays, it is becoming increasingly difficult for parents to arrange marriages. Girls are different now, and they are more prepared to be out in the world. They have their own expectations about the kind of husband they desire. They want to know the kind of man they will be marrying, and many girls are refusing the choices made by their parents."[4] Many women have careers and want to know whether potential husbands will force them to quit working after marriage and remain in the home. In fact, many women stipulate in their marriage contracts (*ʿaqd-e nikāḥ*) that they will be free to divorce their husbands if they refuse to permit their wives to work outside the home. Men possess a unilateral right to divorce according to Islamic law. The criteria according to which women may sue their husbands for divorce are limited, and the violation of conditions included in marriage contracts may theoretically allow women to obtain divorces. The freedom to work and travel outside of the home is an important aspect of Asghar's marriage as well as a reflection of her family history, which is validated by the model established by the women of the *ahl-e bait*'s social engagement in the public sphere.

Asghar's mother always wanted to be a schoolteacher, though she could never achieve that goal. When Asghar's mother was a young wife, working outside the home was seen as a sign of poverty and a husband's inability to provide for his family. Moreover, Asghar's mother bore four children and was a member of a joint family, and the responsibilities of raising children and maintaining the household made it impossible for her seriously to contemplate a career outside the home. Now, however, increasing numbers of Hyderabadi women are coming out of *purdah* and holding professional jobs, and Asghar's mother encouraged her daughter to pursue her educational and professional dreams, saying, "It was my desire to run a school. Now, that talent is in you." Asghar married during her first year of college, when she was twenty years old, and soon had a son. Her mother looked after the baby while Asghar was in school and studying. She obtained her bachelor's degree in education, and in 1995, she went with her husband to Saudi Arabia. She stayed for only one year because she felt stifled, unable to leave the house alone or go anywhere or do anything without a male chaperone. To remain in *purdah* behind closed doors prevented Asghar from cultivating a complete, idealized Shiʿi selfhood modeled on *ḥusaini* ethics–imitable sainthood, which requires active engagement with self, family, faith, and society.

Shiʿism has a deep tradition of women whose public lives are committed to the doctrine of justice (*ʿadālah*) and social service to build a better society. The powerful model of the women of the *ahl-e bait* as embodiments of *ḥusaini* ethics–imitable sainthood supports this tradition and in fact compels women's active contribution to society. The socially sanctioned desire to emulate the women of the Prophet Muhammad's family (especially Fatimah and Zainab) creates a dynamic space in the public sphere for women to cultivate idealized feminine selves and to participate in the public sphere.

In this chapter, I take the example of two women of the Prophet Muhammad's household, his daughter, Fatimah al-Zahra, and his granddaughter, Zainab. Shiʿi women and men particularly revere these figures for their piety and dedication to their family and society, which is manifested primarily through their embodiment of *ḥusaini* ethics–imitable sainthood. In addition to her this-worldly sanctity, Fatimah is endowed with a special feminine form of transcendent sainthood. Fatimah al-Zahra is revered as one of the most holy of Muslim women. The Shiʿa believe that God entrusted Zainab with the responsibility of being the messenger of martyrdom after the Battle of Karbala. Zainab's hagiographers portray her as a spiritual and socioethical exemplar, whose bravery and willingness to sacrifice everything for the sake of religion and justice are admired and emulated by both Shiʿi men and women. Fatimah and Zainab uphold the notion of justice, a central concept in Shiʿi social and religious life. Their intense engagement with religious and social matters in the public sphere compels many Shiʿi women to work for the betterment of society and to cultivate an idealized selfhood based on a Hyderabadi vernacular cultural model.

(De-)Sexing the Saintly Body

Christian and Sufi traditions of female sainthood are founded on transvestic acts and behaviors. Christian hagiographies narrating the lives of female saints are "expressed in terms of physical, male power; it is the attainment of a victory in a drawn-out contest in which the female participants assume the characteristics associated with male fighters."[5] Likewise, hagiographical traditions extol the spiritual mastery and virtues of female Sufi saints, whose exemplary piety places them in the category of "women who achieved the status of men."[6] One North Indian Chishti Sufi, Farid al-Din Ganj-e Shakar (d. 1265 C.E.), described the female saint's spiritual mastery as proving that she is a "man sent in the form of a woman."[7] Nevertheless, female Sufi saints are relegated to the appendixes of biographical dictionaries of saints (*taẕkirat al-awliyā*). Attaining spiritual feats that are coded as masculine denies women the potential to attain sainthood in a specifically female gendered body.

Some Muslim women certainly have lived lives of extraordinary piety and spiritual rigor yet are recognized as saints only when they erase their female gendered bodies through extreme practices of asceticism and celibacy. The Sufi hagiographical tradition is rife with stories extolling the celibacy of female saints such as Mughal princess Jahan Ara Begum (d. 1092/1681), who never married and devoted her life to attaining spiritual mastery.[8] The female sexual body must be controlled and contained, as is emphasized by

Qur'anic injunctions for women to practice *ḥijāb* by covering themselves and to behave modestly (see *Sūrat al-Aḥzāb* [Chapter of the Clans], 33:53, 33:59). After the "descent of the *ḥijāb*," in which God proclaimed, "And when you ask of them [the wives of the Prophet] anything, ask it of them from behind a curtain" (33:53), a new ethical order was established in the Muslim community, with unrelated men and women segregated from each other (a practice known in Indo-Muslim culture as *purdah*).

This practice of sexual segregation created a dilemma for typically male hagiographers who sought to write about the lives of female saints. Much of sainthood is based on control of the body and the public lives of the saints, and for a man to write about a woman's body violates the ethical division of space into masculine and feminine. One way of circumventing the potential violation of the honor of a female saint is to emphasize her celibacy and asceticism, which obliterate any potential for the disorder (*zina*) that her female sexed body might create. Another way for the male biographer of the female Sufi saint to avoid violating religiously enforced gender codes is through "hagiographical transvestism." If the soul of a female saint is actually male, then the biographer may consider her earthly body merely a shell concealing her truly masculine essence. The female saint's body is the clothing covering her essentially male self (soul), which is exactly what a transvestite does when he dresses his male sexed body in the clothing of a woman.

In the Shiʿi tradition, imitable sainthood is located at the nexus where familial relationships and physical bodies are an ontological necessity—that is, this form of sainthood is based on blood relationship to the Prophet Muhammad. This emphasis on marriage and family sets this particular model of Shiʿi sainthood apart from the normative tradition of Sufi sainthood, which places a greater premium on celibacy. The importance of kinship roles is a distinctive feature of Shiʿi sainthood. The bonds of family further distance the ascetic tendency that is such a prominent aspect of Sufi sainthood.

The women of the Prophet's family are embodiments of *ḥusaini* ethics-imitable sainthood, and their model, while exceptional, encourages imitation by both Muslim men and Muslim women. Rather than emphasizing the asceticism of celibacy, male hagiographers explicitly maintain these Shiʿi female saints' gendered status. Male hagiographers emphasize the family roles and identities of Fatimah al-Zahra, Zainab, Fatimah Kubra, and Sakinah, but this process does not necessarily reduce them to mere relatives of the Prophet Muhammad and the Imams. Fatimah al-Zahra is revered as one of the most holy of Muslim women—sinless, spiritually perfected, the lady of sorrows and patience. Fatimah also possesses a form of initiatic knowledge, having received the *muṣḥaf fāṭimah*, a heavenly text revealing all events in her descendants' future.[9] Zainab is venerated as an imitable saint and a socioethical exemplar whose bravery and willingness to sacrifice everything are admired by men and women alike. Sakinah and Fatimah Kubra, daughters of Imam Husain, were young girls at the Battle of Karbala but made sacrifices to preserve their family and religion. Several generations after Zainab, Fatimah Maʿsumeh, the sister of the eighth Imam, Reza, is revered as a woman of great learning and piety, and hundreds of thousands of devotees go on pilgrimage (*ziyārat* [visitation]) each year to her lavish gold-domed shrine in Qom, Iran. Like their male relations, the women of the *ahl-e bait* occupy a distinctive role as imitable saints and socioethical exemplars in the spiritual-devotional life of Shiʿi Muslims. They are respected and portrayed in various hagiographical genres as female, feminine, pious, learned, and brave figures.

Never are the women of the *ahl-e bait* relegated to an appendix of the biographies of saints, nor do they undergo a transvestic inversion that transforms them into quasi-men. Females and the feminine are an integral aspect of Shiʿi sainthood. In fact, the hagiographical tradition amplifies the various models of piety and exemplary socioethical behavior provided by the women of the *ahl-e bait*, particularly Fatimah and Zainab, who are portrayed as models for ideal womanhood.[10] Why are stories about the women of the Prophet's family so frequently invoked in the ritual performance of the *majlis* mourning assembly, and why are feminine voices and emotions, particularly those of Sakinah and Zainab, so effectively employed in Karbala hagiographical literature?

At the most basic level, the women of the *ahl-e bait* are such enduring models because they survived the battle and spent the remainder of their lives spreading the message and keeping alive the memory of Imam Husain's martyrdom. These women sacrificed, suffered, survived, and remained intensely dedicated to the preservation of Islam and to demanding justice for the atrocities committed against their families. This justice is meted out in the Shiʿi collective memory performed in the mourning assembly, documented in martyrdom narratives (*maqtal*) and poetry (*marśiya*, *salām*, and *nauḥa*), and materialized in the sacred architecture and objects of the *ʿāshūrkhāna*. Shamsul Hasan Shamsi extols Zainab as "a second Husain, keeping alive the revolutionary movement of her brother . . . in keeping aloft the banner of Islamic values and in keeping alight the torch of the noble ideals lighted by her martyred brother."[11] Shamsi's reference to Zainab as "a second Husain" is not an act of hagiographical transvestism. Zainab's memorializing role as the messenger of martyrdom is a fundamentally public act that dramatizes the degradation of the Muslim community less than fifty years after Muhammad's death.

According to the principle of complementary pairing, if there are Shiʿi male saints, then there must also be female saints. At the beginning of chapter 1, I tell the story of how M. M. Taqui Khan narrated an account of Qasem's martyrdom through the experience and emotion of Fatimah Kubra. Hagiographical narratives of Qasem's martyrdom are as much about the bridegroom/warrior as they are about his bride/widow, Fatimah Kubra. At the everyday, nonelite level, the Shiʿa of Hyderabad seek guidance from the women of the *ahl-e bait*, whose spiritual attainments are imitable and whose embodiment of the *ḥusaini* ethic is to be cultivated. Many of the hagiographical narratives and poetry that comprise the mourning assembly draw on feminine voices and emotions, reflecting a deep tradition of venerating the feminine in Indo-Muslim religious and aesthetic traditions.

The Feminine Is Powerful Here: Shiʿi and Vernacular Convergences

There are a variety of Hindu traditions, including the *Vedas*, *bhakti* devotional movements, Gaudiya Vaisnavism, and worship of the god Siva, in which the feminine is both an aspect and manifestation of the divine. The feminine exists in a complementary balance with the masculine, as can be seen in the god Siva's dually sexed form of Ardhanarisvara and in the integrated aniconic form of the phallic lingam nested within the gynic yoni. The Gaudiya Vaisnava tradition of North India and Bengal is centered on the figure of Krishna Caitanya (d. 1533), in whose body the god Krishna and his lover-consort Radha are fused. The feminine is an important trope in Gaudiya Vaisnavism, and male devotees often assume ritual roles that are gender coded as female. Like Sufism, the medieval Indian *bhakti* movement has a rich poetic tradition that dwells on emotions of love and longing for the divine. Much of this poetry focuses on mystical love for God, who, as the concealed beloved, is metaphorically described as a woman in *purdah* whom the lover (the Sufi or *bhakta*) has glanced through a window and longs to see once again.

With the advent of Shiʿism on the subcontinent, hagiographical traditions venerating the women of the *ahl-e bait* were easily integrated into vernacular Indic religious and aesthetic traditions. The power and the potency with which the women of the *ahl-e bait* are endowed is manifested through their embodiment of piety, religious knowledge, and the *ḥusaini* ethic. The women of the *ahl-e bait* are potent because they reflect culturally and religiously defined qualities of idealized selves that people recognize and seek to share. Yet in no way are the women of the *ahl-e bait* comparable to the many goddesses of the Hindu traditions. Saints are not goddesses, and God's special friendship (sainthood) is not divinity. Drawing on a wealth of Deccani vernacular religious traditions that venerate goddesses, including the Bonalu festival of Mahankali and the Gangamma *jātarā* (festival), as well as on the transgressive role of the Hyderabadi *hijṛa* (transgender man), who appropriates a Shiʿi identity and works as a ritual practitioner, several natural parallels can demonstrate the ease with which veneration of the women of the *ahl-e bait* as imitable saints has been integrated into everyday practice in the Deccan. Over the past six hundred years, an unconscious assimilation of Indic notions of the supernatural power of the feminine has deeply influenced and shaped the development of Hyderabadi hagiographical literature and ritual practice commemorating the Battle of Karbala.

In South India, the goddess tradition has long had an important role in vernacular religious life. Men and women propitiate a variety of goddesses, both benevolent and destructive; the consorts of the gods Siva (Kali, Durga) and Vishnu (Sita, Radha); and village goddesses (Mariyamman, Gangamma), seeking divine assistance in curing diseases, conceiving children, or removing curses. The goddess is a manifestation of both the positive and negative energies that animate the universe. The goddess tradition is more pronounced in South India, where the imprint of patriarchy is less pronounced than in such North Indian contexts as Rajasthan and Uttar Pradesh, where family (male) honor is tightly bound with control of women's sexuality. Many South Indian goddesses are called *ammā* (mother), rooting these female divinities within the family.[12] Devotees establish intimate personal relationships with the goddess as mother, worshiping and fearing her feminine generative and destructive power (*śakti*). The goddess's *śakti* is an aspect of her divinity in which connection with the raw power of her femininity makes her especially potent and worthy of a devotee's worship.

The women of the *ahl-e bait* in their Hyderabadi vernacular form also possess the potency and power of *śakti*, yet because of the Islamic doctrine of God's absolute uniqueness (*tawḥīd*), they are not goddesses. *Śaktis* are not passive, just as the women of the *ahl-e bait* are not passive in their portrayal in the Hyderabadi hagiographical tradition. Terrible things happen to these women at the Battle of Karbala, but their embodiment of the *ḥusaini* ethic ultimately actualizes a positive emphasis on the present and provides a hope for the eschatological future. The feminine power with which these Shiʿi imitable saints are endowed compels devotees to seek out the saints' intercession to arrange marriages, conceive children, and achieve financial security, among other issues. The women of the *ahl-e bait* are manifestations of potent feminine power that their hagiographers cast into an acceptable expression of God's mercy that is both in keeping with Islam and demonstrated through the saints' intercessory powers.

The *hijṛa*, with her distinctive clapping and ritualized appearance at weddings and births, has a feminine ritual potency that has long had an important role in Hyderabadi everyday practice. *Hijṛas* are men who identify as women, and the most ritually powerful are castrated. Gayatri Reddy observes that Hyderabadi *hijṛas* tend to identify generally as Muslims and specifically as Shiʿa, a phenomenon she attributes to the "significant Perso-Islamic domination of the cultural, religious, and political life of Hyderabad."[13] Reddy's explanation is correct although incomplete. Though the Hyderabadi *hijṛas* self-identify as Muslim, they do not describe themselves as Sufi.

By identifying as Shiʿa and tapping into the feminine power of the women of the *ahl-e bait*, the *hijṛa* gains considerable latitude in which to perform her ritual functions at births and weddings, where she sings and ensures the auspiciousness of a moment that is charged with the potential for black magic, jealousy, and other harm. Even in South Asia, Sufism has tended to express a more ambivalent attitude toward the role of feminine power in the religious realm. South Asian Sufi orders have far fewer female role models in positions of ritual power and leadership, a sharp contrast to the women of the *ahl-e bait*, who are charismatic, powerful saints whose religious example is readily invoked and emulated. Furthermore, as a marginalized community, *hijṛas* share a sense of difference and uniqueness with the Shiʿa, who comprise only 10–15 percent of Hyderabad's minority Muslim population.

When the sun rises on the morning of *ʿāshūrā*, men have gathered at the Bargah-e ʿAbbas (one of the centers of Shiʿi ritual activity in the Old City) to perform bloody *mātam*. Thousands of men affiliated with the numerous Muharram associations (*mātamī gurūhān*) come to publicly flagellate themselves as a symbolic affirmation of their willingness to sacrifice their lives at the Battle of Karbala. Women gather along rooftops to watch this blatant display of masculinity in which the sexual segregation of Muslim men and women is publicly transgressed. Men remove their shirts to more effectively draw blood, and the women watch and carry on a steady stream of commentary. Much blood flows during the several hours that the men whip themselves with chains and strike their heads with knives (*qameh zanī*), but this is not the most important ritual activity of the day.

On 10 Muharram (*ʿāshūrā*), a massive procession of people carrying *ʿalams* and men flagellating themselves with their hands and chains weaves its way through the Old City, eclipsing the masculine performance of self-flagellation (*mātam*) earlier in the morning. Tens of thousands of Hyderabadis line the streets to watch the black-clad mourners pass by. The crowds comprise not only Shiʿas but also Sunnis, Hindus, and Christians, who come to pay their respects and to watch the spectacle. Everyone wants to glimpse the *bībī kā ʿalam* and benefit from Fatimah's intercessory power. People take this final opportunity to reflect on the socioethical meaning of the *ḥusaini* ethic embodied by Fatimah and her progeny.

The most important part of the procession (*julūs*) is the *bībī kā ʿalam*, a large golden battle standard that contains a wooden piece of the plank on which Fatimah al-Zahra received her funerary bath that is carried through the Old City on the back of an elephant. In Hyderabadi Hindu practice, the annual Bonalu festival of the goddess Mahankali is celebrated during the month of Ashadam (July/August) in the Old City and its twin city, Secunderabad. The focal point of the Old City procession is a large statue of Mahankali that rides atop an elephant slowly making its way through the streets and alleys accompanied by thousands of devotees. Groups of women carry pots (*bonam*) decorated with turmeric and neem leaves on their heads. Both the *bībī kā ʿalam* and the *bonam* are taken out in processions that draw huge crowds, ultimately making their way to the Musi River, where the *ʿalams* and Bonalu pots are ritually immersed to cool the potent *śakti* that radiates from them. The river itself is a potent symbol of feminine power. Hindus worship rivers such as the Ganges in the form (*avatār*) of regenerative and life-giving goddesses. Cooling the *bībī kā ʿalam* and *bonam* in the Musi River reappropriates their *śakti*, sustaining and protecting their devotees for another year.

The veneration of feminine power in South India has enabled the women of Imam Husain's family to attain a prominent place in the vernacular Shiʿi hagiographical tradition. The preexisting qualities and criteria for being a Shiʿi imitable saint found their complement in the Indic vernacular religious and aesthetic traditions of the Deccan, where Hindu and Muslim elements have in many ways fully interpenetrated each other. Many of the criteria for

Figure 2. The procession of the bībī kā ʿalam *as it makes its way through the Old City on* ʿāshūrā, *February 2006.*

Shiʿi imitable sainthood are values deeply ingrained in the vernacular culture of Hyderabad, especially the emphasis on family and social engagement rather than ascetic withdrawal.

Female Imitable Saints and Feminine Socioethical Exemplars

In chapter 1, I identified three distinctive qualities that mark the Shiʿi hagiographical tradition's difference from stories about the lives of saints in Roman Catholicism and Sufism. First, Sufi and Roman Catholic hagiographies often emphasize ascetic practices and virtues of the saint; Shiʿi hagiography overwhelmingly lacks any such element. Hagiographers of the Imams and the members of the *ahl-e bait* do not typically depict them as ascetics. Similarly, the Sufi predilection for emphasizing the asceticism and chastity of female saints is not the focus of Shiʿi hagiography. The women of the Prophet's family were mothers, sisters, and daughters and were very much involved in political and social matters. Second, kinship plays a vital role in the construction of Shiʿi female sainthood. Blood descent through the Prophet Muhammad and his daughter, Fatimah al-Zahra, is a prerequisite for imitable sainthood. God has chosen these women as charismatic spiritual exemplars and embodiments of the *ḥusaini* ethic, and society recognizes them as such. The charismatic blood that runs through their veins distinguishes them from everyday Muslims, who lack such pure lineage. Their hagiographers portray the women of the *ahl-e bait* not only as mothers, daughters, sisters, and wives but also as learned in the Qurʾan and religious sciences. The third distinctive feature of a gendered notion of Shiʿi sainthood is that the femininity of these women is positively recognized and venerated by men and women alike. Shiʿi female saints are not considered lesser versions of their male relatives.

Poverty, Piety, and Social Engagement

The embodiment of the *ḥusaini* ethic by the *ahl-e bait* accounts for Shiʿi hagiographers' minimal attention to asceticism. The *ḥusaini ethic* is one of sacrifice and is characterized by the value that "the wants of others should be given preference to one's own wants."[14] It is not a part of the Shiʿi hagiographical imperative that the women of the *ahl-e bait* exhibit ascetic virtues such as excessive fasting, weeping, or sleep deprivation. The difference between poverty, which tends to be both an involuntary state and a consciously chosen ascetic lifestyle, is significant with regard to the hagiographical narratives about the women of the *ahl-e bait*. This approach contrasts with the stories of a sixteenth-century Rajput princess, Mirabai, whose intense love for the Hindu god Krishna caused her to abandon her life of wealth and comfort and to live as a *bhakta* (devotee), alienating her from family and society. A more apt example can be seen in the ecstatic asceticism of Rabiʿa al-ʿAdawiyya (d. 801 C.E.), a freed slave who devoted her life to absolute love of God. By all accounts, Rabiʿa's "love for God was absolute; there was no room left for any other thought or love. She did not marry, nor did she give the Prophet a special place in her piety."[15] Rabiʿa's life was completely otherworldly, focused singularly on God. Rabiʿa introduced the emotional flavor of love to Sufi asceticism, yet such emotion did not embrace the world.

In the Shiʿi context, none of the women of the *ahl-e bait* abandoned either family or wealth to live a life of spiritual detachment. The Prophet Muhammad, his children, and his grandchildren experienced much poverty throughout their lives, and their suffering and endurance are a popular theme in Shiʿi hagiography. Fatimah al-Zahra's hagiographers typically portray her as a pious woman whose life was characterized by grinding poverty and hardship. As was the case for most of the prophets, years of persecution and marginalization had reduced Muhammad and his family to poverty. The feast (*walīmah*) celebrating Fatimah's wedding to ʿAli was a decidedly simple affair, with guests served dried fruit and other simple foods. The *walīmah*, hosted by the bride's family, usually takes place in the days or weeks following the wedding ceremony. In Hyderabad, some Muslim families host a month of wedding feasts, generally on Fridays. As a form of critique against what is seen as the accretion of such Hindu practices as lavish wedding ceremonies, multiple feasts, and the payment of a sizable dowry, some Muslim families consciously choose to imitate the model of the Prophet Muhammad, who could afford to provide his daughter only a modest dowry and simple *walīmah*.

Fatimah did not face her poverty with a smile on her face and willing acquiescence that the situation was God's will. A life of poverty and want was not Fatimah's choice, and she often resented the hardships she endured. Fatimah's poverty is a popular topic for her hagiographers, who tell numerous stories of how both Fatimah and ʿAli were compelled to work extra jobs to supplement their meager incomes. Fatimah's biographers note that she and her family often went hungry, and she was forced to supplement the household income by grinding corn "until she had blisters on her hands." In Hyderabad, the *chakkī* ritual that takes place during the prewedding *manjha* (turmeric grinding) ceremony reenacts Fatimah's ceaseless labor, although instead of corn, the bride's female relatives grind turmeric (*haldī*), which symbolizes fertility and prosperity, and sing joyful songs describing the happiness of Fatimah's marriage to ʿAli. The *chakkī* ritual symbolizes both the difficulties and sweetness of marriage:

> It is reported in *Biḥār [al-anwār]* that ʿAli (A) [peace be upon him] said to a man from Bani Saeʿed: "Should I speak to you about Fatima and Myself? She was my spouse who was the most beloved to the Prophet. Once, she carried water using a waterskin until it scarred her chest, she ground (grain) using a hand mill until blisters appeared on her hands, she swept the floor until her clothes became dusty and lit the fire under the cooking pot until her clothes became mud colored from the smoke.
>
> "Fatima was inflicted by great pain as a result of this, so I said to her: 'Why don't you ask your father for a servant to relieve you from these jobs?'

“When Fatima (A) [peace be upon her] went to the Prophet she found that he had company; and was too shy to talk to him, so she left the house. But the Prophet (S) [peace and blessings upon him] knew that she had come for something.”

Imam ʿAli (A) continued: “The next morning, the Prophet came to the house while we were still under our quilt and said: ‘*Assalāmu ʿAlaikum!*’

“Yet because we were ashamed (of being under the quilt), we preferred to remain silent.

“The Prophet once again said: ‘*Assalāmu ʿAlaikum!*’

“Once again we remained silent. Then for the third time the Prophet said, ‘*Assalāmu ʿAlaikum.*’ Now we feared that he would depart, for it was the prophet’s habit to say *Assalāmu ʿalaikum* three times and then wait for permission to enter or leave.

“So I said: ‘*Wa ʿalaik as-salām*, Messenger of Allah! Come in.’

“He (S) sat near our heads and said: ‘Fatima, what was your need when you came to Muhammad yesterday?’

Imam Ali added: “I was afraid that she (Fatima) would not tell him, so I pulled my head from under the cover and said:

‘I will inform you, Messenger of Allah! Surely she carried water using a water skin until her chest was scarred, she ground (grain) using a hand mill until blisters appeared on her hands, she swept the floor until her clothes became dusty and lit the fire under the cooking pot until her clothes were mud colored from the smoke.’

“So I said to her: ‘Why don’t you ask your father for a servant to relieve you from these jobs?’ ”

“The Prophet (S) upon hearing this, said: ‘Shall I teach you something that is better for you than a servant and a world with everything in it? After every prayer say: “*Allāhū Akbār*” thirty-four (34) times, “*Alḥamdulillāh*” thirty-three (33) times, and “*Subḥān Allāh*” thirty-three (33) times then conclude that with *lā ilaha ilallāh* [there is no god but God]. Surely this is better for you than that which you wanted and the world and its belongings.’

“Thus, Fatima adhered to this glorification after every prayer; and it came to be known as ‘*Tasbīḥ* Fatima.’ ”[16]

This hagiographical account of Fatimah and ʿAli’s desire for a servant to help ease their burden dramatically demonstrates that the Prophet’s daughter did not choose a life of poverty. Fatimah endured but did not accept her impoverished state. Her poverty is not an indexical feature of her sainthood. Her status as the Prophet Muhammad's daughter meant that she must endure hardships for the benefit of other Muslims. Muhammad denied her a servant lest other Muslims suffer or experience want. Fatimah and ʿAli learn a valuable lesson that one must be grateful to God for his mercy and give thanks for that which God has provided. Although Fatimah may lack material wealth, this story demonstrates her spiritual riches and God's love for her.

The songs sung during the *chakkī* ceremony that invoke the sweetness of Fatimah and ʿAli's marriage are intended to offer encouragement to the new couple as they begin their life together. The implicit lesson is that if Fatimah and ʿAli can endure their poverty and suffering, understanding it as a sign of God's love, then any other challenges the new couple encounters can surely be surmounted if they have enough faith. The *chakkī* ritual replicates this hagiographical narrative, recasting it in vernacular terms and thus establishing Fatimah as an idealized Muslim who puts the needs of the *ummah* (community of Muslims) before those of her own family. In a sense, it is the substitution of the larger family and its needs for that of the smaller nuclear unit.

Unlike the ascetic, who has renounced the affairs of the world, both the historical and hagiographical sources on Fatimah al-Zahra document her active participation in public life. One particular event is recounted in all of the histories, both Shiʿi and Sunni: the dispute over the land Fatimah received from her father at Fadak. Fatimah's speech (*khuṭbah*) is recounted in the Sunni *ḥadīth* collections of al-Bukhari and Muslim and in Imam Ahmad ibn Hanbal's *Muṣnad*.

Three years prior to Muhammad's death, he gave Fatimah a parcel of land in the gardens at Fadak. Following the Battle of Khaybar in 629 C.E., the Jews gave the Prophet Muhammad a piece of land, and he, in turn, gave it as a gift (*ḥiba*) to his daughter. After the Prophet's death, Abu Bakr, the first *khalīfah* and Muhammad's successor, seized this property from Fatimah. Abu Bakr argued that the progeny of prophets do not inherit and that Fatimah therefore had no legal claim to the gardens of Fadak. According to the Qur'an, however, a woman has the legal right to inherit from her parents: "From what is left by parents and those nearest related, there is a share for men, and a share for women" (*Sūrat al-Nisā'* [Chapter of the Women], 4:7). As a Muslim daughter and woman, Fatimah invoked her Qur'anic legal right and brought her case to court for arbitration. Although she was ultimately unsuccessful, her knowledge of her legal rights and desire for justice indicates that she was deeply involved in the affairs of society.[17]

Even in death, Fatimah's presence and participation in the spiritual affairs of the world are palpable. One of Fatimah's epithets is *sayyidat nisā' al-ʿālamain* (mistress of the women of the two worlds), and all Shiʿa consider her the patron of the *majlis-e ʿazā*. In the *majlis* assemblies, the Shiʿa of Hyderabad believe that Fatimah is present and gathers up the tears of the mourners for the *ahl-e bait*. M. M. Taqui Khan told me that "in the *majlis*, we offer condolences to Bibi Fatimah because she has suffered the most of anyone."[18] Despite the fact that Fatimah's life was characterized by poverty and political intrigue, she listens to the condolences and grief of the Shiʿa.

Members of the *ahl-e bait* often appear to Shiʿa in dreams and as apparitions, providing solace and advice as well as information about the future. On one occasion, Fatimah appeared in Khan's dreams and praised him for continuing the tradition of mourning for her son, Husain: "Fourteen hundred years have passed, and you are still crying for my son."[19] On the Day of Judgment, she will intercede on behalf of every person who has genuinely wept for the sufferings of her family. As a leader, a role model, and a feminine, nurturing figure, Fatimah is portrayed as anything but ascetic, and the Shiʿa venerate her for her humanity and dedication to family and faith.

The Messenger of Martyrdom: Zainab and the Memorializing Imperative

Fatimah's daughter, Zainab, is likewise committed to a life of public service as the messenger of Imam Husain's martyrdom. Although Zainab is not one of the Fourteen Infallible Ones (*chārdah maʿṣūmīn*), the Prophet Muhammad's closeness to his granddaughter and his role in choosing her name, which means "a beautiful possession or adornment of her father," indicates her significant role as a member of the *ahl-e bait*. According to Shiʿi tradition, the Prophet Muhammad "left clear instructions . . . that Janab-e Zainab should always be respected because he knew what services she was going to render to Islam."[20] Zainab is revered as the messenger of Imam Husain's martyrdom, and she and her brother must fulfill the divinely predestined events of Karbala and its aftermath—each has a God-given duty. Zainab's responsibility is to keep alive the message of Karbala and thus preserve Islam.

Zainab is the living witness to Imam Husain's martyrdom, and she has a divinely ordained responsibility to ensure that the Muslim community never forgets what happened at Karbala. Zainab's public mission reflects the degradation of the Muslim community, and hagiographical accounts of the suffering she and her female relatives endure in Yazid's court instill feelings of shame and anger in *majlis* participants. These narratives provoke feelings of indignation in devotees' hearts, an effective strategy of narrative engagement that plays on patriarchal desires to protect and control women, especially these embodiments of *ḥusaini* ethics–imitable sainthood. In the aftermath of Karbala, Zainab, however, is the protector and preserver of her family's memory.

After the Battle of Karbala, Zainab devoted the remainder of her life to testifying about what happened to her faith and family:

> Weeping, Bashir[21] cried out, "The women's quarters are plundered, Husain is dead."
> The flame of the lamp of Medina has been extinguished, "The women's quarters are plundered, Husain is dead."
>
> That pious attendant of the Prophet's tomb, who was the ornament of Medina;
> His flame was extinguished in the dust, "The women's quarters are plundered, Husain is dead."
>
> In the afternoon, the house was cleared, by the time of *ʿaṣr*,[22] the King's throat was cut.
> Upon killing the King, the tents were set ablaze, "The women's quarters are plundered, Husain is dead."
>
> Alas, that visage of Mustafa, the King has relinquished his life,
> On the battlefield that youthful King has died, "The women's quarters are plundered, Husain is dead."
>
> The powerless ones are in fetters, all of the ladies have become prisoners,
> The House of Mustafa has become shackled, "The women's quarters are plundered, Husain is dead."
>
> The widows were mounted on camels, the hands of that one struck ill[23] were bound to the reins;
> Driven into alien lands, "The women's quarters are plundered, Husain is dead."

By the arrow that pierced and silenced that throat, the bitterly sobbing infant died.
By the fire of tyranny, the cradle was set ablaze, "The women's quarters are plundered, Husain is dead."

"Baqir" laments until the Resurrection, and there was a tumult in Mustafa's grave;
When weeping, Bashir said, "The women's quarters are plundered, Husain is dead."[24]

This *nauḥa* powerfully appropriates Zainab's voice to bear witness to Muslims of what has happened to the progeny of the Prophet Muhammad and the people most beloved by God at the Battle of Karbala. The refrain, "The women's quarters are plundered, Husain is dead," elevates the pathos of the *majlis* participants, increasing the intensity with which the mourners strike their hands on their chests in *mātam* while shedding tears of grief.

By Virtue of the Blood Coursing through Their Veins

ʿAli Shariʿati, a twentieth-century Iranian philosopher, asserts that Imam Husain was predestined to die a martyr so that the women of the *ahl-e bait* could serve as socioethical exemplars for future generations of Muslim women. According to the patriarchal "system which rules history, women had to either [*a*] choose bondage and being toys of the harems or [*b*] if they were to remain liberated, they must become the leader[s] of the caravan of the captives and the survivors of the martyrs."[25] The women of the *ahl-e bait* were captured by Yazid's army and brought to his court in Damascus, but hagiographical narratives counter this captivity narrative with accounts of their defiance. Shariʿati continues,

> Once again, from . . . this little house which is greater than all of history, a man emerges—angry, determined. . . . But no! Walking side by side him, a woman has also emerged from Fatimah's house, step by step with him; she has taken half of the heavy mission of her brother upon her own shoulders. . . .
>
> The second mission is that of the message [it] is to deliver the message of martyrdom to the ear of the world, is to be a tongue which speaks. . . . This message is upon the delicate shoulders of a woman—Zaynab—a woman who [is such that] alongside her, manliness has

learned manliness. And Zaynab's mission is more difficult, more grave [even] than the mission of her brother.[26]

Shariʿati elevates Zainab's role as the messenger of martyrdom to virtually transcend that of the bodily sacrifice of her brother, Husain. Shariʿati juxtaposes the "delicate shoulders" of Zainab with the difficulty, even heaviness, of her mission. Despite the fact that Zainab is a woman, her strength and bravery are a lesson to men. Zainab is not transformed into a woman with manly strength. Bravery and strength are qualities typically coded as masculine, yet Zainab, a woman, embodies these powerful traits.

Zainab's charismatic strength and power are drawn from her descent from the house of Fatimah. Zainab's embodiment of *ḥusaini* ethics-imitable sainthood is based on her direct blood relationship to her mother, Fatimah, who is the progenitor of the Imamate. Imam Husain's sanctity as an embodiment of both *ḥusaini* ethics-imitable sainthood and Imamate-transcendent sainthood is based on the fact that he is the descendant of Fatimah and her father, Muhammad.

Fatimah's honorific title (*kunya*) *umm abīhā* (the mother of her father) is peculiar in Arab kinship because no daughter can be the literal mother of her father, and lineal descent is passed through males. In her study of Fatimah, Denise Soufi notes that "we find traditions that ascribe the lineage of Fatima's progeny to the Prophet: while all other children have their lineage reckoned through their fathers, Fatima's children have their lineage reckoned through her to the Prophet, and the Prophet himself referred to Hasan and Husayn as 'my sons and my daughter's sons.'"[27] Fatimah's *kunya* marks her as the mother of prophecy (*nubūwwah*) and the Imamate, and she connects the line of prophets from Adam to Muhammad and the Imamate—she links the Seal of Prophecy with the divine guides who will lead humanity until the Resurrection (*qiyāmat*).

A. K. Ramanujan has observed that the spiritual achievements of Indian female saints (typically Hindu) are gained at certain social expense.[28] These women tend to forsake marriage and live on the margins of society, qualities that are largely absent from the Shiʿi hagiographical tradition. Shiʿi hagiography centers on networks of kinship, a phenomenon that marks the second distinctive feature of Shiʿi hagiography. In Hindu, Christian, and Sufi traditions of sainthood, female religious exemplars such as the Sufi Rabiʿa and the Roman Catholic anchorites tend to exist at the margins of society because of their refusal to participate in the patriarchal institution of marriage, a subversive act that goes against the natural order. Without a kinship identity defined by the patriarchal family, a woman is transformed into an antiwoman, a rebel against her ascribed gender roles. Without an identity that is defined by the gendered roles of wife, mother, and daughter, a woman poses a danger to both men and women in society. She is dangerous to men because she represents subversion of the masculine order and her sexuality is not contained by marriage or the protection of her father. The female renouncing saint (as almost all of them are) is dangerous to women because she represents an alternative to the patriarchal order.[29]

As members of Muhammad's family, the women of the *ahl-e bait* are required to be consummate socioethical and religious exemplars, upholding the Prophet's Sunnah (lived tradition). To choose not to marry is not a possibility for the women of the *ahl-e bait*. According to one *ḥadīth* found in the ninth-century *Sunān Ibn Mājah*, the Prophet declared, "Marriage is my *Sunnah*. He who does not follow my *Sunnah* does not follow me." Corresponding to the requirement to follow the Prophet's tradition by marrying is the expectation that the married couple will procreate. In fact, lineal descent from Muhammad through Fatimah is the central criterion for belonging to the *ahl-e bait*. According to one *ḥadīth*, ʿAbd al-Rahman ibn ʿAwf said, "I heard the Apostle of Allah say, 'I am a tree, Fatimah is its trunk and ʿAli is its pollen. Hasan and Husayn are its fruits, and our followers (Shiʿah) are its leaves. The roots of the tree are in the Garden of Eden, and its trunk, fruits and leaves are in Paradise.' "[30]

The women of the *ahl-e bait* are portrayed with fullness of femininity because they do not subvert the patriarchal order. The women of the *ahl-e bait* marry, have children, and do not engage in any activities that might make them sexually suspect. Nor are they simplistically reduced to their familial roles. In vernacular hagiographical narratives of Fatimah Kubra, however, we encounter a contradiction because she willingly sacrifices her husband with the knowledge that she will remain a widow for the rest of her life. Fatimah Kubra's status as a widow in Hyderabadi hagiographical literature reflects the Indic vernacular taboo on widow remarriage and social anxieties about the sexual power and inauspiciousness of widowed women. The contradiction lies in the explanations that I heard from many of my Hyderabadi Shiʿi informants, who explained that Imam Husain had his daughter married to Qasem to preserve her honor. If Fatimah Kubra were widowed, Yazid could not force her into marriage. Marriage and widowhood prevent Fatimah Kubra from involuntarily destroying the purity and honor of the *ahl-e bait*, reflecting the extent of her imitable sainthood in the context of India. It is better to be married and then widowed than not to marry at all. Fatimah Kubra upholds her religious obligations and the honor of her family by willingly sacrificing her husband and being widowed. According to the hagiographical narratives, these are the proper actions for her family and faith.

A Saint and a Woman: Shiʿi Sainthood and Positive Femininity

The third indexical feature of Shiʿi hagiography is its inclusion of women as full human beings whose spiritual attainments are expressed in positively gendered terms. The women of the *ahl-e bait* are ontologically complementary to their male relatives. In comparison to the Roman Catholic and Sufi hagiographical traditions, which often portray women as almost like men in their spiritual attainments, the women of the *ahl-e bait* are described with explicitly feminine imagery and vocabulary. Zainab is never relegated to an appendix located at the back of a *taẕkirah* (biographical dictionary of saints), nor is she ever described as being like a man in her spiritual attainment.

John Kitchen has observed that male hagiographers of Merovingian women saints express their sanctity in explicitly masculine terms.[31] For example, in *Life of Saint Monegund*, Gregory of Tours notes that the *inferiorum sexum* (the inferior sex) can be exemplary combatants for the faith; "imitating the previous models of holiness, [they] are not weak opponents but fight like men (*viriliter agonizantem*), attaining the heavenly kingdom after 'sweaty' (*desudantibus*) exertions in battle."[32] However, Gregory faces the ideological dilemma that "with the life of Christian warfare an *imitatio Christi*, the female saint, if she is to be genuinely Christ-like, must be shown as striving in the contest to attain eternal life."[33] But the female is the "inferior sex" and therefore cannot fulfill such an idealization.

In the Shiʿi devotional literature and many Sunni histories, Zainab's femininity is never subordinated. She is a brave woman whose spiritual and psychophysical capabilities are never determined in comparison with those of men. Kashefi vividly portrays Zainab's bravery and spirited temper in his account of her confrontation with the ʿUmayyad *khalīfah*, Yazid, and Ibn Ziyad, the governor of Kufah: "The officials of the court made an attempt to kill Zain al-ʿAbidin, but Zainab stood up and turned toward Ibn Ziyad and said, 'Have you not had your fill of killing the family of the Prophet of God? Was it not enough for you to unlawfully spill this blood? If you wish to kill him, then kill me first!'"[34]

Zainab's request that Ibn Ziyad kill her first is intended as a shock-inducing tactic, compelling one to consider what sort of a tyrant willfully murders a woman. Radiating her *wilāyah* bestowed by God through her spiritual exemplariness and membership in the *ahl-e bait* forces even Zainab's enemies to recognize her special status.

The women of the *ahl-e bait* are refractions of the divine Muhammadan light (*nūr muḥammadī*), which, when combined with the public recognition of their spiritual exemplariness, elevates these figures beyond their typical subordinate status in patriarchal society. Fatimah al-Zahra and to a certain extent her daughter, Zainab, simultaneously possess the qualities of both transcendent and imitable sainthood, which are manifested through their reflection of God's divine radiance (*nūr*). Both Fatimah and Zainab were selected for God's special friendship, and both have been granted power, responsibility, and knowledge that have a complementary function to that of the Prophet Muhammad and the Imams. While Fatimah and Zainab are exceptional imitable saints and Fatimah is endowed with a special form of transcendent sainthood (*walāyat-e fāṭimiyyah*), they are excluded from the Imamate. Nevertheless, God has chosen them to fulfill specific transcendent roles. Fatimah is the mother of prophecy and Imamate and the mistress of the Day of Judgment, where she will have ultimate intercessory power. Zainab is the messenger of martyrdom and a guardian of the *Lauḥ-e Maḥfūẓ* (the Preserved Tablet).[35] At first glance, it may seem that because Fatimah and Zainab are excluded from the patriarchal prerogative of the Imamate, they cannot be endowed with transcendent sainthood (*walāyah*).

If these women appear to occupy a subordinate status because of their gender, we must examine more deeply their roles vis-à-vis the Imamate to illuminate their inimitable qualities. Fatimah's epithet, *al-zahra* (the radiant), is the manifestation of her participation in the *nūr muḥammadī* created preeternally by God. In the *ʿUyūn al-muʿjizat* (The Wellspring of Miracles), eleventh-century Shiʿi historian Husain ʿAbd al-Wahhab describes Fatimah's heavenly radiance as a deliberate act of God: "By My power, My majesty, My generosity, My eminence, I will act." God then created Fatimah's celestial light (*nūr*), which lit up the heavens.[36] Ibn Shahrashub further develops the cosmic-theological meaning of Fatimah's radiance, connecting it to *walāyah*: "God created Paradise from the light of His countenance; He took this light, and threw it; with of a third of it He struck Muhammad, with another third Fatimah, and with the remaining third ʿAli and the People of the House."[37] In an Eliadian sense, Fatimah's manifestation of *walāyah* is the worldly duplication of the celestial model.[38] According to Ibn Shahrashub's description of God's bestowing of the *nūr muḥammadī* on Muhammad and his descendants, Fatimah receives a larger portion than either ʿAli or the twelve Imams, who must share one-third of God's light of *walāyah*.

Seyyed Hossein Nasr's observation that Fatimah is endowed with a partial *walāyat-e fāṭimiyyah* underestimates the pivotal and cosmologically important role God has bestowed on her.[39] Through the generative light radiating from Fatimah in preeternity, prophets and Imams have guided humanity. Fatimah links the Seal of Prophecy with the divine guides, who will lead humanity until the Resurrection. Without Fatimah, the Imams would not be born and God-given *walāyah* could not be transferred. As the mistress of paradise (*khātūn-e jannat*), Fatimah possesses the supreme powers of intercession and condemnation. Fatimah will avenge those who were killed at the Battle of Karbala, and she will intercede on behalf of all who support the *ahl-e bait*. The *walāyat-e fāṭimiyyah* of Fatimah is complete, and her role as *umm abīhā* renders Islam theologically complete; she connects preeternity to eternal paradise or hell through the descent of prophecy and the Imamate, which is made possible through her divine generative radiance. Fatimah Zahra constitutes a human form of divine will exhibited through her embodiment of transcendent sainthood, and she is made human and real through her enactment of imitable sainthood. Fatimah's sanctity, although extraordinary, establishes the necessity for feminine sanctity, both transcendent and imitable.

God's Strong Women

Shiʿi theological and devotional tradition has created a significant space for feminine sanctity. The women of the *ahl-e bait*, whose descent is traced through the house of the Prophet Muhammad and Fatimah al-Zahra, are in some instances transcendent and imitable (Fatimah and her daughter, Zainab); in other cases, they are models of imitable sanctity that are both spiritual and socioethical (Fatimah Kubra, Umm Kulsum, Sakinah). Yet all are venerated by the Shiʿa for their potent femininity, devotion to God and family, and involvement in the affairs of the world. The women of the *ahl-e bait* are God's strong women, and their survival at the Battle of Karbala and their mission to keep the memory of Imam Husain alive make them powerfully imitable social, ethical, and spiritual role models for Shiʿi women and men.

chapter three

The Saddest Story Ever Told

TRANSLATING KARBALA THROUGH FEMININE VOICES & EMOTIONS INTO A DECCANI SHIʿI IDIOM

Learn from the Hindu how to die of love—
It is not easy to enter the fire while alive.
—Amir Khusrau

Beginning in the 1860s, Sayyid ʿAbbas Sahib moved from Madras (Chennai) to the princely state of Hyderabad, the capital of the Sunni Asaf Jahi dynasty. He was a renowned writer of *marṡiya* poems commemorating the Battle of Karbala. ʿAbbas Sahib came to Hyderabad seeking the patronage of the fifth Asaf Jahi Nizam, Afzal al-Dawlah Bahadur (r. 1857–69 C.E.). The observance of Muharram has flourished in Hyderabad since the establishment of the Shiʿi Qutb Shahi dynasty in 1512 C.E. The *mehndī* mourning assembly has been celebrated with much enthusiasm in Hyderabad since the reign of ʿAbdullah Qutb Shah (r. 1626–72 C.E.), who commissioned the construction of the Alava-ye Qasem shrine in Yaqutpura, a neighborhood in the Shiʿi section of the Old City. As he did in his former home city of Madras, ʿAbbas Sahib discovered a reverence for Qasem and the *mehndī* ritual among the Shiʿa of Hyderabad.

ʿAbbas Sahib's house, ʿAbbas Manzil, was initially located at the present site of the ʿAzakhane-ye Zahra *ʿāshūrkhāna* in the Old City neighborhood of Darulshifa. The ʿAzakhane-ye Zahra was commissioned in 1941 by the seventh Nizam, Osman ʿAli Khan (r. 1911–48), in memory of his mother, Amtul Zahra Begum.[1] In this large house sitting on the banks of the Musi River, ʿAbbas Sahib hosted an annual *majlis* mourning assembly on 7 Muharram in which trays of henna and an *ʿalam* dedicated to Qasem were brought out in procession (*julūs*).[2] The "ʿAbbas Sahib *mehndī kī majlis*" quickly became Hyderabad's most popular 7 Muharram mourning assembly.

Following ʿAbbas Sahib's death, the tradition of hosting the *mehndī* mourning assembly was continued, even when the family home shifted to a large plot of land in Yaqutpura, just a few hundred meters from the Alava-ye Qasem shrine. ʿAbbas Sahib's great-grandson, M. M. Taqui Khan, and his family continue to host one of Hyderabad's largest and most important *mehndī* mourning assemblies.[3] Each year, several thousand men gather on the busy road outside the house, and more crowd into the spacious courtyard that connects Khan's house with the family *ʿāshūrkhāna*.

Leading up to the beginning of the men's *majlis*, devotees crowd before the *Qāsem kā ʿalam* (the metal standard bearing Qasem's name) and wait for one of Khan's daughters or sons-in-law to tie a red string around the devotee's right wrist. This mourning assembly is truly a family affair. Khan's wife oversees the preparation of the consecrated food (*tabarruk*) that will later be served to the mourning assembly participants; his daughter, Kulsum, assembles the tray of *mehndī*; and another daughter visiting from the United States ensures the comfort of the female *majlis* participants. Because of the practice of *purdah*, the women and girls remain in the house and watch the men's *majlis* through the living room windows. Hearing the *majlis* is never a problem, as it is broadcast over loudspeakers at deafening levels. As the men and boys arrive and take their places in the courtyard, the anticipation of an encounter with the *ḥusaini* ethic of these imitable saints creates a palpable energy.

For the first six days of Muharram in Hyderabad, the ritual activity builds. On the seventh day, the remembrance of Karbala becomes energized. As Maulana Reza Agha, a high-ranking Shiʿi religious scholar (*ʿālim*) and popular *ẕākir*, declared at the beginning of his discourse (*khuṭbah*), "There are many, many martyrs in this world, but there are two figures whose martyrdom is observed in the *majlis* more than any others . . . Sakinah Bibi and the orphan [*yatīm*] of Hasan."[4] Sakinah was the three- or four-year-old daughter of Imam Husain who, the Shiʿa assert, died from her grief in Damascus following the Battle of Karbala. Qasem is the orphan whose father, the second Imam, Hasan, was allegedly poisoned by one of his wives in 669 C.E. On 7 Muharram, the members of Imam Husain's party found their access to the waters of the Euphrates River cut off, yet the wedding "procession of the thirsty groom and thirsty bride [went] out." According to Agha, however, this was not a joyful event in accordance with the usual Indic wedding procession (*barāt*), in which the bridegroom goes from his home to that of his bride on horseback, wearing a turban (*ʿimāmah*), fine clothing, and a floral veil (*sehrā*). In these wedding processions, the bridegroom is accompanied by a brass band (*bājā*), fireworks, and frolicking boys; there is noise, merriment, and ribald joking, all in celebration of the newlyweds' joyful union.[5]

Agha's discourse conjures dissonant memories in the minds of the *majlis* participants. This dissonance results from the actual auspiciousness and happiness (*shādī*) that a wedding is supposed to inculcate. Every man, woman, boy, or girl who sits in the mourning assembly and weeps for Qasem and his bride, Fatimah Kubra, not only weeps for the tragedies that befell these two but also shares in the anxiety that such a tragedy engenders. A bride should never become a widow so soon after her wedding: these two gendered states ideally should exist along a broad continuum, with motherhood and menopause filling the intervening years.

Fatimah Kubra's status as a fortune-bearing bride and her rapid transformation into an inauspicious widow is an important theme in Agha's discourse. At the midpoint of his recollection of Qasem and Fatimah Kubra's troubles, a part of the discourse known as the *maṣā'ib*, a narratological ellipsis occurs. Agha suddenly makes a narrative leap in his account of the events, so that the wedding—an event that does not require any sort of description or didactic reflection—has already taken place. This is a performative strategy in that such an ellipsis dramatically reinforces for the *majlis* participants the extraordinary and tragic circumstances of this wedding. Qasem approaches his new bride and gives her a piece of his sleeve, reassuring her that it will enable them to recognize each other on the Last Day (*yawm-e qiyāmat*). Drawing the moment of Karbala into the general present, Agha declares,

> Whenever a wedding takes place, people say, "Pray to God that the bride remains a wife. Oh God! Let not separation come between groom and bride!" What kind of a wedding was this? The bride does not even have a living husband [*suhāgan*]! She has become a widow. . . . Alas, what has befallen this Karbala wedding? The bride was imprisoned and the bridegroom, too, was made a prisoner. . . . At weddings, sweet, refreshing drinks [*sharbat*] are usually served, but here, the groom and the bride have gone out in a thirsty procession. Now, the bridegroom has fallen! The bride has fallen captive, and the bridegroom's head rests upon the tip of a spear. Thus was the Karbala procession taken out.[6]

In the memories and imaginations of the mourning assembly participants, the joy of marriage and the deep despair of widowhood are simultaneously conjured by Agha's discourse. Agha's use of the term *suhāgan* further roots his description of Qasem and Fatimah Kubra's wedding in a vernacular, Indic context. *Suhāgan* is an Urdu word that is laden with deep cultural meaning, indicating a woman's status as both auspicious and having a living husband; she is not a widow. In Deccani-Urdu Karbala poetry and discourse, the wifely status of being a *suhāgan* is often set up against its binary opposite, the widow, who is dramatically invoked with the term *rand̄*, meaning both "widow" and "prostitute."

Referring to a widowed woman as *rand̄* reflects deep vernacular cultural anxieties about the perceived rampant sexuality of a widowed woman, particularly one who is young. In her study of nineteenth-century Hindu anxieties about the wretched and inauspicious existence of widows as well as their perceived sexual dangerousness, Charu Gupta notes that many Hindus considered young widows particularly susceptible to converting to Islam to circumvent the Indic taboo on widow remarriage.[7] Popular pseudoscientific literature of nineteenth-century North India postulated that women are naturally eight times more sexual than men; therefore, widows pose a danger to society because they have no socially acceptable outlet, such as remarriage, for their rampant sexual urges. Conversion to a "foreign" religion thus becomes appealing. Agha's discourse indicates that the opposite is customary for Indian Muslim widows, especially those of high status (*ashrāf* or *sayyid*) who have adopted and integrated the Indic taboo on widow remarriage into their everyday Islamic practice.

While Qasem is an integral character in this narrative, the dramatic impulse and the feelings of grief that Agha's discourse provoke in the *majlis* participants are based on the remembrance of his wife and widow, Fatimah Kubra. According to the hagiographical narrative, Qasem must die. Fatimah Kubra will be a widow for the remainder of her life and will bear responsibility for keeping alive the memory of her husband and the other heroes of Karbala among the Shiʿa. Fatimah Kubra's hagiographical persona is that of a bride of one night and a widow forever. In his discourse, Agha acknowledges that the signing of the marriage contract (*ʿaqd-e nikāḥ*) took place, but this is not the point: he wants these men to remember Fatimah Kubra's embodiment of the *ḥusaini* ethic of sacrifice and suffering. Implicit in this narrative is the fact that Fatimah Kubra is consigned to a dual captivity. Not only is she a prisoner of war and taken in the "Karbala procession" to Damascus, where the female survivors were brought as war booty to the court of the

ʿUmayyad *khalīfah*, Yazid, but Fatimah Kubra is also held captive by her widowed status.

Sitting with the women of the Khan family in the *zanāna* (women's quarters), I am enveloped in their keening, which mingles with the male *majlis* participants' shouting and frenzied displays of physical grief outside in the courtyard. Narrating Fatimah Kubra's dyadic embodiment of the bride/widow binary pairing, Agha works the crowd into an emotional frenzy. Time and place become blurred, and Fatimah Kubra's story reminds the men and women in the *majlis* of their relatives and friends who, like the bride/widow of Karbala, have suffered and lost spouses and become the inauspicious *rand̈* or *bevāh* (*be-* [without], *vivāh* [marriage]).

At about three-thirty in the afternoon, directly following the men's *majlis*, the Khan women sponsor the women's *mehndī* mourning assembly. The women's mourning assembly hosted by the Khan family is much less popular than the men's *majlis* because at four o'clock, a popular annual *mehndī kī majlis* takes place at Bait al-Qa'em, the major Khoja Isna ʿAshari *ʿāshūrkhāna* in Purani Haveli. The Bait al-Qa'em *mehndī* mourning assembly attracts several thousand women each year. During the *majlis*, many women seem to pay scant attention to the ritual events, demonstrating more interest in chatting with friends and relatives. Although many women appear not to be paying attention, the structure of the mourning assembly is ingrained in the women's minds: the recitation of Karbala hagiographical poetry (*marśiya* and *salām*) that comprises a major portion of the *majlis*, the *ẕākirah*'s didactic discourse and hagiographical narration of the troubles of the hero(in)es of Karbala, and the chanting of *nauḥa* poems accompanied by women's rhythmic chest beating (*mātam*). Women attend these mourning assemblies in large groups, accompanied by older children, energetic toddlers, and fussing babies. The highlight of the Bait al-Qa'em mourning assembly is the *mehndī* procession. A group of women moves from the partially finished upper floors of the *ʿāshūrkhāna* down an open staircase, carrying trays of henna and bearing a number of *ʿalams*. The procession slowly makes its way through the crowds of women. The female *majlis* participants clamor to view the *ʿalams* and trays of henna, from which they believe emanates Qasem's potent spiritual power (*baraka*).

In 2006, I observed the Khan family women's *mehndī* mourning assembly. Unlike the men's *majlis* and the large women's *mehndī* mourning assembly at Bait al-Qa'em, the event was intimate, attended by fewer than one hundred women. The men of the family retreated into the house—an instance of reverse *purdah*—and had lunch, while several women recited selected stanzas from *marṡiyas* and invocatory *salāms*.

The *ẕākirah*, Sayyidah Maryam Naqvi, sat on a chair in the center of the small group of women and launched into her account of Qasem's martyrdom. As I sat in the crowd of women, I was astonished to discover the differences between Naqvi's remembrance of Qasem and that of Reza Agha. Aside from the modulation of Naqvi's voice—she spoke softly at one moment, then raised her voice into a keening wail to emphasize some particularly tragic or dramatic event—the representation of Qasem's martyrdom in her discourse seemed far less emotionally engaging than Agha's. In fact, as her oration continued, it became clear that she was simply telling a historical narrative of Qasem's martyrdom that would meet the approval of many of Iran's clerical elite. Her narrative was remarkably similar to that advocated by Ayatollah Morteza Motahhari, one of Ayatollah Ruhollah Khomeini's closest allies and an architect of the 1979 Iranian Revolution. In reference to the marriage of Qasem and Fatimah Kubra, Naqvi declared, "Have you ever seen such a wedding, where there wasn't even *mehndī*? Indeed . . . these days we use *mehndī* as a means of remembering, but at Karbala there wasn't *mehndī*. According to the traditions, it is said that Imam Husain by his very own hands prepared Qasem [for his wedding], and it was he who tied the turban to Qasem's head."[8] Naqvi's discourse pedantically informed the female *majlis* participants that the *mehndī* ritual never happened at Karbala and acknowledged that the wedding happened; in her view, however, those aspects are not what people should remember. Naqvi clearly strove to reform and purify the vernacular Shiʿi hagiographical imagination of Qasem's battlefield wedding, describing the event without imaginative or overly dramatic emotional embellishment. Although she wept for Qasem's martyrdom, she wanted her listeners to remember the "correct" aspects of this event.

In these two *mehndī* mourning assemblies sponsored by Khan and his family, Qasem's martyrdom and Fatimah Kubra's sacrifice are remembered and represented in differently gendered and ideological ways. Upon initial consideration, it may seem counterintuitive that Agha's discourse would be so emotional and even sentimental in portraying Fatimah Kubra's wedding and widowhood. In patriarchal societies, particularly those that place a premium on the institution of marriage and systems of exchange such as dowry, weddings and their preparations are typically gendered as women's work.

Men relegate themselves to the background, participating only when necessary. In this instance, Agha is much more concerned with Fatimah Kubra's wedding than is Naqvi. Agha's hagiographical discourse portrays Fatimah Kubra as a religious and social exemplar whose suffering and sacrifice are exceptional. Naqvi gives a far less compelling account that minimizes the wedding event and its rituals to the extent that it merely serves as a didactic, reformist gloss to her discourse. Why does Agha remember and mourn Qasem and Fatimah Kubra's marriage with such fervor? Why does Naqvi deemphasize this wedding and Fatimah Kubra's widowhood? These questions about the nature and meaning of hagiography in the formation of vernacular, Hyderabadi Shiʿi identity are addressed in more detail in chapter 5.

Agha and Naqvi's hagiographical discourses demonstrate that memory is gendered, although not always according to our expectations. In the hagiographical Deccani-Urdu literature and ritual performance of the Hyderabadi mourning assembly, a gendered, vernacular form of religious memory was repeatedly manifested. In many instances, such as the men's and women's mourning assemblies sponsored by the Khan family, hagiographical narratives appear to subvert received understandings about how social memory is gendered for men and women.

I was puzzled by the narrative strategies employed by Agha and Naqvi in their mourning assembly discourses. Like the other *majlis* participants, I felt the anxiety and fear that Agha conjured when he cried out, "Oh God! Do not let this bride become a widow!" Watching the men's mourning assembly, albeit from the concealed space of the women's quarters (*zanāna*), the sorrow and emotional pain that the men expressed as they wept loudly and beat their hands on their heads and thighs was palpable. I had assumed that marriage is more important and anxiety-inducing for Hyderabadi Shiʿi women because of such practices as arranged weddings, dowry, and the taboo against widow remarriage; I had expected Naqvi to emphasize Fatimah Kubra's sacrifice and suffering much more than Agha did. My ethnographic assumptions about women being more concerned or even interested in retelling Fatimah Kubra's sacrifice and subsequent widowhood were incorrect. Why was Naqvi's discourse about Qasem and Fatimah Kubra less vividly emotional?

The *maṣāʾib* is the section of the *majlis* orator's discourse that marks the dramatic peak of the hagiographical narrative in which the Karbala hero(in)es' feats and ultimate sacrifice are told in detail. The mourning assembly enables the Shiʿa to remember the Battle of Karbala, weep for the suffering of the *ahl-e bait*, and integrate the *ḥusaini* ethic of faith and sacrifice into the practice of everyday life. As participants are drawn into the hagiographical realm of Karbala, such remembrance is achieved through the *majlis* orator's improvisational skill and choice of narratives, which are based on strategies of narrative engagement.

In her study of gender and sexuality in the construction of Iranian modernity, Afsaneh Najmabadi interprets a nineteenth-century casket lid painting attributed to Muhammad ʿAli ibn Zaman that shows a small group of women lounging in a garden.[9] Najmabadi observes that all of the women in the painting with the exception of an old woman are gazing directly at the viewer. One woman also has her image refracted through a mirror, effectively doubling her gaze on the viewer. Najmabadi posits that the practice of having this woman both gazing into the mirror and looking directly outward at her viewer is an "engaging strategy" that invites the viewer to participate in the scene and (voyeuristically) to take part in the action.[10] The strategy to which Najmabadi refers is Robyn Warhol's literary critical theory of narrative engagement, in which the narrator seeks "to evoke sympathy and identification from an actual reader."[11] Agha's hagiographical discourse and particularly his *maṣāʾib* employ a strategy of narrative engagement. The narrative structure and the commentarial asides that pepper Agha's discourse compel the mourners (*ʿazādārs*) to step into and voyeuristically participate in the drama of Karbala. At a minimum, the mourning assembly participants feel sympathy if not grief for the young bride/widow.

Female voice and emotion are foundational elements of the Indic epic tradition. Exemplifying the feminine role in the Indic epic tradition is Sita, the wife of King Rama in the *Rāmāyaṇa*, who is much beloved by Indians of all castes and religions. Sita is everywoman in the *Rāmāyaṇa*: the idealized, faithful wife (*pativratā*), potent goddess (*śakti*), powerful ascetic (*yoginī*), devoted mother, and accused adulteress. Unlike the epic hero, the Indic epic heroine is capable of expressing a range of emotions that is distinctively human, and she has the most potential for personal development both within and beyond the text. The author employs the experience and emotion of that epic heroine to draw the audience into the epic arena through a strategy of narrative engagement.

The centrality of feminine voices and emotions in Indic epic traditions generates and maintains audience interest and instills feelings of concern about the protagonist's fate, which finds a close analog in the Karbala hagiographical tradition. The Karbala hagiographical tradition depends on the survival of the women of Imam Husain's family. All of the men, with the exception of Imam Husain's eldest son, ʿAli Zain al-ʿAbidin, died in the battle, leaving the women to bear witness about what happened at Karbala. All subsequent Shiʿi devotional literature about Karbala represents a female perspective, although the typically male hagiographer may not be conscious of this. Most of the historical record of the events of the battle and its aftermath are based on the testimony of Imam Husain's sister, Zainab. All Shiʿi hagiographical writing is therefore a double remembrance: the hagiographers' words are refracted through the feminine voices and emotions of the women of the *ahl-e bait*. As Agha's hagiographical discourse reveals, the feminine emotions and the voices of the Karbala heroines draw the mourning assembly participants into the scene of battle; however, most of the drama takes place in the women's encampment. In the hagiographers' imaginations, the women of the *ahl-e bait* are the embodiment of imitable sainthood (*wilāyah*) and the *ḥusaini* ethic, which is dramatically amplified through their interactions with Imam Husain, the other men of the family, each other, and God.

The heroines of the Indic epic traditions—both Hindu and Shiʿi—occupy what can be classified as ranges of characterization. At the most general level, epics tell grand stories about exceptional figures who are venerated for their high status, piety, good manners, and breeding. The second range of characterization is subtler, because some epic characters are dually portrayed as being extraordinary yet also profoundly human individuals with whom one can identify. Writers of epic and hagiography use both ranges of characterization in the creation of the heroine, whereas the hero tends to occupy a larger-than-life, distanced, static role.

With the advent of Shiʿism in the Deccan, the Karbala epic tradition, with its many heroines, readily adapted in form, idiom, and performance style to the already vital vernacular Indian epic traditions. Examining the portrayal of Zainab in Mohtasham Kashani's mid-sixteenth-century Persian-language narrative poem (*marṡiya*), the *Karbalā-nāmeh* (Karbala Chronicle), we can trace the way in which the female voice became typologized in Karbala hagiographical literature. Mohtasham's use of Zainab's voice and emotions in the dramatic climax of the *Karbalā-nāmeh* intensifies the *majlis* participants' feelings of grief and provokes the perpetual memory of the *ḥusaini* ethic of the *ahl-e bait*. From a literary critical perspective, the popularity of the *Karbalā-nāmeh* can be attributed to Mohtasham's strategy of narrative engagement enacted through Zainab's embodiment of the dual range of characterization: her bravery and the charismatic blood running through her veins make her larger-than-life, yet her suffering is profoundly real and understandable. Mohtasham's feminine imaginaire has deeply influenced succeeding generations of writers of Karbala hagiographical poetry in Iran and the Indian Deccan.

Indian Epic Women: Sita and Fatimah Kubra in the Masculine Imaginaire

Sita, the ideal wife of King Rama, is one of the most beloved heroines of the two great Indic epic traditions, the *Rāmāyaṇa* and the *Mahābhārata*. Sita figures prominently in the Indic epic imagination, particularly for her embodiment of faithful wifely duty (*pativratā*), suffering, and occasional subversion of patriarchal ideals. Indians who grow up hearing and seeing performances of these two epic traditions develop a sympathy for and identification with the heroines as dynamic and real characters, marking the gendered dimension of this literary-performance genre.

Although much of the theoretical scholarship on epic literary and performance traditions, particularly with regard to voice and emotion, has tended to focus on classical Greek and European texts, some of the observations made by scholars such as George Lukács, Mikhail Bakhtin, and Northrop Frye have a degree of applicability in the context of Indic-Karbala hagiographical traditions. Lukács posits that "the epic hero is, strictly speaking, never an individual" because the hero lacks the capacity for personal growth and individuation.[12] In the Indic Karbala tradition and in the *Rāmāyaṇa*, however, not all epic characters lack true individuality. Evidence from the Deccani-Urdu Karbala tradition requires that an expansion of theses regarding the lack of the epic hero's individuality be limited only to the masculine hero. Interpreters of epic literary forms in diverse literary traditions thus confront a particular challenge.

In contrast, the Deccani-Urdu Shiʿi documentary evidence demonstrates genre contiguity with the Indic epic tradition, particularly with regard to the way in which the heroine is individualized, allowing the author narratively to engage with the audience. Lukács, Frye, and others do not seriously consider the role of the female character in European epic traditions. Although Frye assesses the role of the epic heroine in *The Secular Scripture*, he reduces these women to stock types: sacrificial virgin, scheming trickster seductress, and good wife. These women hardly have any of what Lukács might consider true individuality.[13] In the Indic epic tradition, the female character possesses greater individuality because she occupies a dual range of character that is generally not possible for the epic hero.

In the Indic-Karbala tradition, Imam Husain's martyred male family members are revered as heroes, but they are of the static type that Lukács theorizes. Indo-Islamic epic literature shows the personal growth and individuation of the epic protagonist, whereas epic heroes such as King Rama and Imam Husain are portrayed through strategies of narrative distancing. Imam Husain and the other male heroes of Karbala do not experience any sort of personal growth because they cannot narratologically do so. Their individuality and character cannot develop because as male warriors, they are confined to a specific, unitary plot outcome: martyrdom. The male heroes are not supposed to exhibit a novelistic expression of emotion. Instead, the men of Imam Husain's family fulfill an ideal. There is no narrative ambiguity because the reader-listener knows the conclusion of the story before it even begins.

Naqvi's discourse at the ladies' *mehndī* mourning assembly effectively engages in a strategy of narrative distancing to emphasize Qasem's battlefield exploits and his martyrdom. If a strategy of narrative engagement invites devotees to participate in Karbala's unfolding drama, provoking feelings of empathy and grief for these palpably "real" hero(in)es, then a distancing technique elevates the epic hero to the primary range of characterization as a figure who is larger-than-life. Although Naqvi dramatically modulates her voice and weeps, her discourse constructs Qasem as an idealized young warrior dedicated to his family and the ideals of Islam. Naqvi avoids discussing Qasem's marriage to Fatimah Kubra; in fact, Naqvi dismisses the event. Naqvi's grief for Qasem's martyrdom is certainly evident, but she is much more concerned with portraying Qasem as a larger-than-life hero whose sacrifice is to be admired and respected and whose domestic life is not worthy of emphasis in the sacred context of the mourning assembly. Naqvi's strategy of narrative distancing emphasizes Qasem's epic masculine qualities of emotional distance, bravery, and loyalty.

Lukács's assessment of the character stasis of the hero in the Greek epic tradition applies to the heroes of the *Rāmāyaṇa* and *Mahābhārata*, which in turn provide an analog for understanding the gendered strategies of narrative distancing and engagement employed in Karbala epic hagiography. Rama's character in most vernacular *Rāmāyaṇa* traditions presents him as a king responsible for ruling over his kingdom in a properly dharmic manner, although he inflicts considerable suffering on others, especially his wife,

Sita. Rama is a static figure in virtually all vernacular recensions of the *Rāmāyaṇa*, whereas Sita is a dynamic character diversely portrayed as a powerful ascetic, a benign goddess, a goddess in her "terrible" form, and the embodiment of dharma (doing one's duty according to caste and life-cycle stage).

In the *Rāmāyaṇa*, the young prince, Rama, son of King Dasaratha of Ayodhya, has lost his claim to the throne through a series of palace intrigues. Exiled by his stepmother for fourteen years, Rama heads to the forest, accompanied by his wife, Sita, and loyal brother, Laksmana. The ten-headed demon, Ravana, learns of Sita's incomparable beauty and falls in love with her. Ravana creates a ruse to lure Rama and Laksmana away from Sita, allowing the demon to kidnap her to his kingdom of Lanka. Rather than going to Lanka, Rama sends the monkey-god, Hanuman, to rescue Sita, much to her chagrin. In the *Sundarakāṇḍa* (Beautiful Chapter) of Valmiki's Sanskrit *Rāmāyaṇa*, Sita rejects Hanuman's rescue effort and implores him to send her husband:

> If Rama kills Ravana, his family and his relatives,
> Takes me in pride and returns home, that's an action that befits him.
> . . . .
> So bring him here and make me happy
> With his army, his commanders and his powerful brother.
> I grieve without him, alone in this island.
> Great monkey, do this for me.[14]

Insulted, Sita goads Rama into rescuing her through a speech of eloquent reproach:

> You know your weapons; they are the best.
> You are strong and truthful, for certain, but
> Why not use these weapons on this demon,
> If you really care for me?[15]

Chastened by Sita's words, Rama comes to Lanka to rescue his wife, who has repulsed her amorous kidnapper with ascetic practices that generate dangerous amounts of yogic heat (*tapasyā*). Rama lays waste to Lanka, kills Ravana, and takes Sita back to India. A happy ending to a dramatic story, or so Valmiki leads us to believe. But Rama doubts Sita's chastity and asks her to undergo the *agniparīkṣā* (trial by fire), which will either prove her guilt (infidelity) or innocence (chastity). In the performance context of the *Rāmāyaṇa*, Sita's compulsion to prove her innocence to her distrusting husband provokes men and women to feel sorry for her, since they know she has resolutely resisted Ravana's advances. Valmiki's gendered strategy of narrative engagement causes the audience to feel discomfort when Sita is humiliated by Rama's initial unwillingness to rescue his wife, further compromising her honor, and to experience shock and disbelief when he demands that his wife prove her fidelity. Sita enters the fire and emerges unscathed, yet her trial is not yet over.

After Sita and Rama return to Ayodhya and Rama is restored to the throne, a period of *rāmrājya* is established, and all appears well and dharmically balanced in the kingdom. To maintain perfectly dharmic order during this period of *rāmrājya*, Rama dispatches spies throughout the kingdom, and one day he learns of a washerman (*dhobī*) who has questioned Sita's chastity. At this point, the narrator reminds the audience that Sita has already submitted to and passed one trial by fire. Rama is horrified to discover that Sita's chastity and honor remain in doubt, thereby potentially lessening his power.

To reaffirm his authority, Rama asks Sita to undergo a second trial by fire, which he promises will decisively prove her chastity. This event is narrated in the *Uttarakāṇḍa* (Concluding Chapter),[16] where Sita acquiesces to her husband's request: "I have never set my mind on any man other than Rama, so may the goddess of the earth open up for me. I have served only Rama in thought, word and deed, so may the goddess of the earth open up for me. If all that I have spoken is true, and if I do not know any man other than Rama, may the goddess of the earth open up for me."[17] Rather than submit yet again to the indignity of the trial by fire, Sita creates her own test, asking Mother Earth to swallow her up if she has remained loyal to Rama. A strategy of narrative engagement is employed in which the audience shares Sita's suffering. As the epic hero, Rama is so monodimensional, limited to only doing what is "correct," that he is compelled to make Sita prove her honor. Sita, however, exhibits the qualities of the narratively engaging epic heroine, experiencing personal growth, emotion, and individuation, which she demonstrates by returning to Mother Earth rather than be humiliated one more time.

This outline of the significant events of the *Rāmāyaṇa* illustrates certain narratological elements and strategies that reflect a gendering process in Indic epic traditions. Lukács observed that the epic hero is never an individual—he cannot step outside the character that has been constructed for him. This narratological rigidity of characterization is limited to the male hero of the epic. Rama's kingly persona and voice are never used to draw the audience into the drama through shared emotions, so it is incumbent on male narrators and writers to assume a "transvestic" role by imagining and becoming the active female agent of the epic.[18] In a study of *rekhtī*, a genre of Urdu poetry in which men imagine themselves and speak as women, C. M. Naim asserts that this is a specifically Indic genre.[19] *Rekhtī*'s transvestic quality allows a male writer to free himself from patriarchal controls that inscribe the expression of emotion as a feminine trait. At first glance, this observation seems to reinforce a gendered inscription of rationality and emotional control on the masculine body, further strengthening patriarchal claims to authority; however, it is perhaps more useful to understand this transvestic strategy as further evidence of the unnaturalness of masculine and feminine in the binary system of gender. Vulnerability, a trait that is coded feminine, is expressed through Sita and her various trials and in the case of Karbala through the female members of Imam Husain's family, who are taken as prisoners to Damascus after the battle.

It is neither accurate nor fair to state that men lack emotion, because just as women are socialized to perform certain types of socially sanctioned feminine emotion (tears), men are conditioned to be reasonably passionate. Naqvi appeals to the socially acceptable expression of masculine emotion. Naqvi's discourse is transvestic; she weeps, yet her narrative of Qasem's martyrdom emphasizes Qasem's heroism, distancing the female *majlis* participants through the strategy of passion in the service of reason.[20] Likewise, Agha cries and assumes a feminine voice and emotions in his *mehndī* mourning assembly discourse. His plaintive cry, "Oh God! Don't let this bride become a widow," is intended to cast the male *majlis* participants into the throes of intense crying. Naqvi's narrative distancing and emphasis on factuality limits the extent to which one can enter into the hagiographical realm of Karbala, pointing to her tendency to use the mourning assembly for "correcting young people on matters of the commands of Islamic law [*sharīʿah*] and Shiʿi doctrine."[21]

Two possible explanations for why these two discourses exhibit the transvestic performance of voice and emotion can be found in the strategies of narrative engagement and distancing employed by the *majlis* orators. Hagiography constitutes a form of epic literature that is predicated on simultaneous strategies of narrative engagement and distancing, compelling the Shiʿa to enter the drama of Karbala and cultivate an idealized selfhood that is informed by the religious and vernacular social values and gender roles that are refracted through the embodiment of the *ḥusaini* ethic of Imam Husain's family. The Indic imaginal inhabitation of the contours of female emotion is based on a narratological strategy of engagement, drawing listeners into the story so that they identify with and feel sympathy for the protagonist(s). As Najmabadi notes, the direct gaze compels interaction between the viewer and the subject/object being viewed, effecting a relationship in which neither party is passive and distant.[22]

In the *Rāmāyaṇa* and Karbala narratives, the audience connects with the female characters, who speak directly to the other actors in the story and emotionally engage the listeners/readers through a range of narratological devices that accomplish a variety of goals. In the case of Karbala hagiographies, both in text and performance, devotees are drawn into the action of several settings, most notably the cosmopolitan[23] sites of Karbala and Damascus that are transformed into "real" vernacular sites to which devotees can relate. Zainab, Fatimah Kubra, and the other heroines of Karbala draw *majlis* participants into the action and elicit appropriate expressions of emotion from them by compelling them to enter the tableau. As a distant epic hero, Qasem's role is to die and become a martyr, whereas Fatimah Kubra survives the battle of Karbala; her fate as a "widow forever" leaves her in a state of narratological suspension into which the Shiʿa may insert themselves.

Reflecting the vernacular context of the Deccan, the events of Karbala are expressed in a feminine idiom, and the emotional contours of the event are truly female-centered. The image memory of Karbala is refracted through a women's universe because the women survived the battle. In particular, Zainab was the messenger of martyrdom and provides a powerful role model for both men and women. Sixteenth-century Persian *maršiya* writer Mohtasham Kashani employs a narrative strategy that engages hagiographical transvestism. At the climax of the *Karbalā-nāmeh*, Mohtasham transvestically assumes Zainab's voice when she speaks in apostrophic form, first to her grandfather, the Prophet Muhammad, and then to her mother, Fatimah al-Zahra. Testifying to the deceased members of Husain's family, Mohtasham uses Zainab's voice to foster emotions of intense grief in the Shiʿa that are amplified by the exceptional qualities of the members of this family and their love for one another and faith in Islam. Engaging Zainab's voice, Mohtasham powerfully and effectively draws the listener into the moment. Everyone, male and female alike, can share in Zainab's anxiety in this terrible situation and weeps for her vulnerability, yet Mohtasham's strategy of hagiographical narrative engagement also compels his audience to follow her example and remain steadfast in faith and persevere in even the most trying circumstances. In the *Karbalā-nāmeh*, Zainab simultaneously occupies a dual range of characterization in which she is larger-than-life yet a real and imitable model of the *ḥusaini* ethic of faith and sacrifice. In Mohtasham's poem, Zainab is both a social and religious role model for Shiʿi Muslims; more important, her voice and emotion effectively instructed sixteenth-century Iranians in how to be properly Shiʿa. Zainab is a dynamic heroine: her emotion and modes of speech teach the Shiʿa how properly to remember and mourn Imam Husain.

Setting the World Aflame: Mohtasham's Zainab and the Message of Karbala

In chapter 10 of *Rowẓat al-shohadā* (The Garden of the Martyrs), a sixteenth-century Persian-language Karbala hagiography, Mullah Husain Vaʿez Kashefi repeatedly exhorts the Shiʿa to remember the faith and sacrifice of Karbala's hero(in)es. At this moment in Kashefi's hagiography, the penultimate battle has taken place, Imam Husain has been martyred, and the women and children have been taken as prisoners to Damascus, Syria, where they are paraded before the ʿUmayyad *khalīfah*, Yazid. The surviving women captives go neither meekly nor silently. At Yazid's court, Zainab bears witness to what happened to her brother, family, and supporters at Karbala. Brought before the Kufan governor, Ibn Ziyad, Zainab strides past him and takes her seat, giving neither an oath of allegiance (*bayʿah*) nor a greeting. When Ibn Ziyad chastises her insolence, in a tone redolent with sarcasm, Zainab warns,

> You have done a good deed. You have done something important, on account of which you are hoping for freshness, enjoyment, and peace of mind. From this baseless wisdom, and from the spine of deception, you have become drunk. Through pride and vainglory, the transient has escaped your hand. "Prepare for the hangover tomorrow; you are drunk today." Do you not know that you have killed the best of the Family of Prophecy? You have cut off the root and the branch of the tree in the orchard of prophecy. If this message is the remedy of your heart, then it will soon become your daily repentance. Its imprint will remain on the page of time. You shall receive a compensation for your own unacceptable behavior:
>
> The tyrant thought that he had oppressed us,
> It remained on his neck and passed us by.[24]

Zainab's public and incessantly repeated account of what happened at Karbala makes it impossible for any person to forget about her family's sacrifice and embodiment of the *ḥusaini* ethic.

Because of this experiential dimension to Shiʿi devotional mourning literature, such poetic forms as the *marṡiya*, *nauḥa*, and *salām* as well as the more expansive prose narratives serve a dual function: First, this literature compels the audience to remember the Battle of Karbala. Second, and more important, the *majlis* participants remember the events of Karbala through the perspective of Imam Husain's sister. Zainab's statement that Karbala's "imprint will remain on the page of time" dramatically amplifies the meaning of social memory for the Shiʿi community. Zainab's speech is a powerful form of moral communication that produces a social sensibility and moral community through the devotional literature and ritual performance of the *majlis*.

In Yazid's court (*darbar*), as well as every other place that she visits, Zainab instantiates the Shiʿi tradition of remembrance and mourning that keeps alive this calamitous moment through a mode of ritualized recollection of her family's suffering at Karbala (*maṣāʾib*). The Shiʿa have attributed to Zainab the composition of the first *marṡiya*, a narrative poem eulogizing the Battle of Karbala and an emotionally engaging form of *maṣāʾib* that draws devotees into a Shiʿi moral universe. *Marṡiya* is a shorthand term used by the Shiʿa of South Asia to refer to a broad range of hagiographical literary styles, both prose and verse, that narrate the events of Karbala. Whether *marṡiya*, prose narrative, or the chanted *nauḥa*, this devotional literature seeks to draw the Shiʿa into the spirit of the *ḥusaini* ethic of faith and sacrifice and to cultivate an idealized self based on the imitable socioreligious model of Imam Husain and his family.

The *marṡiya* originated in an oral tradition in which rhymed and rhythmic laments celebrate the merits (*rithā*) of the deceased. In pre-Islamic Arabia, the female relatives traditionally commemorated the activities and heroic qualities of deceased male family members. The Arabic *marṡiya* tradition has tended to be cultivated and transmitted within a woman's world. Women composers and performers of the *marṡiya* have found an abiding place in this deeply religious history, and this place became further solidified after the martyrdom of Imam Husain, particularly because of the large number of *marṡiyas* about the tribulations of the *ahl-e bait* that are openly acknowledged to have been composed by women, especially Zainab.

The use of the feminine voice and emotions in the Shiʿi hagiographical literary tradition provides an important ritual context in which the female relatives of Imam Husain adequately and appropriately mourn the loss of their beloved spiritual leader, father, husband, and brother. Lynda Clarke argues that what is most significant about the various forms of hagiographical literature commemorating the Battle of Karbala is its "beauty and deep feeling," which "has something of the force of memory" for the intended audience.[25]

The highly conventionalized style that emerged from the *marṡiya* compositions of these pre-Islamic professional female mourners has become an important element of the Shiʿi hagiographical tradition, especially as it developed in Persian and other Islamicate languages such as Urdu. The *marṡiya* provided women with not only a socially acceptable means for mourning deceased family and tribe members but also a conventionalized and highly stylized genre of religious literature.

Mohtasham Kashani's twelve-stanza *marṡiya*, the *Karbalā-nāmeh*, offers one of the best examples of how the Battle of Karbala is remembered from a feminine perspective in both voice and emotion.[26] Mohtasham cleverly translated the genre of the Arabic *marṡiya* into a vernacular Persian language and idiom. Mohtasham's *marṡiya* served as a model for Iranian Shiʿa, narrating the historical events of Karbala through vivid words and imagery, guiding the Shiʿa to experience the emotions of *gham* (grief), *mātam* (lamentation),[27] and *giryān* (weeping). Following the established conventions in Arabic literature and ritual practice of women remembering the dead and through the narrative strategy of literary transvestism, Mohtasham utilizes Zainab's voice to great emotional effect as she speaks to the Prophet Muhammad and Fatimah al-Zahra in their graves. Zainab's voice is important not only because she was endowed with the responsibility of spreading the message of Husain's martyrdom but also because as a woman, she is an important embodiment of the *ḥusaini* ethic.

Because Zainab's suffering and testimony are the centerpiece of Mohtasham's poem, we can identify the *marṡiya* and all other types of Karbala literature as a form of hagiography. As such, the *Karbalā-nāmeh* serves several didactic functions. In particular, this *marṡiya* compels active remembrance of the Battle of Karbala and instructs devotees in proper emotional behavior, such as self-flagellation (*mātam*) and grief (*soz*). In its performance context, the *marṡiya* eliminates both time and place: every place and every moment is Karbala. In this sense, the *marṡiya* is experiential because it is predicated on Zainab's act of remembrance.[28] As hagiography, the *marṡiya* constructs the women of the *ahl-e bait*, particularly Zainab, as imitable saints (embodiments of *wilāyah*) and paragons of the *ḥusaini* ethic. The women of Karbala exemplify ideals to which all may aspire.

Since hagiography chronicles the lives and experiences of saints, who exemplify particular religious ideals, the genre must be both didactic and experiential. Although the many forms of Karbala literature function as hagiography, the vocabulary, themes, and highlighted characters must constantly change to "chronicle the ways in which followers experienced the saint as a saint."[29] Hagiographies are sacred biographies that tell saints' life stories. In this regard, Karbala devotional literature corresponds in part to Hippolyte Delehaye's classic definition of hagiography as "writings inspired by religious devotion to the saints and intended to increase that devotion."[30] We must, however, take care not to strive too much to determine the actual or true historical life of the saint. Hagiographies should not necessarily be read as works of history; rather, they are literary works that emplot the saints' lifetimes in specific social and historical contexts. Thus, at its most basic level, hagiography is "the history of how the saint's followers have chosen to remember him or her," and hagiographers "serve as mediators, creating a bridge between the saint and his followers through their texts."[31]

Hagiography, like epic, is experiential because it is an interactive genre that is based on strategies of narrative engagement and distancing. As a form of Shiʿi moral communication, the *Karbalā-nāmeh* served an important didactic function in teaching Iranians about the Battle of Karbala by employing a strategy of narrative engagement reinforced by Mohtasham's use of vivid vocabulary and imagery. In the *Karbalā-nāmeh*, Zainab's memorializing function calls both women and men to remember Karbala according to how their individual gendered selves construct the salient features of this remembrance. In particular, men might emulate Zainab's willingness to die to protect Islam from injustice, and women might emulate Zainab's fierce dedication to family and faith.

Zainab's apostrophic speech to Muhammad and Fatimah in their graves illustrates Mohtasham's two characterizations of Imam Husain's sister. Zainab is the larger-than-life heroine who survived the battle, and she understands that she and her brother share a divinely bestowed responsibility to spread the message of Karbala. Husain's role was to die for the dual causes of familial justice and religion, and Zainab's responsibility was to spread the message of his martyrdom and to preserve the Imamate. This aspect of Zainab's characterization reflects her role as an epic heroine, yet the grief and anger she expresses over the carnage and death that she has witnessed make everyday Shiʿa identify with her and understand her feelings of anguish:

Suddenly, among the dead the eyes of the daughter of the Radiant [*zahrā*]
Fell upon the noble body of the Imam of the Age.

Impulsively, she cried, "This is Husain [*Haẕā Husain*]!"[32]
So hot, that this cry set the world aflame.

Then with tongue of reproach, that part of Fatimah [*baẓʿat al-batūl*]
Turned her face to Medina, saying, "O Messenger!"

"This man slain and fallen upon the plain—this is Husain!
This prey that is covered from head to foot in blood—this is Husain!

"This verdant palm, from which the smoke of the life-burning fire of thirst
Was borne up from the earth to the heavens—this is Husain!

"This fish, fallen in a sea of blood,
Upon whose body are wounds more numerous than the stars[33]—this is Husain!

"This one drowned in the ocean of martyrdom, the waves of whose blood
Have stained the face of the desert red—this is Husain!

"These parched lips, prohibited from the banks of the Euphrates,
From whose blood the earth has become like a mighty river—this is Husain!

"This king of a small army, whose troops of tears and sighs
Decamped from this world—this is Husain!

"This quivering body that was left like this on the ground,
The unburied King of the Martyrs—this is Husain!

When she turned to address Zahra in the Everlasting Cemetery
She roasted the beasts of the earth and the birds of the air:

"O! Intimate friend of the brokenhearted, behold our state,
Behold us, exiled, forlorn, and without companion.

"Your children, who will be the intercessors at the Resurrection,
Behold them in the abyss of the torment of the People of Oppression.

"In eternity, beyond the veil of both worlds, open your arms wide!
And in the world, behold our misfortune out in the open.

"No, no! Come to Karbala like a weeping rain cloud.
Behold the seditious flood of rebellion and the wave of affliction.

"Behold all of the slain bodies in the dust and blood.
Behold, the heads of commanders all set upon spears!

"The head that always rested on the Prophet's shoulder,
Behold it separated from its shoulders by an enemy's spear.

"That body which was nurtured in your embrace,
Behold it wallowing in the dust of the battlefield of Karbala

"O! Part of Fatimah, give us justice from Ibn-e Ziyad,
For he destroyed the People of the House of Prophecy and cast them
in the dust."[34]

Mohtasham deliberately employs Zainab as the familiar female voice of the *marśiya* tradition and does so in a way that is multivalent. First, Mohtasham establishes a literary connection with the Arabic *marśiya* tradition by using Zainab's feminine voice and Arabic phraseology to mark the emotional climax of the poem. Second, and more important, by adopting Zainab's voice, Mohtasham's poem fulfills two functions of hagiography. First, the Karbala narrative conveys the political-historical dimension of Shiʿism, particularly the idea that Zainab was endowed with her brother's political legacy. Moreover, through her embodiment of the *ḥusaini* ethic and imitable sainthood (*ḥusainiyyat-wilāyah*), she safeguards the survival of the *ahl-e bait* and Islam. This is her role as the epic heroine who is a religious exemplar. Second, by using Zainab's voice and emotions, Mohtasham makes his *marśiya* a powerful form of moral communication, instructing people how to remember Karbala and reminding them to emulate the social and religious model of Imam Husain and his family.

By tapping into the tradition in Islamic culture of women as the primary eulogizers and memorializers of deceased male relatives and by utilizing Zainab's voice in the *Karbalā-nāmeh*, Mohtasham not only created a dramatic climax in his Karbala narrative but also transformed the genre into a distinct form of epic hagiography.

Karbala's Deccani Idiom: The Ahl-e bait *Becomes Indian*

Just as texts and performances commemorating the Battle of Karbala were translated into an Iranian idiom by sixteenth-century Persian writers, most notably Kashefi and Mohtasham, these texts were brought to the Deccan, where they acquired distinctive South Indian cultural, ecological, and linguistic forms. As early as the fourteenth century, Iranians began to immigrate to the Deccan in large numbers to serve in the court (*darbar*) of the Bahmani king, Muhammad II (r. 1378–97). S. A. A. Rizvi notes that the Iranians "practiced *taqiyya* [dissimulation] although they did not miss any opportunity to prepare the ground for the growth of Shiʿism in the Deccan."[35] The ʿAdil Shahis of Bijapur were enthusiastic patrons of the foreign (*āfāqī*) scholars and writers who filled their courts.[36] In 1585 C.E., an Iranian *āfāqī*, Mir Muhammad Muʾmin Astarabadi, was appointed to the court of Muhammad Quli Qutb Shah in Golconda (on the outskirts of the modern city of Hyderabad). This appointment proved significant for the development of Shiʿi devotionalism in the Deccan. According to Rizvi, Mir Muʾmin was astonishingly successful in introducing and propagating Shiʿism in the non-Muslim communities of the Deccan: "As if the construction of Hyderabad itself was not enough, Mir Muhammad Muʾmin founded many villages as centers of Shiʿi and Islamic life. In them he constructed reservoirs, mosques, caravanserais, *ʿAshur-khanas* and planted gardens. The mosques and *ʿAshur-khanas* brought the Hindu villagers into contact with the Islamic and Shiʿi way of life. The *ʿalams* and other symbols of the tragedy of Karbala were introduced by Mir Muʾmin into these villages where they aroused Hindu curiosity and helped to convert them to Shiʿism."[37] Although he was an Iranian and an outsider to the diverse religious traditions practiced by the people of the region, Mir Muʾmin thus contributed to the creation of a complex multicultural environment in which Hindu, Shiʿa, Persian, Telugu, and Deccani came into dynamic contact.

With the movement of scholars, poets, and merchants between Iran and India, both Mohtasham's *Karbalā-nāmeh* and Mullah Husain Vaʿez Kashefi's *Rowẓat al-shohadā* were being read in the mourning assemblies at Golconda and Bijapur by the end of the sixteenth century.[38] The *Karbalā-nāmeh* was recited in the *majlis* mourning assemblies, particularly under the patronage of ʿAli ʿAdil Shah I of Bijapur (r. 1558–80) and Muhammad Quli Qutb Shah of Golconda (r. 1580–1611). To make the recitation of the Karbala narrative understandable to those who knew only the local languages of Deccani and Telugu, Mohtasham's and Kashefi's writings were translated and vernacularized to reflect the tragedy of Karbala through a distinctively Indic idiom and worldview. This does not mean that these writings experienced a brief moment of popularity and then faded into obscurity. In fact, quite the opposite occurred. Just as in Iran, the *Karbalā-nāmeh* "became a source of elegy emulation for . . . Indian poets of ensuing generations."[39] The repeated imitation and translation of the *Karbalā-nāmeh* and *Rowẓat al-shohadā* attest to the fact that these two styles of Shiʿi hagiographical literature created a literary and imaginary link that enabled the Shiʿa to remember the events of Karbala through vernacular idioms and as a sacralized modality through which the hero(in)es of Imam Husain's family teach religious and social values.

Rowẓat al-shohadā appeared in the Deccan sometime in the mid-seventeenth century, and within a couple of decades, countless writers were translating the Karbala narrative into Deccani-Urdu. One of the Deccan's earliest composers of Shiʿi hagiographical literature was a Hindu, Rama Rao, who wrote under the pen name (*takhalluṣ*) Śaiva. As the first Hindu writer of *marśiya* in the Deccan, Rama Rao received the patronage of ʿAli ʿAdil Shah of Bijapur. In 1681, Rama Rao also completed one of the first Deccani-Urdu translations of *Rowẓat al-shohadā*. With non-Muslim practitioners of Hindu traditions participating in the composition of Shiʿi devotional literature, the remembrance of Karbala in the Deccan was bound to reflect an Indic vernacular worldview and its attendant social, aesthetic, and gender values.

Shiʿi devotional literature continued to flourish in all parts of the Deccan. With the collapse of the Qutb Shahi dynasty following Mughal emperor Aurangzeb's lengthy siege of Golconda Fort in 1687, the succeeding Asaf Jahi dynasty (1724–1948 C.E.) was Sunni, although the Nizams exhibited a predilection for Shiʿism in both governance and aesthetics. Under the reign of Asaf Jah II Nizam ʿAli Khan (r. 1762–1803) and Asaf Jah III Sikandar Jah (r. 1803–29), Shiʿi institutions, religious practice, and literature experienced a period of revival. The Nizams and other senior members of the government supported renovation projects and the construction of new *ʿāshūrkhānas*, which many observers considered official acknowledgment of Shiʿism's indelible religiocultural imprint on the Deccan.

If Hyderabad's archives may serve as an indicator of the sorts of Shiʿi hagiographical literature commissioned and composed in the eighteenth and nineteenth centuries in the Deccan, Kashefi's *Rowẓat al-shohadā* was one of the most popular Shiʿi devotional texts of the period. Writers in the Deccani-Urdu dialect found the work a malleable text in which the entire world of Karbala was transformed from seventh-century Arab Iraq to early modern Hyderabad and its surrounding countryside. Some authors chose to retain the Persianate title of Kashefi's work, while many others assigned new titles to their translations as part of the process of vernacularizing the hagiographic text (and related performance traditions).

Most vernacular recensions of *Rowẓat al-shohadā* were composed in verse form. Around 1717, Vali Vellori composed one of the most famous South Indian versions of Kashefi's Karbala hagiography, ascribing to it the title *Dah majlis* (The Ten Assemblies). Vali Vellori retained the contents of Kashefi's Karbala hagiography but appealed to local aesthetics by composing the text in rhythmic metrical form that facilitated its dramatic recitation in the mourning assemblies. Composition of Shiʿi devotional literature remained a popular pastime for the governing elite during the Asaf Jahi dynasty, with two significant manuscripts produced during this period. The first, a different manuscript also titled *Dah majlis*, was written by Mir ʿAlam, the prime minister (*dīwān*) to Asaf Jah III Sikandar Jah in Muharram 1196 A.H./1781 C.E. The same year, Mir Vali Khan Munis composed *Riyaẓ al-ṭāhirīn*[40] (The Gardens of the Chaste), a Karbala hagiography written in prose form. In both of these hagiographies, Karbala and its hero(in)es were thoroughly vernacularized through the integration of Indic practices, clothing, and forms of speech as well as descriptions of the area's physical landscape.

As a genre of Shiʿi literature, Deccani-Urdu Karbala hagiographies maintained their distinctively Islamic tone despite their otherwise thorough vernacularization and absorption of Indic epic forms and gendered conventions of characterization. By the end of the nineteenth century, Karbala hagiographies had clearly become another type of Indic epic literature in which male heroes conform to rigid roles that preclude them from emotional development and engagement with the audience. The female characters figure prominently in Karbala hagiographers' imaginaire—in fact, the female characters become the emotional focus of the drama, and through strategies of narrative engagement, the women of the *ahl-e bait* come to embody the *ḥusaini* ethic of moral communication that instructs men and women how to cultivate idealized selves.

Men Mourning Widows:
Fatimah Kubra in Mir ʿAlam's Masculine Imaginaire

In his *mehndī* mourning assembly discourse, Agha expressed true grief for Fatimah Kubra's widowhood and suffering so soon after her battlefield marriage. Weeping and raising his voice to a crescendo, Agha cried out, "Oh God! Do not let this bride become a widow!" In the discourses that I heard Agha deliver at the Khan family's men's *mehndī* mourning assemblies in 2005 and 2006, the memory of Fatimah Kubra that he invoked is of a bride whose wedding is anything but *shādī*. The conventional Urdu word for "wedding" is *shādī*, but its more literal meaning is "joyfulness," the emotional state that a wedding is supposed to produce. Of course, there is nothing joyful about Fatimah Kubra's wedding, over which death and destruction loom darkly. Listening to Agha's discourse, I wondered whether his extremely passionate narrative of Fatimah Kubra's suffering is typical of male *majlis* orators in Hyderabad.

In his role of *majlis* orator, Agha, too, is a hagiographer, drawing on the complex, vernacular devotional Karbala traditions of the Deccan. Engaging a transvestic voice, Agha speaks as a woman, cries, and beats his breast to convey his identification with and embodiment of Fatimah Kubra's *ḥusaini* ethic. In his discourses, we can see that Agha employs a sophisticated strategy of gendered narrative engagement, drawing the *majlis* participants into the feminine world and emotions of the wedding chamber. In the Indian epic traditions of *Rāmāyaṇa* and *Mahābhārata* (as well as many other vernacular narrative performance contexts), the audience identifies the heroine as both extraordinary and imitable. Sita is a good wife yet also is a subversive example of how women can resist systems of patriarchal oppression and violence. Imam Husain's sister, Zainab, is a similarly dynamic epic heroine and imitable saint: a dedicated mother/wife/sister, she also fulfills God's will to uphold the Imamate and spread the message of Karbala in the aftermath of the battle. For many hagiographers who depict the hero(in)es of Karbala in text and performance, the female survivors are easier to transform into saints with distinctly mimetic qualities. For Agha, Fatimah Kubra is special and real because despite being just a young girl, she willingly sacrifices her husband for the political and spiritual cause of Islam.

Agha's dramatic portrayal of Fatimah Kubra as both a strong and pathetic bride/widow draws on an established Deccani tradition. The widowing of Fatimah Kubra is a popular theme for writers of Karbala literature in the

Deccan. Usually, however, Fatimah Kubra's experience is a subplot in texts such as *Rowẓat al-shohadā* and the various recensions of the *Dah majlis*. One text I encountered during my archival research differed from the twenty other Deccan-Urdu manuscript sections I examined. This manuscript offered a unique hagiographical depiction of Qasem and Fatimah Kubra; moreover, only one Hyderabad archive possessed a copy of this document.[41] This particular manuscript attracted my attention for two reasons: first, this manuscript was composed by Mir ʿAlam, prime minister (*dīwān*) from 1804 to 1808, during the reign of Nizam Sikandar Jah; and second, this chapter on Qasem's martyrdom actually says very little about the bridegroom/warrior.

Sayyid Abu al-Qasem Mir ʿAlam Bahadur (b. 1752) was the son of Sayyid Reza, who immigrated to the Deccan from Iran. In his youth, Mir ʿAlam studied Persian literature and the fundamentals of Shiʿi thought and belief.[42] This early education instilled in Mir ʿAlam a deep knowledge of Shiʿism and love for the *ahl-e bait*. In addition to patronizing Muharram mourning assemblies and poets, Mir ʿAlam also composed *Dah majlis* in the poetic form of a *qaṣīdah* (narrative encomium). Mir ʿAlam was a prominent supporter of Hyderabad's Shiʿi community, and he wrote one of the most significantly vernacularized and Indianized of the Deccani-Urdu Karbala hagiographies composed since the seventeenth century. Mir ʿAlam's account of Qasem's martyrdom has little to do with the hero of the chapter's title; rather, in a striking act of literary transvestism, the author narrates this event through Fatimah Kubra's voice and perspective. Mir ʿAlam focuses almost exclusively on the vernacular rituals of an Indian wedding, Indic anxieties about widowhood, and the articulation of the gender roles to be cultivated and embodied by Hyderabadi men and women. Qasem is peripheral to the narrative; his only real role is to be martyred. Mir ʿAlam transvestically inhabits Fatimah Kubra's emotional world and status as a bride/widow. Mir ʿAlam engages his audience by channeling Fatimah Kubra's speech, emotions, and actions, thereby compelling *majlis* participants to share in her experience, to weep for her sacrifice of her husband, to be inspired by her faith in Islam, and to connect with her as both a religious and vernacular social role model. Both Mir ʿAlam and Agha use engaging narrative strategies that transform Fatimah Kubra into a woman who is as real and intimate as audience members' sisters, mothers, or aunts.

Mir ʿAlam introduces the chapter on Qasem's martyrdom with a dramatic statement that he is about to tell the story of a wedding unlike any other:

In this manner, the *majlis* of the seventh day has been written, in which,
By this grievous event, the customary rituals of the wedding were changed.
In the place of gaiety, there is bloodshed.

The first fifteen lines of the chapter, composed in verse form, continue to set the scene. The members of the *ahl-e bait* are invoked, and their suffering is brought into focus when Mir ʿAlam asks his audience,

How can I describe the effulgence of the Holy Five,
Whose wedding garments are like a shroud?
O! Lovers [of the *ahl-e bait*], here is an account of their death;
Now, Listen! This is the moment of the bridegroom Qasem's *shahādat*!
This lament is for the martyrdom of this newly fledged bridegroom,
Just as it is for the new bride Fatimah Kubra.

The narrator calls on the Shiʿa, the loyal devotees of the *ahl-e bait*, to participate in and celebrate Qasem and Fatimah Kubra's wedding. The narrator sets up a metalepsis that draws the *majlis* participants into the drama of the battlefield wedding. In the ritual context of the *majlis*, the use of narrative metalepsis enacts a vernacular transformation of Karbala in which each man and woman imagines his or her participation in the battlefield wedding, where Fatimah Kubra's crimson bridal *sāṛī* is transformed into a widow's shroud.

The narrator next extols the extraordinary qualities of Qasem ("the best of humanity") and Fatimah Kubra (Husain's beloved daughter). These two youth are superlative embodiments of faith and honor. Their wedding attains a supernatural and transcendent quality that is foreshadowed by Qasem's father, Imam Hasan, and the joining together of these two exceptional people is necessary to fulfill his will and testament (*waṣīyat*). Qasem and Fatimah Kubra are described as *maʿṣūm* (innocent children) who have been forced into a situation that requires maturity far beyond their years. The narrator creates a dramatic tension that juxtaposes Qasem and Fatimah Kubra's youth with their embodiment of the *ḥusaini* ethic:

At that moment, the son of Shabbar[43] dismounted from the horse,
and fell at the feet of that lord [*sarvar*] Husain.
He said, "Oh King, will everyone achieve martyrdom?
I am an orphan [*yatīm*], so please grant me permission to go to battle."

Qasem's statement that he is an orphan marks a transition in the narrative by which he simultaneously emphasizes his parentless state and his recognition of the fatherlike role that Imam Husain has assumed. Imam Husain's deference to the wishes of his elder brother and his desire to protect his favorite nephew elevate the pathos of this moment:

"How can I give my approval, alas!
　By God when I remember my brother.
If you populate the battlefield with your corpse,
　How will I hold myself accountable to Hasan?"
Hearing the king's words, Qasem was disheartened,
　He said, "Uncle, this is my lament,
How will it be possible for me, your majesty,
　That I might see your martyrdom with my own eyes?
How can I not lose my neck in this fashion?
　Oh King, my fate has been written on my forehead!
This affliction has become such a sign
　That my head does not appear to bear any burden at all."
"If you go before me into battle,
　How can I show this face of mine to Hasan?"

Imam Husain is rendered powerless in this impossible situation. How can he allow his nephew to go into battle, where he will most certainly be martyred? How will Imam Husain face his brother on the Day of Judgment? These questions torment Husain, yet he feels worse seeing his beloved nephew yearning to go into battle and fight for the dual cause of religion and family. At this juncture in the drama, the epic hero exhibits the maximum amount of emotion possible, and the narrator releases him from the responsibility of solving this dilemma.

Incapacitated by his grief, Imam Husain summons his sister, Zainab, to take control of this situation with Qasem. The narrator effects another transition in the action by introducing Zainab, whom hagiographical strategies of gendered narrative engagement portray as a far more practical and action-oriented character than her brother. Zainab heaves a sigh, speaks, and moves Qasem along his fated path toward matrimony and martyrdom:

When Imam Husain summoned his sister, Zainab,
　In such a manner she was consumed with sighs and began to say,
"Now, Hasan's house is destroyed,
　Qasem has gone to battle so that he may lose his head.

I had but one wish for this marriage,
That I could see the garlanding [*sehrā bandhānā*] of the bride and groom.
Now, go and take him to the encampment
Make my Qasem into a bridegroom.
Quickly, make the wedding preparations for the bride,
She will burn terribly from that bloody shroud.[44]
This bridegroom is a guest for but a moment;
I shall see him again when he is in the grave."

Imam Husain is effectively removed from the action, but Zainab's voice is increasingly poignant as she speaks of her futile wishes and aspirations for the wedding of her niece and nephew. Zainab's wish to see the bride and groom garlanded with flowers (*sehrā bandhānā*) reflects an Indic vernacular practice that marks the completion of a Muslim wedding after the couple signs the marriage contract (*ʿaqd-e nikāḥ*). The bride and groom then perform the postwedding ritual of *ʿarsī muṣḥāf*, sitting side by side as the groom sees his bride's face for the first time in a mirror. Women from both families approach the couple and place heavy, fragrant garlands of flowers around their necks (fig. 3).

During the garlanding ceremony (*sehrā bandhānā*), the bride and groom are seated together and adorned with roses, jasmine, and marigolds. They are fed sweets, and family and friends wish the newlyweds a happy and fruitful marriage. While a joyous, laughter-filled event for onlookers, it is a somber occasion for the new couple, marking the final event in the lengthy wedding ceremony. Zainab laments not witnessing this event, thereby provoking the grief of Hyderabadi *majlis* participants, who understand the value and meaning of such vernacular wedding rituals.

Zainab's words establish another inversion in which this wedding is not the joining together of a man and woman in a permanent relationship but rather a fleeting and tragic union, and the audience can find consolation only from the extraordinariness of the situation. Zainab's speech exaggerates the transience of this marriage, in which the "bridegroom is a guest for but a moment / I shall see him again when he is in the grave." Despite the fact that this most unusual marriage takes place in extraordinary circumstances, lacking any of the vernacular ceremonies and rituals that are customary in respectable South Asian Muslim weddings, Fatimah Kubra and Qasem must get married.

*Figure 3. The garlanding ceremony (*sehrā bandhānā*) that marks the end of a Hyderabadi Shiʿi wedding, Bait al-Qaʾem* ʿāshūrkhāna*, Purani Haveli, Hyderabad, 15 December 2005.*

Now the mother's offspring was snatched away,
  To whom she came in order to make into a groom.
"Now, make the daughter, too, a bride
  Bring her quickly to the place of the bridegroom Qasem!"
Bano[45] said, "How can I bring Kubra?
  Woe! How can I make her a bride?"
She groaned, "What kind of a marriage is this to be?
  He has gone and is about to lose his head!"
Saying this, she went to Kubra.
  She said, "All of my hopes for my daughter are dashed.
I have come in order to tie the bracelet [*kaṅgnā*] to your wrist,
  I have come to make you a bride, my dear."
Kubra said, "Now, I desire nothing else.
  The marriage contract ceremony is enough for me."

This vignette reflects the tension caused by Qasem's and Fatimah Kubra's mothers' desire to provide their children with all of the customary rituals necessary for a respectable vernacular South Asian Muslim marriage. Fatimah Kubra understands the direness of the situation and implores the women to perform the minimum requirements for the marriage—that is, signing the

ʿ*aqd-e nikāḥ*. The narrator speaks almost exclusively through the voices of the women of the *ahl-e bait*, expressing emotions that are distinctly feminine, almost to the exclusion of all men except Qasem. In India, women usually arrange marriages and organize and plan the variety of customary events. As in North America, men are often peripheral to the planning and organizing of a wedding. The narrator removes Imam Husain from this vignette so that he will conform to his gendered role as epic hero of the *ahl-e bait*. One might assume that he is tending to more pressing matters of strategy and battle rather than to the "women's work" of arranging a wedding.

The women busy themselves with wedding preparations. Although many of the rituals and customs of marriage cannot be performed in this battlefield wedding, the women of the *ahl-e bait* do their best to make the ceremony conform to the requirements of an idealized South Asian Muslim wedding. The clothing of the bride and groom and the wedding rituals performed are completely vernacularized, thereby making this upside-down wedding much more poignant and meaningful for Deccani *majlis* participants. One can vividly imagine such a tragic wedding in culturally relevant terms. Considering Qasem's imminent martyrdom, wedding participants' greatest wish cannot be fulfilled:

> The moment at which the bride approached her groom,
> Their love was sacrificed.
> Everyone began to pray, "Oh God!
> Do not bring widowhood upon the bride!
> May not the home of the bride become ruined!
> Nor should the groom sleep in the place of death!"

At the moment of marriage, Imam Husain returns to the scene to perform the ceremony (*nikāḥ*). He remains just long enough to officiate; to maintain his role as an epic hero whose emotions are contained, he then flees to the battlefield. His daughter is about to become a widow, and his nephew, whom Imam Husain loves as a son, is about to die. To conform to the strategy of narrative distancing in this Indic epic hagiography, Imam Husain cannot fully express his grief or stress. When he feels overcome with grief, he cries out to God, an act of narrative distancing that reinforces the Imam's role as an epic hagiographical hero whose deepest connection is with God:

> Going to the bridegroom [*naushāh*], Shahrbano cried out,
> "The bride Kubra has come; look at your bride!

Come into the tent, Lord, and listen,
  Please consent to this."
Hearing these words, Husain then came to the tent.
  He looked at the bride and groom,
Consider, at that very moment Shah Husain was overcome,
  And he cried out an appeal to the Prophet of God [*yā nabī Allah*].
Having given her away to Qasem, Imam Husain said,
  "Now, bridegroom, this bride is yours, take her.
Either leave her here or take her and go, beloved.
  This is your trust, for which you are responsible."
Saying this, he left Qasem in the women's quarters.
  He stood his ground, thirsty-lipped among the people of oppression.

Qasem then asks for leave from his wife to go into battle. Fatimah Kubra is saddened, asking how he can abandon her so soon after their marriage. She tells him that she knows that he will be martyred and proclaims her willingness to sacrifice herself for him. Qasem lies to Fatimah Kubra, telling her that he is not going to die and that he will soon return. Fatimah Kubra's frustration and fear are palpable in her response to her bridegroom:

"Today you are going to battle and claim that you will not be killed, so
  Why are you giving me such a bridewealth?"

This discussion about Fatimah Kubra's bridewealth (*mahr*) refers to a common explanation given by Hyderabadi Shiʿa for the necessity of Qasem and Fatimah Kubra's battlefield wedding. According to many of my informants, Fatimah Kubra married Qasem because she had reached the age of maturity and could be forced into marriage by Yazid or any other person in his court unless she was widowed. As a widow, Fatimah Kubra was legally free to refuse any marriage alliance that was not agreeable to her. This discussion refers to the fact that her widowed status would save her from the even greater suffering that she would experience if she were forced to marry Yazid.

"If there is no matter of separation in the heart,
  then why has my mother given my hand [to you in marriage]?"

Despite the logic of Fatimah Kubra's marriage strategy, this is a grievous moment, and she feels frustration that her bridegroom is so eager to martyr himself. In good epic heroic fashion, Qasem is unable to handle his wife's feelings, summoning his mother to reason with Fatimah Kubra. Just as Mir ʿAlam removes Imam Husain from the narrative at emotional moments, the author likewise distances Qasem's participation by introducing his mother, Umm Farwa. But Qasem's mother reacts in much the same way as Fatimah Kubra. Umm Farwa promises to sacrifice her life for her son: "Any blow that will befall you / I will first take it upon myself."

Qasem tries to reason that martyrdom is his fate, seeming at least to reconcile his mother to this inevitability. As Umm Farwa and Fatimah Kubra lament the loss of their son/husband, another female character is introduced into the scene. Four-year-old Sakinah, the youngest daughter of Imam Husain, enters in a state of grief. She is upset that she cannot fulfill her ritual responsibilities in her role as Qasem's sister-in-law and receive the privileges to which she is entitled. Again, the narrator further vernacularizes Karbala when he introduces Sakinah:

> Then, in a state of grief, the sister-in-law [*sālī*], Sakinah, approached.
> She grabbed his sleeve; she cried, weeping and wailing,
> "Ay brother, give me my *neg*!
> O! Brother, what kind of a wedding is this today?
> That your sister-in-law is standing around bereft of her *neg*."

This same sense of grief at being denied the opportunity to demand a ransom from a future brother-in-law is found in a popular *salām*, "Come home, brother." Sakinah is particularly upset that she will not participate in the fun of *jūtā chhupāʾī*, a prewedding ritual in which the sisters-in-law steal the bridegroom's slippers, refusing to return them until he provides a ransom of sweets and money (*neg*). Sakinah's sadness is another way in which feminine emotions are a strategy of narrative engagement that draws *majlis* participants into the drama of Karbala, emphasizing the strength, resilience, and faith of the women of the *ahl-e bait*. No woman is unscathed by this event, but the women's embodiment of the *ḥusaini* ethic compels both men and women to imitate such actions and cultivate their exemplary selves.

As the domestic drama builds, the audience knows that Qasem's martyrdom is imminent. The narrator devotes minimal attention to this event because it is inevitable and because this is really a hagiographical account of the women of the *ahl-e bait*. Mir ʿAlam devotes approximately ten couplets to Qasem's participation in the battle and his death before shifting the narrative focus of the chapter and engaging the heroic warriors, who are simultaneously brave and emotionally vulnerable. Imam Husain rushes onto the battlefield to gather up his nephew's body, crying out,

How can I bring you back to the encampment?
   How can I show your corpse to your bride?
How can I go crying in the tent?
   When your mother will ask me the question as soon as I arrive?

Imam Husain's exclamations indicate his deep anxiety about delivering the news of Qasem's martyrdom to the women's encampment. When Imam Husain returns, the women will know that the bridegroom of Karbala is dead. Imam Husain grieves for his nephew, although his sorrow is controlled.

When Qasem's mother sees her son's corpse approaching on horseback, she cries out in anguish. She curses fate and wonders what she could have done wrong as a mother and a human being to deserve such pain and suffering. Although the women of Imam Husain's family know that their male relatives must die to save the lineage and religion of the Prophet Muhammad, the narrative strategy of engagement draws this heroic sacrifice into the present, compelling *majlis* participants to keep the memory of this event alive and to cultivate the *ḥusaini* ethic of these saints. The women know that the battle must happen so that Islam can be preserved, yet they cannot accept the slaughter taking place before them. Umm Farwa bewails her fate and her son's corporeal silence:

Lamenting over her son's corpse,
   Wringing the hands, she lamented "Alas, Fate!
What is my crime? Oh Darling! Alas!
   Woe to me that you are not able to speak!
Why are you angry with your mother?
   This night in which you are sleeping has now passed."
She cried out, "Grant justice to the oppressed!
   My grown son has been ruined, what can I do?
Alas, how this hour of my son's death afflicts me!"

Fatimah Kubra has now become a widow, and the women of Imam Husain's family must address this inauspicious woman. Just as Agha cried out in his discourse that God should forbid a woman from becoming widowed, the worst thing that can happen in Indic society is for a woman to become *bevāh*, especially so soon after being married. As Khan explained to me, this was Fatimah Kubra's sacrifice. Fatimah's marriage to Qasem accorded her widow's status, protecting her from the predations of men. According to Khan, the marriage did not need to be consummated: the act of signing the marriage contract brought her into the presence of her husband and, in the Indic vernacular context, provided sufficient qualification for her to be considered a widow.[46]

Fatimah Kubra is not easily consoled by her widowed status and the protections it is intended to give her. Indic vernacular culture treats the widow as a socially dead individual. Fatimah Kubra's mother realizes that her daughter has died, too.[47] Fatimah Kubra affirms her social death when she says to her mother, "I am joining now with his corpse."

This chapter has focused on the bride/widow's sufferings and the lamentations of the women of Imam Husain's family over this joyless and tragic wedding. The male epic hero, Imam Husain, is all but absent. Qasem is present only in martyrdom; he has fulfilled his role as epic hero idealized as a bridegroom, sacrificing himself for the preservation of his wife's honor. He is also an idealized male warrior of the *ahl-e bait*, unhesitatingly sacrificing himself for the cause of Islam. Through strategies of narrative engagement and distancing, Mir ʿAlam's use of the female epic heroine as a dynamic character who is exceptional yet real transforms hagiography into a powerful form of moral communication that effectively engages *majlis* participants in the world of Karbala as it is reflected through a Hyderabadi socioreligious vernacular.

Epic Hagiography and Its Feminine Voices and Emotions

Feminine voices and emotions construct the religious heroine—exemplified by the bride/widow Fatimah Kubra—in the Karbala epic hagiographical tradition as it has developed in Hyderabad. By virtue of surviving the battle and living to tell the story, the dynamic epic heroine of Karbala articulates the values of Indian culture and society and the ideals of Islam through the filter of sainthood that is embodied in the *ḥusaini* ethic.

Mir ʿAlam's account of Qasem's martyrdom reflects the centrality of feminine voices and emotions in the construction of the genre of Karbala epic hagiography. This account is supposed to be about Qasem, but the author instead focuses with terrific emotional intensity and sympathy on Fatimah Kubra's extraordinary battlefield wedding and nearly simultaneous widowing. Each time a moment in the narrative involves the expression of emotion and the imparting of vernacular values, the male protagonists exit the scene, leaving the women to speak and to act—to engage the *majlis* participants. Just like Sita, Fatima Kubra teaches Indian women how to be ideal wives (*pativratās*). At its most basic level, Indic epic hagiography has an ethical function. Listeners/readers learn their duty (*dharma*) through the exploits of the hero(in)es of Indic epic hagiographies. The women of Karbala provide such compelling ethical and religious role-models for Hyderabadis because the story is never finished: as long as the voices of the *ahl-e bait* continue to be spoken in the devotional literature and ritual performance of the *majlis*, they are powerful, living models for how to properly be in the world.

chapter four

A Bride of One Night, a Widow Forever

TEXT & RITUAL PERFORMANCE IN THE CONSTITUTION OF AN IDEALIZED SOUTH ASIAN SHIʿI SELFHOOD

Marriage is my sunnah.
He who does not follow my
sunnah does not follow me.
—Prophet Muhammad

In the Yaqutpura neighborhood in Hyderabad's Old City, Dr. M. M. Taqui Khan's family has been hosting the *mehndī* mourning assembly for nearly sixty years.[1] In the early 1950s, this area was comparatively sparsely populated. The members of the Khan family had relocated from their residence on the banks of the Musi River to their current location near Nawab Shawkat Jang's palace. One year, Khan's grandmother remarked, "We have such a big house and this open space. Why don't we host the seventh of Muharram *majlis* here?"[2] Around 1955, the Khan family began sponsoring an annual *mehndī* mourning assembly. The family's first *ʿāshūrkhāna* was a simple structure built of canvas tents and bamboo screens; the members of the Khan family subsequently replaced this modest structure with a permanent *ʿāshūrkhāna* located in the spacious courtyard behind their large house, which sits on Yaqutpura's main road. Every 7 Muharram around one o'clock in the afternoon, more than one thousand men and boys flock to the Khan family *ʿāshūrkhāna* for the men's *mehndī* mourning assembly. Thousands of other men participate while standing in the street outside.

Inside the *ʿāshūrkhāna*, the blaring of horns, the buzz of traffic, and the shouts of vendors and children are diminished. Stately palm trees (*nakhl*), symbolic of Imam Husain and the youths of Karbala, wave in the breeze, their fronds rustling in accompaniment to the chanting of *marṡiya* and *nauḥa* poems.[3] The present *ʿāshūrkhāna* features a large hall where the *ʿalams* (metal battle standards symbolizing various members of the *ahl-e bait*) are displayed during Muharram and where the action of the *majlis* takes place: mourning poetry is recited, the *majlis* orator (*ẕākir*) narrates the events of Karbala, and devotees slap their chests in time to the chanted poems. Behind the main hall, several rooms are curtained off, enabling women to observe *purdah* yet still participate in the men's (*mardāne*) mourning assembly. When the *ʿalam* is brought out for procession, a certain degree of relaxation of the *purdah* regulations occurs, and women stand in doorways or move the curtains to better observe the activities of the men's *majlis*.

I first met Khan during Muharram in 2005. A retired chemistry professor at Osmania University, Khan has also been a *ẕākir* (*majlis* orator) for several decades. Such mixing of careers is not unusual in the Hyderabadi Shiʿi community, where both men and women with doctorates in various fields (including the sciences, Urdu literature, geography, and Persian history) have pursued careers as professors, lawyers, and scientists while becoming acclaimed *ẕākirs* and *ẕākirahs*, speaking at countless assemblies during the mourning period, which lasts two months and eight days (known in Urdu as *ayyām-e ʿazā* [the days of mourning]), from 1 Muharram to 8 Rabiʿ al-Awwal. Khan enthusiastically responded to my inquiries about the Hyderabadi observance of Fatimah Kubra and Qasem's wedding, and he invited me to come to his house to observe his family's preparations for the *mehndī* mourning assembly to be held later in the day.

Preparations for the afternoon mourning assemblies were well under way by late morning, with a steady stream of devotees coming to "visit" (*ziyārat*) the *ʿalams* installed along the center of the *ʿāshūrkhāna*'s back wall.[4] The central and largest *ʿalam* is dedicated to Qasem (fig. 4). Tied to the pole supporting the *ʿalam* is a red cloth (*ḍhaṭṭī*), over which multiple garlands of roses and jasmine have been placed. In front of the *ʿalam*, a silver tray sits on the ground—devotees will leave offerings of fruit, which others will subsequently take as blessed food (*tabarruk*).

Devotees light incense, and its smoke rises and mingles with the heady sweetness of the jasmine and rose garlands. The smell of the smoke is pleasing, bringing to mind the purity of the *ahl-e bait*. Men, women, and children approach the *ʿalam*, making their offerings and lighting incense; they bend and kiss the *ʿalam* as a sign of their respect for the *ahl-e bait*. Each person cups the grace (*baraka*) emanating from the *ʿalam* in his or her right hand and wipes it over his or her face. Mothers apply the *ʿalam's* healing and protective power to the babies slung over their hips. Khan's daughter and son-in-law

Figure 4. The Qasem ʿalam (center) installed on 7 Muharram 2005 in Taqui Khan's ʿāshūrkhanā.

stand on either side of the *ʿalam*, tying red cords (*lāl nārā*) around the wrists of the devotees to protect them against the evil eye. Even while waiting in line to approach the *ʿalam*, men and women continue to observe a form of *purdah*—Khan's daughter ties strings on the women's wrists, while her husband does so for the men.

After an hour or so, some of the garlands are removed from the principal Qasem *ʿalam* so that it can be "dressed" in its wedding attire. At the emotional climax of the *majlis*, the Qasem *ʿalam* will be taken out in a symbolic wedding procession to his bride's house (*barāt*). According to South Asian wedding custom, the groom typically rides on horseback to his bride's home, accompanied by music, the banging of drums, and great fanfare. Taqui Khan and his daughter, Kulsum, were busy with their preparations, yet they took great care to explain the elements of the *mehndī* tray and their meaning in the context of the *majlis* as well as in contemporary Hyderabadi Shiʿi marriage rituals. Kulsum lined two large wooden trays with shiny gold paper and then summoned a household servant to deliver plates of henna paste. Later, when the Qasem ʿ*alam* goes out in procession, participants will grab at the tray of *mehndī* in an attempt to possess this physical memorial of Qasem's sacrifice.

Just as *mehndī* is the primary symbolic element in the 7 Muharram mourning assemblies, the application of henna to the hands and feet of the bride and bridegroom is also an important South Asian wedding ritual. For Indian Muslims, *mehndī* is the final event before the ceremonial signing of the marriage contract (ʿ*aqd-e nikāḥ*). The custom of applying henna to the arms and feet of the bride is an Islamicate ritual, and Muslims in many Arab countries as well as Iran have similar customs of bodily decoration; however, the adornment of the bridegroom with *mehndī* is an Indic practice. The vernacular non-Muslim cultural and religious environment has influenced many South Asian Muslim wedding rituals. The influence of Hinduism is palpable, and most Indian Muslims with whom I have spoken candidly acknowledge the influence of their vernacular environment on wedding practices, whether or not they approve.

In December 2005, I participated in several rituals celebrating the wedding of Riaz Fatima's son, ʿAbbas. Fatima, who holds a doctorate in Urdu literature from Osmania University, is a prominent member of the Shiʿi community in Hyderabad's Old City. A couple of days before the wedding, I spent an evening with a multigenerational group of fifteen women preparing for the *sāchaq* (a prewedding ritual in which the groom's family presents gifts and a tray of henna paste) for the bride, Shafath. One of the bedrooms was set aside for decorating the trays and gossiping, providing me with the opportunity to learn about the requisite (and respectable) number of trays of *mehndī* and outfits that the groom's family customarily gives the bride. We worked for more than two hours preparing fourteen trays for the *sāchaq* ceremony, which was to take place later that night, following ʿAbbas's turmeric-grinding ceremony (*manjha*). Indian women and men customarily apply turmeric to the skin to make it glow and thereby enhance their attractiveness.[5] Although the women are working slowly, the room hums with energy and voices talking and laughing.

The process for preparing the *mehndī* tray is time-consuming. Just as Kulsum Khan decorated a plain wooden tray for the *mehndī* mourning assembly's symbolic plate of henna paste, the wooden wedding *mehndī* trays (*kishtī*) are covered—in this case, with shiny Mylar wrapping paper. The women engage in lively deliberations regarding the arrangement of gifts, often resulting in

Figure 5. Mehndī tray containing sweets that symbolize aspects of a happy marriage: (clockwise from top right corner) turmeric paste, henna paste, coconut, rock sugar, betel leaves, and betel nuts. From the wedding of ʿAbbas and Shafath, December 2005.

much laughter and joking. Ten trays contain outfits for the bride—a *sāṛī* or "suit piece" (uncut fabric to make a tunic and a pair of baggy trousers), a pair of fancy sandals, matching bangles, and chocolates. Tens of thousands of rupees have been spent on these gifts for the bride, yet many times more rupees will go into the bride's dowry (*dahej*).

Fatima's eldest sister has been assigned the task of preparing the all-important tray of henna paste. As the senior member of the group, she oversees all of the preparations. One tray contains a plate of turmeric (*haldī*), on which I was assigned to spell out the groom and bride's first initials in confetti. I decorated a different plate of henna paste, also bearing the initials A and S, that was placed on a tray with the plate of turmeric paste, twenty-two betel nuts, sugar cubes (*miṣrī*) symbolizing a sweet marriage, shredded coconut, a container of sandalwood powder, and one sweet *pān* (a popular digestive made of areca nuts and spices wrapped inside a betel leaf). The items on the second tray symbolize the aspects of a successful and happy marriage.

The *sāchaq* ceremony is one of the two prewedding rituals that involve decorating the bride and the groom with *mehndī*. Approximately two days before the wedding, the bridegroom's family comes to the bride's house bearing gifts and trays of *mehndī*. One day before the wedding, the groom's *mehndī* ceremony is held. Reflecting the patriarchal nature of marriage as a form of property exchange, the *mehndī* ceremony is often bigger and characterized by more pomp and circumstance than the *sāchaq* ceremony. Along with the tray of *mehndī*, all of the articles of the bride's dowry (*dahej*) are delivered to the groom's home, a public display of the material wealth and respectability that the bride brings to her new home.

Dowry (also known as *jahez*) is another South Asian vernacular wedding practice that Muslims have adapted. According to Islamic law, the groom bears responsibility for providing the bride with a gift (*mahr*), which is agreed upon and stipulated in the marriage contract: "And give the women (on marriage) their dower as a free gift" (*Sūrat al-Nisā'* [Chapter of the Women], 4:4). *Mahr* demonstrates the husband's trust that "Allah will grant him the power and ability to shower his wife, in future, with sufficient sustenance through the *baraka* (blessing) of the sacred *ʿaqd*."[6] The *mahr* is provided in exchange for the wife's legal obligation to have sexual relations with her husband. Although Islamic law stipulates that a husband must provide *mahr* to his bride, it is legally permissible (*jā'iz*) for the bride's parents to provide a dowry to the husband's family. S. K. Husain observes that "the Prophet of Islam had himself offered a few things of domestic use as dowry on the occasion of his daughter's marriage although no demand was made by his son-in-law Ali."[7] Husain agrees with the spirit of dowry yet trenchantly critiques the "Hindu" custom of dowry for inculcating "selfishness and materialism."[8] The customary practice of *dahej* reflects the vernacularization of Islam in its South Asian context, where the bride's presentation of dowry is culturally compulsory to secure a good marriage alliance and, more important, to advertise publicly the respectability of the bride's family.

The Value of a "Good" Marriage

The ritual preparation of the *mehndī* trays for Shafath's *sāchaq* was replicated in Kulsum and Taqui Khan's pre-*majlis* activities. While Kulsum prepared the *mehndī* tray, her father searched through a wooden trunk and removed an ornate cloth, brilliant red with gold threads woven through. This *ḍhaṭṭī*, he explained, symbolizes Qasem's wedding outfit. For approximately half an hour, Taqui Khan chatted with his daughter and me as he lovingly applied rich-smelling amber oil to his hands and then slowly rubbed it into the cloth. The bride and groom traditionally wear essence of amber on their wedding day. After Khan finished scenting the cloth, he folded it and placed it next to the tray of *mehndī*. The final element included on the *mehndī* trays is the floral veil (*sehrā*) with which the bridegroom covers his face—a form of masculine *ḥijāb*. Two of Khan's sons-in-law removed the *sehrā* from its basket and unfurled a fragrant cascade of roses and jasmine. With preparations thus completed, the final task is wrapping the trays containing the plates of henna and *ḍhaṭṭī* in a dark red cloth and tightly tying it with string. The young men of the family take great care in securing the tray, although it will soon be ripped apart in the frenzy of emotion during the wedding/funeral procession (*barāt-julūs*) that marks the emotional climax of the *majlis*.

At the midpoint of the *majlis*, the trays go out and devotees violently grab at the plates of *mehndī*. People crowd around the bearers, jostling, thrusting their hands to get just a little bit of this mixture. Single men and women customarily daub this henna paste onto their right palms (*mehndī lagānā*) in the belief that it is imbued with Qasem's spiritual power (*baraka*) and will result in good marriage alliances. The frenzy that the procession of the *mehndī* tray incites dramatically highlights the premium Indic culture places on the institution of marriage, which is intensified by the Islamic imperative for all men and women to marry and by Fatimah Kubra's compelling model of faith and sacrifice—her embodiment of the *ḥusaini* ethic. The vernacular practices of arranged marriage and dowry and the taboo on widow remarriage reinforce the fact that for many women, marriage is a high-stakes endeavor in which making a good alliance is of the greatest importance. In South Asian culture, marriage is a social and familial obligation. Beyond cultural expectations, religious mandates in the Qur'an and in the Sunnah (lived tradition) of the Prophet Muhammad make marriage a religious duty. For South Asian Shiʿa, both cultural community and religion exert pressure to marry, often making it unclear which exerts more of a coercive force.

In the summer of 2005, I was discussing various domestic issues with Lizzie, a Catholic woman who worked as our maid. Lizzie, a widow, was feeling profound stress about arranging her youngest daughter's marriage. She had already married off three daughters, but her son and her youngest daughter remained unwed. Still paying for her other daughters' weddings, Lizzie did not see how she would come up with 1.5 lakhs (approximately $3,000) in cash to provide her youngest daughter with a dowry that would bring her a husband of higher economic status. When I asked Lizzie why she was in such a rush to arrange this marriage, especially since the effort was causing her so much stress that she was becoming ill, Lizzie spoke words that revealed the chasm between our worlds: "Everyone marries here; it is not a question of if we marry, but of how good the alliance can be." Marriage may be religiously compulsory for Muslims, but it is a cultural, social, and familial obligation for the majority of South Asians. Just as Lizzie was overwhelmed by her duty to marry off her daughters, Sarah, the twenty-seven-year-old Muslim woman I met at Yadgar Husaini, felt excluded from society because she could not find a husband.

With such religious, cultural, and familial pressures to marry, asking for the intervention of the bridegroom of Karbala is one of the most important events in the Muharram cycle for unmarried men and women. On 7 Muharram, women and girls conspicuously display small circles of *mehndī* drying on their right palms. While preparing for the *majlis*, Kulsum Khan explained that after applying *mehndī* to the palm, a garland of flowers must be tied to Qasem's *ʿalam* to complete the votive request for a successful marriage arrangement. In earlier years, Kulsum performed *mehndī kī mannat*, and she attributes her marriage to the ritual. Kulsum believes that she indeed has a good husband, and she feels truly grateful to have made a good marriage alliance. She is convinced that a miracle (*muʿjizah*) had taken place—a manifestation of Qasem's saintly and intercessory power. Echoing Lizzie's words, Kulsum stated that it is easy to get a husband but that finding a good husband is a real challenge.[9] According to Kulsum, countless weddings have been arranged after would-be brides sought Qasem's intervention through the *mehndī kī mannat* ritual. Although many women emphasized the necessity of finding a good husband, what that means is individualized and highly subjective.

The final preparation of the props for the *mehndī kī majlis* is the removal of the shroud (*kafn*) from the trunk. At the midpoint of the mourning assembly, following the *majlis* orator's narration of Qasem and Fatimah Kubra's sufferings (*maṣāʾib*), the *ʿalam* is taken out in procession. The Qasem *ʿalam* is heavily wrapped to prevent injury to participants as well as to protect the standard from damage. The *ʿalam* leaves the *ʿāshūrkhāna* in a vertical position and returns in a horizontal position, a ritual act with a dual symbolic meaning: the vertical departure of the *ʿalam* from the *ʿāshūrkhāna* represents both the *barāt* and Qasem's departure for the battlefield, while the horizontal return represents Qasem's martyrdom. Returning in its *julūs*, the Qasem *ʿalam* is covered

importance of marriage shows why symbols & rituals are followed

Julia Quote

in a blood-smeared cloth—a burial shroud. This cloth also represents a symbolic dyad that profoundly affects the already overwrought crowd. Red symbolizes marriage in Indic culture, but Qasem's clothing is red from his blood, not in celebration of his wedding. This nested symbolic dyad of the *ʿalam*'s procession enacts the dual aspects of Qasem's hagiographical persona: Qasem as bridegroom (*naushāh*) and warrior (*mujāhid*). In Hyderabad, Qasem's persona of tragic bridegroom is more popular, and he and his ill-fated bride are a popular topic for local Muharram poets. One particularly popular *salām* (short rhythmic poem with a refrain) that is recited at all 7 Muharram mourning assemblies (as well as at most prewedding ritual events) has Sakinah imploring her future brother-in-law, Qasem, to come home for his *mehndī* ceremony:

> Coming to the field of battle, Sakinah calls out: "Come home, brother, so that I may apply the *mehndī*.
> O, Bridegroom Qasem, your sister is devoted to you! Come home, brother, so that I may apply the *mehndī*.
>
> "The bride and groom are separated, what an extraordinary marriage this is!
> I could not demand the groom's ransom [*neg*]. Come home, brother, so that I may apply the *mehndī*.
>
> "Brother, how quickly you have departed this house—the wedding rituals are not yet complete.
> The wedding guests are waiting for you. Come home, brother, so that I may apply the *mehndī*.
>
> "The bride wears the garment of widowhood and, crying, she has removed her bangles and nose pin.
> In grief, I am weeping here. Come home, brother, so that I may apply the *mehndī*.
>
> "On that body you wear a colorful wedding gown, upon that head is a floral crown [*sehrā*].
> Over that moonlike face, blood flows. Come home, brother, so that I may apply the *mehndī*.
>
> "Someone has buried you in the dust; someone has untied the nuptial knot.
> Come home, brother, so that I may apply the *mehndī*."

When the chorus chants the refrain, "*Ghar chalo bhā'ī mehndī lagā'uṅ*," the emotional effect is profound. Participants at the women's *majlis* keenly feel this poem, singing the refrain at a high pitch that imitates the sound of a young girl's voice—that is, the voice of Fatimah Kubra's youngest sister. Four-year-old Sakinah has already internalized the rituals of a proper (South Asian) Muslim wedding.

Sakinah is disappointed that she has been denied her due in the playful *neg* ritual. During the *mehndī* ceremony, the bride's sisters steal the groom's shoes (*jūtā chhupā'ī*), holding them for ransom and joking with and teasing their future brother-in-law. Through an inversion of gender roles and ribaldry, this joyful event draws the two families together, providing a socially acceptable outlet for their collective anxieties over the approaching wedding. In the South Asian Shiʿi community, the families of the bride and groom typically know one another well, as paternal cross-cousin marriage is the preferred practice. The fact that the participants already have blood ties further adds to the joyousness of the occasion, although the bride and groom and their families certainly feel some anxiety, which is alleviated by such prewedding rituals.

Even in her youthful inexperience, Sakinah understands the impossibility of celebrating such a joyful event as a wedding in the unfolding catastrophe of Karbala. Here the double meaning of the Urdu word *shādī* is particularly poignant: *shādī* means "joyfulness" and is commonly used for "wedding." The first line of the poem can be understood in two ways: "How can there be joy in such distress?" and "How can there be a wedding in such distress?" As in the procession of the Qasem *ʿalam*, joy and grief are inextricably linked in the ritual performance of poetry invoking the memory of the battlefield wedding. For the Shiʿa of Hyderabad, the joy of a wedding cannot be celebrated without first remembering and mourning the suffering of the *ahl-e bait*.

In both the preparations for the *mehndī* mourning assembly and the preparations of the fourteen trays of clothing and ritual objects for the *sāchaq* ceremony, the participants take joy in the rituals and feel a keen sense of anticipation and anxiety for the future of bride and groom. The hero(in)es of Karbala embody the *ḥusaini* ethics of sacrificial spirit and exemplary faith, which infuses and shapes the everyday practices of the Shiʿi men and women of Hyderabad. The story of Fatimah Kubra and Qasem is so popular in Hyderabad because marriage is nearly universal and arranged, and the couple's sacrifice and suffering resonate deeply with young men, women, and their parents. Fatimah Kubra's marriage at a young age and her almost immediate widowhood constructs her into an imitable role model for Hyderabad's women and men.

Although the events of 7 Muharram appear at first glance to focus primarily on Qasem's martyrdom, the hagiographic impetus of the remembrance of Karbala is predicated on the voices and experiences of the female survivors of the battle. As bride/widow, Fatimah Kubra teaches Hyderabad's women and men how to be good Muslims, husbands, and wives. Listening to narratives about the sacrifices and feats of the hero(in)es of Karbala, Shiʿi men and women are compelled to cultivate a "set of practices [and values] by which [they] can acquire, assimilate, and transform truth into a permanent principle of action."[10] Here, in Michel Foucault's articulation of a positive ethics or technology of the self, the word "truth" may be applied in the context of Karbala and *ḥusaini* ethics. Shiʿi men and women transform the "truth" of Karbala into a permanent set of actions based on the construction of a shared sensibility and ethical order that create a moral community through the events of the mourning assembly.

Saba Mahmood's study of women's participation in the mosque movement of the Islamic revival in Cairo illustrates the gendered dimension of Foucault's technology of the self. Mahmood observes with regard to women's veiling and prayer practices that "the specific gestures, styles, and formal expressions that characterize one's relationship to a moral code are not a contingent but a necessary means to understanding the kind of relationship that is established between the self and structures of social authority, and between what one is, what one wants, and what kind of work one performs on oneself in order to realize a particular modality of being and personhood."[11] In the poem "*Ghar chalo bhāʾī mehndī lagāʾuṅ*," Sakinah assimilates the values of Shiʿi marriage over which the vernacular values of idealized wifehood and widowhood are overlaid. In this *salām*, Sakinah's lament articulates a positive ethics that has actively cultivated the proper practice of Indian wedding rituals, particularly with regard to introducing the bride and groom to a proper state of relations in married life. In the hagiographical literature and ritual-performance context of the *majlis*, Fatimah Kubra (and to a certain extent her female relatives involved in the marriage preparations and in the aftermath of her widowhood) teaches Hyderabadi women how to cultivate the gendered state of being an idealized wife (obedient, sacrificing, loyal to faith and family), which is based on her exemplary yet imitable model. Fatimah Kubra teaches men how to be kind, self-sacrificing husbands and sympathetic fathers to their daughters. After her bridegroom/

warrior, Qasem, is killed, Fatimah Kubra transforms her gendered state into the renouncing inauspicious widow, removing her adornments and accepting her abject status. Fatimah Kubra's gendered performances fulfill a crucial hagiographic function: her didactic actions show Hyderabadi men and women their proper gender roles, which are life-cycle specific and are mediated by the religious model of *ḥusaini* ethics.

Embodied Ideals: Stylizing Fatimah Kubra as the Model Indian Bride/Widow

Deccani-Urdu hagiographical literature and ritual performance presents Fatimah Kubra as an imitable saint whose willingness to sacrifice her bridegroom, Qasem, at the Battle of Karbala is connected to her exemplary spiritual status, which is derived from her direct blood relationship to Imam Husain. Unlike Wahab ibn ʿAbdallah al-Kalbi (see chapter 1), the other warrior/bridegroom of Karbala, and his martyr bride, Fatimah Kubra realizes the cosmic responsibility she embodies in her roles of bride and widow, deliberately assuming them despite her heavy heart. Like all of the hero(in)es of Karbala, Fatimah Kubra's elevated status is recognized by her devotees as the embodiment of two ideal types—or, more specifically, two *gendered states*: the ideal Indian bride and the perfectly renouncing widow. Through the hagiographical narratives and ritual structure of the *majlis*, devotees are encouraged to cultivate—as life-cycle appropriate—Fatimah Kubra's idealized embodiment of the gendered states of bride and widow. The repeated iteration of Fatimah Kubra's wedding to Qasem inspires devotees to cultivate themselves to be the best possible wives and later widows. Fatimah Kubra's model is to be imitated and integrated into everyday life practices. As Muharram poetry, discourse, and ritual performance endlessly repeat, her example compels women to imitate and actualize an idealized vernacular Shiʿi self.

Judith Butler's theoretical work on gender and embodiment as a socially powerful form of performance provides a useful hermeneutic framework for understanding how the hero(in)es of Karbala are constructed in Hyderabadi hagiographical literature and ritual. Butler's theory of the performativity of gender creates an interpretive space in which the materiality of gendered being may be manifestly expressed yet is not reified by its own significations. Butler defines gender "as a shifting and contextual phenomenon [that] does not denote a substantive being, but a relative point of convergence among culturally and historically specific sets of relations." That is, gender is "performatively produced" through the "repeated stylization of the body, a set of repeated acts within a highly rigid regulatory frame."[12] The performativity of gender allows women to embody and cultivate idealized gendered states through clothing, mannerisms, bodily adornments, speech, and ethical values. While a girl may become a woman at a culturally determined moment in her life cycle (onset of menstruation, marriage), the same individual also potentially embodies a broad range of gendered states during her lifetime (bride, wife, mother, menopausal woman, widow). While we may classify a female as a woman because of her attainment of some culturally determined status, the specificity of her gendered state actually shapes her identity as a social being, particularly if she participates in the patriarchal system of power and privilege that maintains the semblance of a gender framework.

A performative theory of gender in which the body is consciously stylized and engaged in performative acts to attain public recognition requires that the body be something materially real and not inert or passive. The body in its gendered performance and stylization must be cognizant and complicit in what it is doing to itself. These very conscious markings and performances transform the body into a material, meaningful, social being. For some feminist critics and scholars of Shiʿi devotional literature and practice, the stylized marking of gender on Fatimah Kubra's body when she is made into an Indian bride and a widow reflects a system of patriarchal domination and control, a process that is axiomatic of a Foucauldian inscription of oppressive gender signs on a passive, oppressed body.

Scholars who study the texts and ritual-devotional performances that invoke the events of Karbala in both South Asian and Iranian contexts frequently comment on Fatimah Kubra's marriage and widowhood. Some observers see this episode as yet another tragic vignette in the Karbala cycle, while others view it as an example of how hagiographers depict women as lacking agency. For still others, at least in the case of South Asia, the incident represents the "syncretic"[13] dimension of Indian Islam that is characterized by its admixture with Hinduism. Rather than understanding the heroines of Karbala as victims on whom the narrative is enacted, it is more useful to identify the ways in which these narrative and ritual performances teach men and women their proper religious and vernacular social roles.[14]

Karbala hagiographical narratives and ritual performances are powerful, productive iterations generating different meanings for individuals as they move through various parts of the life cycle and gendered states. The devotional texts and the performance of the *majlis* must be read and observed as the Shiʿa do: The hero(in)es of Karbala suffer, yet they are powerful and active religious role models and socioethical exemplars whose embodiment through literature and performance constructs a vital vernacular moral community.

Writing Women's Bodies in the Deccani Hagiographical Imagination

The Shiʿa of Hyderabad do not see Fatimah Kubra as a victim. She certainly feels anguish at being in such a terrible situation; who would not? But Fatimah Kubra's grief does not make her a passive body on which the events of Karbala unfold. Similarly, Mir ʿAlam, author of an eighteenth-century Deccani-Urdu Karbala hagiography, *Dah majlis* (The Ten Assemblies), does not portray Fatimah Kubra as a victim, lacking agency. She may suffer as a result of her willingness to let her husband fight and die in battle, but she makes this choice consciously to preserve her family and faith. Mir ʿAlam's Fatimah Kubra is a strong young woman with a sharp tongue, fully aware of her important role in this cosmic "battle of good versus evil."[15] When Qasem tries to sneak off to the battlefield, Fatimah Kubra chastises her husband for trying to deceive her. Qasem dissimulates, tries to placate his irate bride, and finally calls his mother to deal with her new daughter-in-law.[16] When Fatimah Kubra reprimands her husband, she asserts her right to be treated with respect and fully to participate in the *ḥusaini* ethic of sacrifice: she too is a full actor in this cosmic drama. Fatimah Kubra expects Qasem to be a "good" husband, treating her with honesty and respect. Hagiographical Karbala literature such as *Dah majlis* does not inscribe the gender roles of a "proper" bride/widow on the inert, passive body of Fatimah Kubra; rather, she actualizes the South Asian Shiʿi wife, who is pious, honest, faithful to her husband, devoted to her family. A doormat she is not.

Certain ruptures in Butler's theory of gender as a nonbinary, performatively produced stylization of the body allow us to expand our understanding of how a theory of Shiʿi sainthood and hagiography depend on vernacular embodiments of the religious ideal. Butler's critique of structuralist binary theory applies to the interpretation of gender in a Euro-American context but has distinct hermeneutical limitations in Indic vernacular hagiographical depictions of Fatimah Kubra's gendered roles.

Butler's critique extends beyond the nature-female-body/culture-male-mind binaries to examine the bride's role as a passive object of patriarchal exchange who is an ontological lack in that she "does not *have* an identity, and neither does she exchange one identity for another. She *reflects* masculine identity precisely through being the site of its absence."[17] Butler further elucidates the bride's absence of identity, declaring that women even lack names for themselves: "As the site of patronymic exchange, women are and are not the patronymic sign, excluded from the signifier, the very patronym they bear."[18] Butler's critique is again constrained by the particularities of the Euro-American patriarchal institution of marriage. In the Muslim world, women typically do not assume their husbands' last names. Textual and ethnographic evidence gathered in Hyderabad does little to reinforce Butler's assertion that the bride is merely a passive body on which masculine desires and identities are inscribed and enforced through the institution of marriage. Such trenchant critiques of marriage as a form of patriarchal oppression are counterproductive and reinforce fetishistic fantasies of Muslim women.

The ethnocentric focus of Butler's critique significantly points to the limits of the hermeneutic frameworks that scholars of religion employ to explain religious practices, beliefs, and texts. Such ethnocentric interpretations force Muslim women to inhabit a state of false consciousness in which their lack of identity is reinforced through the patriarchal institution of marriage. Despite the cultural specificity of Butler's theory of gender, aspects of her theoretical work are applicable cross-culturally. The nonabsoluteness of gender in Butler's theoretical framework is especially useful for understanding the ways in which gender is culturally, linguistically, and religiously contingent. Fatimah Kubra is portrayed in the mourning assembly and Deccani-Urdu hagiographical Karbala literature as the structural dyad of bride and widow, gendered states that exist along a nonbinary gender continuum.

The rituals and verbal performances of the *majlis* tell a powerful story that does not necessarily create an opportunity for the potential subversion or disruption of the South Asian Shiʿi religiocultural ideal. With every act of remembrance created in the hagiographical narrative and ritual events of the mourning assembly, men and women develop strategies for cultivating themselves on the practical, imitable model of Karbala's hero(in)es. The incessant repetition of the imitable sainthood and exemplary *ḥusaini* ethic of the *ahl-e bait* enables "very different configurations of personhood [to] cohabit the same cultural and historical space."[19] Furthermore, an idealized Shiʿi selfhood that is multiply situated and constantly changing is "both *enacted through* and *productive of*, intentionality, volitional behavior and sentiments."[20] Hearing hagiographical narratives extolling the virtuous qualities of the *ahl-e bait* is not sufficient for cultivating an idealized selfhood; individuals must actively and willingly participate on their own terms and according to their own subjectivity.

In the two years that I spent in Hyderabad, I participated in a number of *mehndī* mourning assemblies and interviewed and had casual conversations with many people, all of whom generally expressed feelings of deep respect for and a desire to imitate the model of faith and resoluteness embodied by Fatimah Kubra. Urdu literature eulogizing this battlefield wedding is distinctly hagiographical, as it establishes the wedding between these two spiritual heroes as atypical and idealized. The first stanza of the *marsiya* written by North Indian poet Mir Muhammad Rafiᶜ Sauda (1706–81) calls devotees to share in the tragic fate of Qasem and Fatimah Kubra:

> Friends! Hear of the injustice wrought by the celestial orb!
> For the son of Hasan, it has set its heart on an unnatural wedding;
> That bride and groom have joined together in such a union,
> The shroud's inauspicious thread has been tied to this wedding.
>
> . . . .
>
> What else can I tell about the *naubat* [drums] played at the wedding?
> Day and night, men and women beat their breasts in grief.
> Instead of lamps, the house has been set ablaze;
> Never will the thread be saved from the inauspicious cord.[21]

The impasse that results from literal interpretations of structuralist binary theory in the construction of gender as well as assumptions of feminine passivity and ontological lack caused by the patriarchal institution of marriage necessitate a different hermeneutic framework for understanding the powerful roles that the heroines of the *ahl-e bait* possess in Shiᶜi hagiographical literature and ritual. Hagiography creates a space in which the audience can interpret how Fatimah Kubra actively performs the gendered roles of bride and widow without being denied her own agency or identity.

Shiᶜi hagiography centers on the Battle of Karbala, and because the women of the *ahl-e bait* survived and told the story, the lessons that are learned are necessarily imparted from a feminine perspective. Deccani-Urdu literature eulogizing the wedding of Fatimah Kubra and Qasem is distinctly hagiographical, establishing the wedding between these two spiritual heroes to be atypical and idealized. The wedding takes place on the battlefield, and the love and sacrifice shared by Fatima Kubra and Qasem is redolent with symbolic religious meaning:

It was that severed head that was the family's henna ceremony,
Like *sāchaq* pots bound about an elephant, such are the wounds around his neck.
In this vile circumstance, the bridegroom's gift to his bride was his sleeve,[22]
In what land is there such a tradition of *sāchaq*?

The bride's tray of *mehndī* has come,
The in-laws have been congealed in brother-in-law's blood;
The bride has smeared her hand in her husband's blood,
This color is the mode of the wedding season.

No sooner was the bride adorned for the union with her husband,
Then she said, "There is no remedy from God for this state of widowhood.
For whom he gave everything, he went to battle and was slain
Now, what is the point of this passion and love?"

Removing her nose ring, she surrendered it over to me,
She admonished herself, pouring dust over her head in grief.
The corpse is coming, where are his mourners?
Now is not the time for words and discourses.[23]

Only exemplars such as Fatimah Kubra and Qasem, by virtue of the spiritual and socioethical charisma bestowed by their blood relationship to the Prophet Muhammad, can endure such tribulations. The narration of these events in the form of hagiographical discourses has a subjective, didactic function. Kirin Narayan notes, "The cross-cutting points of view and ambiguity with a story can generate multiple meanings, and so audiences may take away different interpretations of what is being told and why. Listeners who screen these stories with the expectation that they will provide counsel, actively appropriate meanings that speak to their concerns and conflicts."[24] Shiʿi devotional life is based on hagiographical stories about the men and women of Imam Husain's family who are recognized for their consummate personification of *ḥusaini* ethics–imitable sainthood.

The women of the *ahl-e bait* are venerated as saints and are accorded their sanctity and status because of the positive gendered roles that they occupy. The narratives and poems about the men and women of Karbala teach the Shiʿa how to be good Muslims. In the Urdu hagiographical tradition, Fatimah Kubra and Qasem are portrayed as honorable individuals who do what is socially correct despite their tragic situation:

In its place, a canopy of brokenheartedness has been spread over
humanity,
The king has been anointed with arrows instead of turmeric oil.
Instead of a bridal gown, she has been clothed in widow's garb, and
The robe of honor for the bridegroom [*naushāh*][25] is the shroud of
grief.[26]

Bride and groom endure their wedding gone awry, and each styles his or her body in gender-appropriate attire. This gendered attire is ritually inverted in Khan's 7 Muharram *majlis*, when the Qasem *ʿalam* is dressed in a bloody shroud (*kafn*) as it returns to its place of honor in the *ʿāshūrkhāna* in its symbolic funeral procession. Despite the inversion of the proper order of the world, the bride substitutes, in honorable Indian fashion, her heavily embellished red *sāṛī* for the widow's white mourning dress, and the groom trades his wedding whites for a bloody shroud.

In Shiʿi Urdu hagiographical literature, both prose and verse, Fatimah Kubra is stylized as the ideal Indian bride, wearing the traditional henna on her hands, the nose ring (*nath*), and wrist bangles (*chuṛiyāṅ*). A *marśiya* written by a nineteenth-century Urdu poet, Dilgir, portrays Fatimah Kubra in a touching vignette with her mother, who laments her inability to provide her daughter with a marital bed on which she will sleep with her husband or any of the rituals so essential to any respectable Indian wedding, whether Hindu or Muslim.[27]

This time of separation that has come is Kubra's,
In the encampment it is a tenderhearted moment for all.
Truly, this time of separation is calamitous,
Bano had said this is a time of affliction;
She said, "Under trial, there is separation,
Today my daughter belongs to another."

She said, "Kubra, my rosy-cheeked one,
I will not meet you again,
I cannot offer you protection.
Daughter! I am stricken with shame for your condition!
Do not lament my plight,
Even in exile from our homeland, I will give you your right!"

"Daughter, accept my advice,
Understand that which is the mother-in-law's right,
For me, too, increase your affection,
And resolve not to turn away your heart from anyone.
Battle with floral sticks,[28] go to your husband's home, and in these
customs,
Do not speak out of turn."

"A great desire is lodged in my heart,
That I might provide you your marital bed!
But alas! Such a debased time is this!
My innermost heart has become paralyzed with emotion,
That your marriage has happened in such place as this.
Where nothing can be attained, alas!"
. . . .
"Daughter, many people blame women,
To your face, such words they will say.
My daughter, this is not the behavior of a daughter-in-law!
Hush! Your in-laws have come.
From your maternal home such a burden will be borne!"[29]

Dilgir's *marśiya* is fascinating because of its emotional tone, complexity, and multiple levels of possible interpretation. Read from a Euro-American feminist critical perspective, the words of Fatimah Kubra's mother may appear to reaffirm the patriarchal order and feminine helplessness with regard to what is enacted on women's bodies and lives. In light of the features of hagiography and the use of voices and emotions of the heroine, which is effected through a strategy of narrative engagement that draws the devotee into the sacred world of Karbala, a different interpretation is possible. Dilgir dramatically demonstrates that the wedding of Fatimah Kubra to Qasem is not routine. This sort of wedding can be undertaken only by exceptional people who understand the cosmic consequences of their choices. This poem enforces the inverted nature of this wedding (*ʿurs*), which is the marriage of Qasem to his faith and family through the sacrifice of martyrdom and Fatimah Kubra's defense of her religion by willingly sending her husband to the battlefield. This wedding does not join together two people; rather, it is the marriage (in a mystical sense) of the bride and groom to God. From a hagiographical perspective, Fatimah Kubra's mother's declaration, "This is not the behavior of daughters-in-law," can be interpreted to reflect the fact that she is an extraordinary young woman who must exhibit bravery and forbearance, giving honor to her family and religion. Fatimah Kubra teaches men and women how to be resolute and brave when confronting the unknown, whether marriage or battle.

At the moment of Qasem's martyrdom, Fatimah Kubra is transformed to embody the gendered state of the ideal Indian widow: she breaks her bangles, removes her veil (*ghūṅgaṭ*), and takes out her nose ring as expressions of her grief and to indicate her status as a widow, no longer entitled to wear ornaments or display her fecundity. Although she is just eleven years old, Fatimah Kubra fully understands the requirements of honorable widowhood as it is defined by the elite *sayyid* class of Muslim South Asia. In her autobiography, Bibi Ashraf, a nineteenth-century North Indian Muslim, recalls the story of a woman who comes to teach the girls of the household how to read and write. The teacher is a young, widowed Muslim woman who broke the Indic taboo against widow remarriage, much to the consternation of Ashraf's grandfather, who feels that the woman has committed a dishonorable act:

> I have heard it said that our teacher had been eleven at the time of her first marriage, and fifteen when she became a widow. Twelve years had passed before she was married again. And during that entire time she had lived with utmost modesty and propriety—may God bless her soul! She was full of virtue and piety, and remained devoted to prayers and fasts till her dying day. The second marriage, which was clearly her religiously allowed privilege [*ḥaqq-i sharʿ*], was not in fact something she had wanted—she had merely given in to the pressure mounted by her mother.
>
> Be that as it may, my grandfather was shocked when he heard the news. Out of his sense of shame, he didn't step out of the house for a whole month. Everyone reasoned with him: "Why must you feel so bad? She was only a hired teacher in your household; she wasn't, God forbid, a kin." My grandfather always replied, "She was, nevertheless, the tutor to my girls. It shames me greatly if my girls' tutor should marry a second time. When I think of it I want to hide my face from the world."
>
> He sent word to our teacher never to cross our threshold again. He also wouldn't allow the Syed who had married her to come before him; he kept that vow as long as he lived.[30]

Ashraf's memory reinforces the fact that Fatimah Kubra, who reflects a sacralized modality of Hyderabadi social values, cannot remarry because she is the most *ashrāf* (noble) of all Muslim women, a direct blood descendant of the Prophet Muhammad. Here, we can discern the tension between *sharīʿah* and customary practice on the one hand and the diminution of orthodox law on the other. The subordination of orthodox Islamic law by local custom and law, particularly in the realm of personal law, is a site of contestation between the universal, cosmopolitan values of Islamic doctrine and the vernacular, local practices that characterize everyday Shiʿism.[31] A number of traditions attest to the high esteem the Prophet Muhammad placed on marriage, most notably his declarations that "marriage is my *sunnah*. He who does not act upon it shall not be mine" and that "there is no scope for celibacy in Islam." In the context of Muslim South Asia, however, the Indic taboo of widow remarriage has effected too significant a cultural imprint.[32]

Fatimah Kubra's socially circumscribed status in Indic vernacular hagiography as a sanctified bride/widow compels her to be gendered in ways that are in tension with normative Islamic doctrine. Fatimah Kubra flouts the Prophet Muhammad's normative injunction for Muslim men and women to remarry after their spouses' deaths; she renounces the world and remains Qasem's widow. Like the Prophet's widows, Fatimah Kubra and her other female relatives never remarried. In the poem "Whose Wedding Banquet Is This?" (Bazm-e shādī kī hai), "Rasheed," a popular Hyderabadi *nauḥa* composer, portrays Fatimah Kubra as the idealized Hyderabadi, Shiʿi widow (*bevāh*), stripped of all adornment; she is the embodiment of the properly gendered inauspicious (female) body:

> Alas! That young bride must wear widow's dress . . .
> Neither an anklet nor bracelet will Kubra wear,
> Lament, for the bond of widowhood is now fastened to the bride.[33]

Fatimah Kubra will not wear any of the jewelry or clothing that constitutes an important part of gendered everyday life for married women in South Asia. She will not wear the anklets and bracelets she receives on her wedding day. Nor will Fatimah Kubra ever wear the auspicious *maṅgalsūtra* necklace that marks her status as a married woman in her vernacular Indian context. In Sauda's *marśiya*, Fatimah Kubra removes her nose ring and pours dust over her bare head, signifying both her grief and the fact that she need no longer protect her modesty in her gendered state of widowhood. Fatimah Kubra must uphold her *ashrāfī* status and perform the gender roles that she embodies in Karbala hagiographical literature and ritual performance. Hyderabad's Shiʿi brides and widows have no better role model than Fatimah Kubra.

Imitable Sainthood in Hyderabad: The Culture-Gender Matrix in Shiʿi Hagiography

This chapter has traced the ways in which Fatimah Kubra teaches Hyderabadi Indian women and men how to enact an idealized South Asian Shiʿi selfhood. In the hagiographical literature and ritual performance of the Hyderabadi mourning assembly, Fatimah Kubra is transformed into a "real" woman, Indian in dress, custom, idiom, and values. Hyderabadi Shiʿi women and men integrate the hero(in)es of Karbala into a number of aspects of their everyday lives, including their fictive kin networks. For example Taqui Khan emotionally explained that Sakinah is like another daughter to him. How, he asked, could he not feel intense grief for the four-year-old orphan of Imam Husain? No father wants to see his daughter suffer.[34] Fatimah Kubra, whether gendered as a bride or widow, fits into the literal and imaginative genealogies of Hyderabadi Shiʿa. Such close relationship to Fatimah Kubra makes her real and relevant, like a sister or daughter, while maintaining her authority as an exemplary Muslim saint whose power and charisma reside in the blood of the *ḥusaini* ethics flowing through her veins.

In the mourning assembly, the collective memory and representation of Karbala constitute an expression of the community's identity (both cosmopolitan and vernacular); in addition, this social frame also contains space for individual women to make meaning for themselves.[35] How the Shiʿa of Hyderabad remember the events of Karbala in both hagiographical literature and ritual performances is a form of collective autobiography, for the modes of commemoration and representation can be read as a "purposeful, intentional, and institutionally supported" articulation of group identity.[36] We can extend this line of thinking to accommodate the function and meaning of the performance of gendered becoming in the hagiographical literature and performance of the Hyderabadi *majlis*. Within this religio-social frame, the individual's act of memory makes the past meaningful and transforms these hero(in)es into culturally relevant figures through whose model gender roles and states for women and men are made, applied to the present, and projected into the future. The remembrance of Qasem and Fatimah Kubra's wedding does not construct a subversive space in which the structures of patriarchal marriage and family can be resisted and critiqued; rather, the mourning assembly and its ritual activities cultivate the potential for the Shiʿa to construct idealized selves that aspire to the models embodied by the *ḥusaini* ethic of saints such as Fatimah Kubra and Qasem.

chapter five

Who Could Marry at a Time Like This?

DEBATING THE *MEHNDĪ KĪ MAJLIS* IN HYDERABAD

Burning sand in the body.
Everyone lives in sorrow's shadow.
—*Kabir*

I arrived in Mashhad, Iran, in October 2004 to conduct research and visit the tomb of the eighth Shiʿi Imam, Reza. It was the middle of the fasting month of Ramadan, and the pilgrimage scene in the city was quiet, unlike most of the rest of the year, when the bazaars, hotels, and restaurants surrounding the shrine/tomb complex burgeon with pilgrims from all over the Shiʿi world. It was much quieter in Mashhad than it had been when I went to Qom to visit the tomb of Imam Reza's sister, Fatimah Maʿsumeh, Iran's second-holiest site. In 925 A.H./1519 C.E., Shah Begum, the daughter of the first Safavid king, Shah Ismaʿil I, commissioned the construction of a large shrine and tomb dedicated to Fatimah Maʿsumeh.[1] At the shrine, I was caught up in the wave of elderly Iranian women pilgrims who travel from their villages to pay their respects to this holy woman. I was alternately exhilarated and terrified by the process of being elevated, crushed, and rapidly propelled forward by short, sturdy women possessing astonishing strength. I briefly grasped the silver grille surrounding Fatimah Maʿsumeh's tomb. There was no time for the ritual actions of greeting the saint: no kisses on the screen or bowing the head while whispering greetings and prayers.

As soon as I touched the tomb, the throngs propelled me back into the melee and toward the exit. The enormous crowd had to pass through the threshold (*āstāna*) separating the sacred space from the profane. Standing in the doorway, further narrowing the exit, were women volunteers known as *khwāharān* (sisters), shouting and pushing. Ostensibly working in the service of order, these women were causing further chaos by constricting the doorway. As the surge of pilgrims struggled to pass through the opening, my ribs were squeezed, and I was afraid they would break. When I popped out on the other side, I felt as if I had been reborn through this threshold. I returned to the everyday world just a little bit touched by the experience.

Unlike the raucousness of the Fatimah Maʿsumeh shrine/tomb complex, Imam Reza's tomb and the city of Mashhad felt almost somnolent yet spiritually awake. The Imam Reza shrine/tomb complex has long been an important place of pilgrimage for Iranian Muslims. Sunni and Shiʿi Muslims have visited Imam Reza's tomb since his martyrdom after being summoned by the ʿAbbasid *khalīfah*, al-Maʿmun (r. 197–218 A.H./813–33 C.E.), to the city of Marv in the eastern Iranian province of Khorasan. Imam Reza fell ill en route, most likely by poisoning, and died in the city of Tus (located near present-day Mashhad) in 818 C.E. With the exception of the shrines dedicated to Imam Husain and other heroes at Karbala and the shrine of Hussain's father, Imam ʿAli, in nearby Najaf, Iraq, the Imam Reza shrine/tomb is the holiest site in the Shiʿi world. Each year, between 15 million and 20 million pilgrims perform *ziyārat* (visitation, pilgrimage) to the tomb of the eighth Imam.[2]

I got off the train in Mashhad early in the morning after an overnight journey from Tehran and took a taxi across town to a hotel on the other side of the Astan-e Qods (Sacred Threshold) shrine/tomb complex. I went for a walk to get a sense of Mashhad and was impressed by its peacefulness. On that late October day, the sunlight was a bit diffuse; ancient Paykan[3] cars puttered along the streets, and the clothing and other durable goods seemed unfashionable after my time in chic North Tehran.

Entering the gates of Astan-e Qods, I passed through the tented entrance marked for women for the security check. Visitors can come and go amid the raucousness at the Fatimah Maʿsumeh shrine with relative ease, but security is much more stringent at Astan-e Qods. The *khwāharān* examined my bag, frisked me for weapons, and thoroughly inspected my clothing to ensure that my *ḥijāb* was modest enough. All being in order, I entered the enormous marbled courtyard (*ṣaḥn*) surrounding the tomb complex. I wandered for hours around the sprawling courtyards and finally asked one of the volunteers where I could locate the Islamic Research Foundation (Bonyad-e Pazhuhish-e Islami). I was escorted to the Office of Foreign Relations, where I was promptly put into the care of a young woman whom I will call Shireen. After I explained my business to her, Shireen offered to show me around and assist me in my research activities. While I recognized that this "assistance" was also a means of keeping track of me, I was nevertheless grateful for the presence of an interested and genuinely helpful woman.

I was looking for a professor, whom I will call Dr. Ghulam ʿAbbasi, a scholar at the Islamic Research Foundation with whom I had been in e-mail contact and had arranged to meet while I was in Mashhad. Shireen made some phone calls, and we set off for another part of the shrine/tomb complex—she had located a Dr. ʿAbbasi, although I quickly realized that he was not the man I sought.[4] Nevertheless, he was another cleric with whom I could discuss my project and ask questions. While conducting research in Tehran, I had encountered surprising reactions to my project focusing on Mullah Husain Vaʿez Kashefi's *Rowẓat al-shohadā* (The Garden of the Martyrs). I had arrived in Iran with the assumption that Shiʿi scholars universally accepted *Rowẓat al-shohadā* as part of the canon of Karbala hagiography, but several mullahs promptly challenged my assumptions about the work's authority, expressing distaste for the text.

The first religious scholar with whom I discussed my research responded, "Why are you studying this text? Don't you know that it is full of lies and it is not a true historical study of Karbala?" Feeling deflated, I spent several days reflecting on this summary discountenance of *Rowẓat al-shohadā*. This scholar's reaction reminded me of a previous discussion with a colleague about the critique offered by a late Iranian religious ideologue, Ayatollah Morteza Motahhari, of *Rowẓat al-shohadā*, which he considered a "perversion" and "made up of lies" (*dorūgh-gū*).[5] As I read through Motahhari's critique of Kashefi's "distortions" (*taḥrīf*) of the true sequence of events at the Battle of Karbala, I gained a better understanding of the negative reactions my research was generating.

By the time I had this scholarly encounter in Mashhad, I was prepared for my interlocutor's dismissal of *Rowẓat al-shohadā*. Perched on the edge of a large sofa with Shireen by my side, I explained my research to ʿAbbasi, who sat behind a large wooden desk more than ten feet away from me. As I spoke, his eyebrows rose, and he folded his hands together. His body language prepared me for what he said: "*Khānom* [madam], how did you ever come across this topic, and why are you studying *Rowẓat al-shohadā*? Surely you know that this text is full of lies and superstition. Did you know that Kashefi did not even refer to the authentic *tārīkhī* [historical] sources?"[6] By now I had prepared a respectful counterargument: "Shaheed Motahhari never read *Rowẓat al-shohadā*.[7] I have read *Rowẓat al-shohadā* and have analyzed the text and translated sections of it into English. In fact, *Rowẓat al-shohadā* is an interesting text because in many sections, Kashefi translated Shaykh al-Mufid's *al-Irshād*. Kashefi's Persian translation from this Arabic history of Karbala is almost verbatim in parts." ʿAbbasi was nonplussed that I had not only identified the source of his critique but also critiqued his critique. He was particularly surprised by my familiarity with the Shiʿi textual tradition, further compelling him to try to correct what he considered to be my misguided interest in a problematic text.

ʿAbbasi reiterated that *Rowẓat al-shohadā* is not a truly historical account of Karbala. Even worse, he explained, Kashefi had put "words into the mouths of the *ahl-e bait*."[8] I then asked two questions: "Do you think that *Rowẓat al-shohadā* should be read as an objective history of the Battle of Karbala? If we agree that this text is not truly historical, then what is wrong with Kashefi creating dialogue? It seems unlikely that we might have actual transcripts of every conversation that took place over the many days of siege and battle." ʿAbbasi evaded my question about reading *Rowẓat al-shohadā* as something other than a historical text, retorting that verifiable recordings exist of what was spoken at Karbala. When I asked whose speech had been recorded, he told me, "Hazrat Imam Zain al-ʿAbidin remembered what was said, and so did Sayyidah Zainab." But, I asked, how could Imam Zain al-ʿAbidin have remembered everything, especially since he lay sick in a tent during the Battle of Karbala?

ʿAbbasi was clearly not pleased with the direction that our discourse had taken. Our meeting came to a close, and he wished me best of luck with my research but again encouraged me to reconsider my topic: "There are many other authentic books about Karbala that you should study instead of *Rowẓat al-shohadā*." Neither of us had persuaded the other about the function or authority of *Rowẓat al-shohadā*'s place in the canon of Karbala hagiography, and I realized that interactions such as this forced me into a liminal state. As a non-Muslim scholar of religious studies and not a theologian, how can I argue that Kashefi's *Rowẓat al-shohadā* is an important and authoritative hagiographical text? Were these discussions, which were later repeated in India, of a theological, religious studies, or literary critical nature? Was I overstepping boundaries and entering into the realm of constructive theology by arguing for a critical reconsideration of *Rowẓat al-shohadā* as a work of hagiography and not history?

In retrospect, my discussions with Iranian mullahs engaged a disputational methodology that is employed as a teaching and learning tool in the *howzehs* (religious colleges) of Qom and Mashhad. In *Mantle of the Prophet*,

Roy Mottahedeh describes a class in which a professor at the Faiziyieh, one of Qom's most prestigious *howzehs*, engaged with his students about Mullah Abdollah's commentary on *The Ultimate Rectification of Speech in Writing about Logic*.[9] Following the professor's introduction and interpretation of the text, he opened a lengthy discussion in which he expected his students systematically to question and dispute his presentation of the text. The students were supposed to find flaws with the professor's logic and to outline alternate interpretations. Such public displays of mastery of the religious sciences and philosophy will enable students gradually to ascend the intellectual hierarchy of the Shiʿi *ʿulamā*. Students prove their arguments by engaging explicitly with texts and are expected to employ the knowledge gained in other courses. Teachers may often prove their students wrong or deficient in their reasoning or rhetorical or argumentative skills, yet the teacher is often encouraging: "You are here to learn to reason, not just to learn to read. Think about the basic text and commentary on your own, and master it by asking about it in class."[10]

Michael M. J. Fischer has also written about the seminaries of Qom and the dialectical teaching style employed by the mullahs. Fischer begins his book with a vivid account of one of his first experiences in Isfahan in 1975. Having seated himself in the Madrasah Jada Buzurg, Fischer was approached by "a couple of mullahs [who] immediately came to ask who I was and to sit and debate."[11] The mullahs began to question Fischer about the nature of the Trinity, and the men engaged in a series of arguments, ending in a draw. Fischer realized that he could not fully participate in the discussion until he "learned more of the tradition of argumentation invoked against" him.[12] Although I was not a seminary student, I had studied the important Shiʿi texts and was learning the intellectual, theological, and devotional traditions, and I could engage with the mullahs.

My disputational dialogue with ʿAbbasi was certainly an unexpected and new experience for him. My conversations with him and other religious and literary scholars demonstrated that one of the keys to understanding the divergent processes of constructing hagiographical and historical canons in Shiʿism is understanding why Kashefi has been so profoundly discredited and why so many scholars offer the Qasem–Fatimah Kubra marriage as the most significant example of why *Rowẓat al-shohadā* is not an authentic Karbala history.

Mullah Husain Vaʿez Kashefi: A "Muslim" Devotee of the Ahl-e Bait

Kamal al-Din Husain ibn ʿAli Kashefi was born sometime during the 1420s C.E. in the town of Sabzevar in eastern Iran. Prior to the founding of the Safavid dynasty in 1501, Sabzevar was already known as a Shiʿi town, influenced by the shrine town of Mashhad forty-three miles to the east. Kashefi spent his youth and completed his early studies in Sabzevar. As a young man, he was already well known for his speaking skills, and he trained to become a preacher (*vāʿeż*). As Kashefi's later prolific literary output demonstrates, he obtained a broad education in the disciplines of mysticism (*taṣawwuf*), chemistry, literature, poetry, traditions (*ḥurūf*), and astronomy.[13] In 1456, Kashefi left the nearby town of Nishapur and moved to Mashhad, where he stayed briefly before settling in the Timurid capital of Herat, in Afghanistan. There, Kashefi became acquainted with an influential and well-known Naqshbandi[14] Sufi, ʿAbd al-Rahman Jami (d. 898 A.H./1492 C.E.). Kashefi and Jami developed such a close relationship that Kashefi not only was initiated into the Naqshbandi order but also married the *shaykh*'s sister.[15]

Members of the Timurid court were Kashefi's patrons, and "the star of good fortune shined" on him.[16] Among the works in various genres he was commissioned to write was *Rowżat al-shohadā*, which was commissioned by a Timurid sultan, Husain Bayqara (r. 875–911 A.H./1469–1506 C.E.). Husain Bayqara was a Sunni, although he possessed strong ʿAlid sympathies, not an unusual stance in the Sunni communities of the frontier zones in eastern Iran and the Indian Subcontinent, especially before the hardening of religious and sectarian identities in the succeeding centuries. The Safavid kings solidified the crystallization of Sunni and Shiʿa as religious categories demarcating theological, doctrinal, and spiritual difference in the decades following the composition of *Rowżat al-shohadā*. The Safavids appropriated Kashefi's Persian and Persianizing hagiography of the hero(in)es of Karbala, and new and elaborate rituals of recitation of the Karbala narrative (*rowżeh-khwānī*) were promoted in the *majlis* mourning assemblies at the royal courts.

Nineteenth- and twentieth-century scholars of Shiʿi devotional literature have struggled to characterize and categorize Kashefi. Was he a Sunni living in a Shiʿi environment? Was he a Shiʿa living in a state of dissimulation (*taqiyya*)? Most of the scant English-language scholarship on Kashefi and *Rowżat al-shohadā* tends to be devoted primarily to trying to solve the puzzle of Kashefi's sectarian identity. For example, in "Husayn Vaʿiz-i Kashifi: Polymath, Popularizer, Preserver," Maria Subtelny notes that "the question of his religious leanings has long been the subject of lively debate."[17] According to Subtelny, some scholars have asserted that Kashefi must have been Shiʿa because he was born in the "traditionally Shiʿite region of Sabzavar, and particularly because his ʿAlid martyrology, *Rawżat al-shuhadā*, achieved near-canonical status under the Safavids."[18] Other scholars posit that Kashefi must have been a Sunni because he was initiated into the Naqshbandiyya, one of the few Sufi orders that do not place ʿAli as the spiritual source of the lineage. Tellingly, however, Kashefi's contemporaries "did not even address the question."[19] Why, then, do contemporary scholars obsess about Kashefi's sectarian identity? Does it ultimately change who he was as a writer or his devotion to the *ahl-e bait*?

For many scholars, the most logical conclusion is that Kashefi wrote a "Shiʿi" hagiography, ergo he was Shiʿa. The fact that Kashefi wrote *Rowẓat al-shohadā* at the request of a Sunni sultan is often overlooked. For a Muslim living in sixteenth-century Herat, ʿAlid devotionalism was an integral aspect of both Sunni and Shiʿi Muslim spiritual life. Whereas most Sufi *silsilahs* (lineages) esteem the Prophet Muhammad's cousin and son-in-law, ʿAli, as their founding father, the Naqshbandiyya attribute the roots of their *silsilah* to the first *Rāshidūn* (Rightly Guided) *khalīfah*, Abu Bakr, further muddling Kashefi's sectarian identity.[20]

With the exception of a very few orders, Sufis in Iran and the Indian Subcontinent have traditionally venerated Imam Husain and have used his martyrdom at Karbala as the idealized spiritual model of sacrifice of the ego (*fanā*). Many Sufis compare al-Hallaj, the ecstatic mystic who was martyred in Baghdad in 309 A.H./922 C.E., to Imam Husain. Both suffered greatly because of their self-annihilating love for God.[21] A twelfth-century Chishti *shaykh*, Muʿinuddin Chishti, of Ajmer, India, is credited with a brief poem praising Imam Husain's spiritual exaltedness:

> Husain is the king, Husain is the sovereign
> Husain is religion, Husain is the refuge of religion
> He gave his head, not his hands, to Yazid
> Verily, Husain is the foundation of "There is no god."[22]

The penultimate line invokes a dual symbolic meaning, one physical, the other reflecting loyalty to God rather than kingly authority. Imam Husain preferred to give his head—that is, to die—rather than give his hand in allegiance to Yazid. *Bayʿah* is an oath of allegiance that is formalized through the act of shaking or giving one's hand. Thus, the Persian compound verb *dast dādan* literally means "to make an agreement" or "to give one's hand." More significantly, the line alludes to *bayʿah*, the allegiance that Yazid demanded and Husain refused to give.

The authorship of this eulogy to Imam Husain is not clear. Over time, this poem has come to be attributed to Muʿinuddin Chishti, which is significant because the pro-ʿAlid sentiments expressed in these verses reflect a Sufi conviction that the Imams are the spiritual heirs of the Prophet Muhammad. This poetic encomium to Imam Husain remains popular in India today, with these words commonly adorning exterior walls or forming a calligraphic border near the ceilings of *ʿāshūrkhānas*. The Shiʿa and most Sufis venerate Imam Husain as an idealized lover of God (*muḥibb*). Therefore, although Kashefi was a Naqshbandi, the pro-ʿAlid milieu of Timurid Herat; the Shiʿi culture of his hometown, Sabzevar, and nearby Mashhad; and his devotion to the *ahl-e bait* further demonstrate that Kashefi's hybrid sectarian identity reflects the fluid nature of Islam in the sixteenth century.

In the quest to establish a model of modernity based on reason as well as on the desire to ascribe unambiguous sectarian identities and obvious categories of belonging, Kashefi is an enigma. Kashefi was comfortable living in the pluralist Sunni and Shiʿi environments of Khorasan and Herat and in the mixed genres of writing that he produced. We can thus surmise that he did not conceive of himself as either Sunni or Shiʿa. Further evidence of the congenial northwestern Afghanistan environment in which Kashefi lived comes from the fact that his patron, Sultan Husain Bayqara, commissioned the renovation of Imam ʿAli's tomb in Mazar-e Sharif in 1481 C.E.[23] The positivist scholarly ideal of allocating people, ideas, behaviors, and ideologies into neatly circumscribed ontological categories is limiting and exclusivist. While scholars have struggled to draw a conclusive picture of Kashefi's religious identity, *Rowẓat al-shohadā* has received far less ambiguous and more negative receptions.

From a scholarly perspective, *Rowẓat al-shohadā* is a befuddling text that few scholars have engaged as part of the canon of Karbala hagiography. For example, not one of the nine essays in the December 2003 special issue of *Iranian Studies* devoted to Kashefi's scholarship focused on *Rowẓat al-shohadā*. Subtelny, who edited the issue, states that scholars have sought "to 'rehabilitate' Kashifi, who has usually been regarded merely as a compiler or popularizer, and to present him as a figure who was instrumental in the preservation of the state of the art of knowledge in a wide variety of fields in late medieval Iran."[24] After listing the forty or more works written by Kashefi in his lifetime, most notably in the fields of Qur'anic hermeneutics (*tafsīr*), ethics, traditions (*ḥadīth*), astronomy, the sciences, and belles lettres, Subtelny explains why *Rowẓat al-shohadā* was excluded. The editorial board believed that "the essays in this issue [should be] devoted to works that are less well-known in Western scholarship than his famous ʿAlid martyrology."[25] In fact, two of Kashefi's books have been translated into English and are the subjects of a sustained body of scholarship: *Akhlāq-e moḥsinī* (Moḥsin's Ethics) and *Futūwwat-nāmeh-ye sulṭānī* (The Royal Book of Spiritual Chivalry). *Rowẓat al-shohadā* has not received such sustained analysis, nor has it been translated into English in its entirety. Although it is a famous and important text, as so many European and American scholars briefly attest in their studies of Shiʿi devotional practices or early Safavid Persian literature, the minimal sustained study of Kashefi's *Rowẓat al-shohadā* indicates our post-Enlightenment need to categorize all things and beings, which is complicated by the fact that the popularizing qualities of *Rowẓat al-shohadā* provoke scholarly suspicion.

Missing the Genre for Text: Is Historical Authenticity Necessary?

While perplexing on the surface, the intellectual anxiety that Kashefi's religious identity and scholarship have induced in contemporary Euro-American and Iranian scholars reflects deeper epistemological struggles about the form and function of hagiography. This anxiety is exacerbated by vernacular/popular commemorations of Karbala, particularly in places where the Shiʿi community has resisted the homogenizing, devernacularizing impulse of the postrevolutionary Iranian clerical-political establishment. ʿAbbasi's assertion that the text is "full of lies and superstition" reflects the marginalized status of *Rowẓat al-shohadā* in the estimation of many Shiʿa of certain intellectual or ideological persuasions who are uncomfortable defining Kashefi's Karbala narrative as an authenticated history.

In the nineteenth century, Iranian and Indian debates about *Rowẓat al-shohadā* emerged as increasing numbers of scholars began to approach history and religious studies as rational and scientific disciplines of academic inquiry. In particular, the study of religious texts mandated and privileged a positivist, rational-scientific methodology for determining the authenticity of a number of genres of literature, including sacred biography and scripture. One of the earliest of the positivist-rationalist critics of *Rowẓat al-shohadā* was Shaykh Hajji al-Nuri al-Tabarsi (1838–1902), who castigated Kashefi in *Lūʾlūʾ wa marjān* (Pearls and Corals), a handbook outlining proper etiquette and subject matter for *majlis* orators (*rowẓeh-khwān*). Motahhari relies on Hajji al-Nuri's critique of *Rowẓat al-shohadā* in a series of lectures on the distortions (*taḥrīfāt*) that have infiltrated the literary and ritual-devotional commemorations of Karbala. Motahhari extols Hajji al-Nuri's trenchant critique of the *rowẓeh-khwāns* for telling lies, being ignorant of true history, and being greedy for fame and fortune.[26] Motahhari cites an incident narrated by Hajji al-Nuri in which a religious scholar from India sought advice about the degradation of Muharram rituals in his homeland: "He complains that in India, the *rowẓeh* narratives are falsehoods. He has requested that I do something, that I write a book revealing how the *rowẓehs* there have been overcome with lies. . . . This Indian *ʿālim* thought that after the *rowẓeh-khwāns* came to Hindustan they began telling lies [about Karbala]. He does not know that the water is polluted from its very wellspring. The center of the false *rowẓehs* is Karbala, Najaf, and Iran! The very centers of Shiʿism are the source of these lies."[27] Such accounts indicate that increasing numbers of the Shiʿi clerical classes were becoming deeply concerned with how to verify and authenticate the Karbala narratives recited in the mourning assemblies by the *rowẓeh-khwāns*. While Hajji al-Nuri does not directly discredit *Rowẓat al-shohadā*, he does so indirectly, in his critique of the narrations of Karbala that diverge from the "official" history. Thus, Hajji al-Nuri's critique of the "distortions and lies" told by the *rowẓeh-khwāns* in the *majlis* rejects *Rowẓat al-shohadā*, which is the source of most of the narratives told in the mourning assembly.

Contesting the Vernacular in a Cosmopolitan World

The critiques of Shiʿi scholars such as Hajji al-Nuri and Motahhari indicate several sites of contestation (Iranian versus Indian, elite Shiʿa versus everyday Shiʿa, cosmopolitan versus vernacular) that came to focus on the most visible marker of Shiʿi identity: the ritual commemoration of the Battle of Karbala. In the nineteenth-century struggle to define what it meant to be Shiʿa—a debate that continues today—Iranian mullahs found *Rowẓat al-shohadā* to resonate with their desire to articulate a distinctive national identity that fused political ideology with Shiʿism. At the time, Egypt, the Indian Subcontinent, and the Levant (Syria, Lebanon) were sites of contestation in which European colonial rule and Islamic revival and reform movements struggled for hegemonic ideological and political power. In the Indian Subcontinent, reform movements such as Deoband endeavored to cleanse Islam of the Hindu accretions that were believed to have emasculated Islam and thus enabled the British to establish their dominion over all Indians, both Hindu and Muslim. Many reformists believed that the restoration of a more masculine, vigorous, and "pure" Islam would enable Indian Muslims to overthrow their British colonizers.

Maulana Ashraf ʿAli Thanawi's *Bihishtī zewār* (Heavenly Ornaments) exemplifies the Deobandi reformist impulse to cleanse Islam of vernacular Indic practices. *Bihishtī zewār* targets Muslim women in particular, condemning their vernacular, everyday practices, which Deoband reformists considered superstitious and contrary to Islamic law and which ultimately supposedly contributed to the dissolution of Indian Muslim piety and orthodoxy. Such rhetoric indirectly blames India's colonial predicament on Muslim women, identified as the principal practitioners of everyday, vernacular Islam and lacking in knowledge of the intellectual traditions of theology and law. According to British colonial systems of classifying Indian religions, Hinduism was a mystical, spiritual, and effeminate religion; consequently, Islamic reformists argued, the diffusion of Hindu practices into Islam had changed a masculine, vigorous, tribal religion into a dissolute and effeminate faith. Islam could be reformed and its vigor (and purity) restored only by teaching women the principles of true Muslim practice. This gendered blame, however subtle and implicit, neglects to acknowledge several complicating issues: Muslim men, too, participated in and promulgated vernacular practices such as visiting shrines, flying kites, practicing wedding rituals, and enforcing taboos against widow remarriage. Over the course of more than a millennium of Muslim presence on the Indian Subcontinent, these were no longer Hindu practices but rather Indic vernacular practice.[28]

Further complicating the already contested arena of Muslim religious identity was the ambitious Wahhabi revivalist movement in the Arabian Peninsula, which promulgated a distinctly cosmopolitan Sunni religiopolitical ideology. Because the Wahhabi movement was centered in the holy cities of Mecca and Medina, pilgrims from all over the Muslim world were exposed to an interpretation of Islam that forbade the veneration of the graves of Fatimah al-Zahra and several of the Shiʿi Imams in Medina's Jannat al-Baqiʿ (Everlasting Cemetery).[29] The Wahhabi movement is named after its founder, Muhammad ibn ʿAbd al-Wahhab (1703–92), who rejected adherence to any one school of law (*maẕhab*), declaring the Sunnah (lived tradition) of the Prophet Muhammad, in conjunction with the Qur'an, to be the most important source of law. The Wahhabis assume a literalist stance with regard to issues such as listening to music, praying at shrines, and celebrating the birth and death anniversaries of holy figures, all of which are considered innovation (*bidʿah*) and are therefore prohibited. Such proscriptions of devotional and vernacular practice fostered Wahhabi antagonism toward Shiʿism, which is based on loyalty to and veneration of the *ahl-e bait*. With the founding of the Saʿudi kingdom in Arabia in 1932 and its co-optation of Wahhabi ideology, *ḥajj* pilgrims from all over the Muslim world were exposed to a staunchly literal interpretation of Islam that condemned many of their vernacular religious practices and beliefs as un-Islamic and unacceptable and instead sought to teach "proper" Islamic doctrine and practice. The Wahhabis intended these newly enlightened pilgrims to return home and teach their family members how to be good Muslims by eschewing innovative, vernacular practices. The Wahhabi interpretation of Islam is anathema to the Shiʿa, but the revitalizing and hegemonizing potential of reforming Shiʿism certainly appealed to the scholars of Qom, Najaf, and Karbala.

At this contested nexus of revival, reform, and colonialism, late-nineteenth-century religious scholars in Iran and Iraq struggled to define a cross-regional, cosmopolitan Shiʿi identity, with Muharram and its vernacular hagiographical literature and practices becoming the focal point of the debates about authentic Shiʿi religious identity. The Indian religious scholar who wrote to Hajji al-Nuri seeking advice about the etiquette for reciting Karbala narratives and especially about how to avoid distortions and embellishments was a bellwether. Hajji al-Nuri's inclusion of this letter in *Lūʾlūʾ wa marjān* reveals a number of underlying and important issues with regard to the global reform movement to devernacularize Islam. First, many Shiʿa felt a strong desire to construct a version of their faith that was global and universal—that is, purified of the perceived taint of vernacularism. Second, to purify and articulate a global Shiʿi identity, the source of Karbala's vernacular elements had to be identified, vilified, and purged from the canon. Third, by establishing a canon of Karbala literature (both historical and hagiographic), a set of authentic pan-Shiʿi devotional practices might be delineated, thus expurgating all un-Islamic vernacular practices that were perceived to dislocate the Shiʿa from the cosmopolitan (universal) history of Karbala that further weakened the global Shiʿi community.

Nineteenth- and twentieth-century Persian critical scholarship of Karbala literature singles out *Rowẓat al-shohadā* as the source of the distorted vernacular practices that had crept into Shiʿism since the Safavid period. ʿAbbasi's belief that the "text is full of lies and superstitions" echoes the critique of *Rowẓat al-shohadā* leveled by such Shiʿi scholars as Hajji al-Nuri and Motahhari. Hajji al-Nuri notes that Qasem's nuptials (*ʿurs*) were mentioned for the first time in *Rowẓat al-shohadā*, more than eight hundred years after the Battle of Karbala.[30] In short, *Rowẓat al-shohadā* is not true history (*tārīkh*). Many Iranian religious scholars asked me the same questions and gave me the same critiques of Kashefi's corrupted history of Karbala. According to Motahhari, before *Rowẓat al-shohadā*, "people used to refer to the original sources. . . . Shaykh al-Mufid [*riẓwān allāhu ʿalayhī*] wrote *al-Irshād* [The Book of Guidance] and many other pious works. If we ourselves refer to the *Irshād* of Shaykh al-Mufid, we haven't any need to refer to other sources."[31] Thus, reform-minded religious scholars have ascribed the role of authentic history of Karbala to *Kitāb al-irshād*, Shaykh al-Mufid's (d. 1022) Arabic-language history of the Imamate.

Kitāb al-irshād's elevated status is based on its Arabic-language composition, its retention of Karbala's Arab milieu, and its retention of the Arab ethos and worldview of the *ahl-e bait*. *Kitāb al-irshād* is the ideal universalizing history of Karbala—localizing no place, except Karbala, the site of the Shiʿi cosmopolitan. Kashefi's *Rowẓat al-shohadā* may have translated the events of Karbala into the Persian language, making Imam Husain's martyrdom understandable to a broader Shiʿi audience, but concomitant with the act of translation was vernacularization. Innovative elements such as the addition of characters or events reveal significant changes in the practice and meaning of Shiʿism as the tradition spread further from its Arab homeland. From the positivist historical perspective of modern Iranian intellectual thought, al-Mufid's historical account of the Battle of Karbala is authentic because of its objective, rational style, devoid of florid emotionality and rhetorical flourish. *Rowẓat al-shohadā* is none of these things.

Critiques of Qasem's battlefield wedding, one of Kashefi's plot innovations, reflect deeper anxieties about the nature of a unified, global Shiʿi community, an especially important concern considering the Shiʿa's minority status in most places outside Iran, Iraq, and Lebanon.[32] A universal narrative of Karbala that devernacularizes Muharram hagiographical literature and ritual reveals a dual strategy employed by the Iranian clerical elite to exert regulatory control over the practices and beliefs of the global Shiʿi population and to create a singular identity around which the Shiʿa may assert their authentic Muslim identity.

Since at least the mid-nineteenth century, the distinctly Indian flavor of the *mehndī* mourning assembly has prompted Shiʿi communities in South

Asia and beyond to debate the ceremony's authenticity and permissibility. Why has this event become the subject of such intense debate? What is at stake for both the global network of devotees of Imam Husain and vernacular communities in such geographically and culturally distinct places as India, Lebanon, and Iran? Whether to participate in the *mehndī* of Qasem is an emotionally charged decision in Shiʿi communities. In Lebanon, for example, failing to observe Qasem's battlefield wedding is a symbol of the Shiʿi community's progressiveness and modernity.[33] In Iran, Qasem's martyrdom continues to be observed on 7 Muharram, but it is now a special day for the martyrs of the Iran-Iraq War (1980–88). In South Asia, the *mehndī* of Qasem is steadfastly observed by the majority of Shiʿa in Hyderabad, Mumbai, Chennai, the state of Bihar, and Lahore. In 2005, Mumbai's Khoja Twelver community invited Tahera Jaffer, a *ẕākirah* from Mombasa, Kenya, to speak at a 7 Muharram *majlis*, where she declared that the *mehndī* of Qasem should not be observed because it is not a historically authentic event. In the wake of considerable community outrage, Jaffer was expelled from India, and the event has been extensively debated in various Internet chatrooms.[34] Understanding the nature of these conversations can teach us much about the dynamic tension between the imaginary hegemony of the Shiʿi cosmopolitan and the practical realities of vernacular Shiʿi social and religious life as it is mediated through a variety of cultural values, politics, and gendered norms.

Focusing on the events of the 7 Muharram performances in Hyderabad as a single snapshot of the much larger Karbala cycle provides several theoretical insights regarding the tensions between the universal-cosmopolitan event of Imam Husain's martyrdom and its emplotment in local contexts. The narrative frame of the Karbala narrative is universal and exists as part of a Shiʿi cosmopolitan that links the global community together in remembrance of the sacrifice of Imam Husain and his family. Of interest is the question of how Shiʿi communities in particular local contexts emplot—that is, place historical data (facts) into familiar plot structures—the Karbala frame narrative and make it meaningful through a process of vernacularization.[35] This emplotment is achieved through a dual process of equivalence, which ultimately links together the values of the global Shiʿi community (the cosmopolitan) and the worldview and ethos of the Shiʿa in myriad cultural contexts (the vernacular). The debates about the authenticity of the 7 Muharram *mehndī* ceremonies illustrate how the practice of making equivalence mediates the interdependent relationship of the cosmopolitan and the vernacular in the transmission and performance of sacred phenomena.

Establishing Equivalence in the Shiʿi Cosmopolitan and Vernacular

In his theoretical outline of the role of mappings and crossings in the hermeneutic positioning of the interpreter of religion, Thomas A. Tweed notes that place is critical. He observes that Miami, Florida, became a center for exiles "who were consumed with place or, more accurately, with being out of place."[36] The ethos of Miami's inhabitants reflects a nostalgic longing for some lost place. The Shiʿa, too, are obsessed with a place: Karbala. This geographical preoccupation is of an altogether different nature, however. Whereas Miami's exilic Cubans yearn for the political restoration of their homeland with the death of Fidel Castro, the Shiʿa do not long for Karbala as a lost land. Karbala is a physical, geographical location in Iraq that is the site of the tombs of Imam Husain; his half-brother, ʿAbbas; and other heroes of the *ahl-e bait*. Perhaps more significantly, it is also a place that occupies the hearts and imaginations of the Shiʿa. A saying attributed to the sixth Imam, Jaʿfar al-Sadiq, indicates the Shiʿi focus on the site of Imam Husain's martyrdom: "Every place is Karbala, every day is ʿĀshūrā." We can interpret a deeper meaning of this saying through the interrelation of the cosmopolitan (the site of Imam Husain's martyrdom in Iraq) and the vernacular (every place, for every Shiʿa). Karbala can be remembered and must be remembered and mourned by every Shiʿa, and the performance of ritually representing this event is refracted from its universal source into vernacular expression (literary and ritual). The third feature of the Shiʿi preoccupation with Karbala is eschatological. Karbala reminds the Shiʿa that Imam Husain fought for justice (*ʿadālah*) as well as that on the Day of Judgment (*yawm-e ḥashr*) those who shed tears for the *ahl-e bait* will be rewarded with the intercession of Fatimah al-Zahra and the pleasures of paradise.

Karbala is a universal location, idea, and ideal for the global Shiʿi population. Its hero(in)es populate the Shiʿi sacred landscape. Every place, whether in India, Iraq, or South Africa, can be Karbala, and its hero(in)es are transformed linguistically, culturally, and morally into idealized citizens of these disparate locations. These transformations reflect the interdependent relationship of the universal Shiʿi cosmopolitan and its infinite variety of vernacular expressions. The cosmopolitan is not only linguistic but also locative. Edward Simpson and Kai Kresse's description of the cosmopolitan helps us to interpret the role of the universal narrative of Karbala in connecting the Shiʿi community across geographical space and time: "Whatever else it may signify, the term clearly, and etymologically, refers to the idea of being part of a broad social project that exists outside the confines of kinship, ethnicity or nationality. Importantly, for us, 'cosmopolitanism' envelops a consciousness of human diversity. It refers to a sense of living beyond the mundane collective boundaries of everyday life and is suggestive of a trans-communal society."[37]

As part of a sacred cosmopolitan, the members of the global Shiʿi community share a fictive kinship predicated on loyalty to the *ahl-e bait*. How this loyalty is expressed reflects the human diversity of living in different places where Shiʿi values coalesce with those of the local environment. Tony K. Stewart observes that "Islam claims for itself a transnational and universal status. . . . [T]he sublime object of [Muslims'] religious world is transportable across all national and cultural boundaries."[38] This statement holds especially true in the case of Shiʿi Islam: every place *is* Karbala.

Much scholarly discourse sets up the cosmopolitan and the vernacular in binary opposition or into a hierarchy of inequality in which the cosmopolitan is the classical source (of language) and the vernacular its corrupted, common expression. Instead, it is more useful to understand the vernacular as the practice of making equivalence. In the context of Hyderabad's ritual commemoration of the *mehndī* of Qasem, the practice of making equivalence is enacted in two different yet intimately related ways, one linguistic and the other locative.

The practice of making equivalence is deeply rooted in linguistics. As we shift linguistic codes, the words that we use to explain a particular concept or thing also effect a transformation in the process. In analyzing the enculturation of Islam in Bengal, Stewart outlines a theory of linguistic equivalence that naturally encompasses religious language, which ultimately transforms the cosmopolitan ideals of Islam into a vernacular Bengali form. According to Stewart, all forms of translation are a search for equivalence in which "when the 'translation' is successful, the new term becomes a part of the target culture's extended religious vocabulary."[39] All religious encounters are acts of translation and therefore integrate a practice of making equivalence. In the case of India's observance of the *mehndī* of Qasem, the universal message of Karbala shared by the Shiʿi cosmopolitan is translated in the encounter with practitioners of Hindu traditions. Equivalences are made through the act of translating the cosmopolitan event into a South Asian vernacular.

The practice of making equivalence through linguistic devices is best understood in its relationship to its locative practice. Economic historian K. N. Chaudhuri proposes a "theory of equivalence" that is consonant with the locative definition of the cosmopolitan presented by Simpson and Kresse: "In the way we understand [Chaudhuri's] use of a theory of equivalence it means that sailors grow up on one littoral and when they travel somewhere else the new coast they encounter reminds them of their home; this creates visual and therefore emotional and psychological bonds that people share, or, in the language we have been using, have in common. In our view, it might not only be the coastline however that creates the sense of an imagined community through the experience of equivalence."[40] Simpson and Kresse offer the example of sailors from the Indian state of Gujarat who traveled to East Africa, where they observed the same door style and decoration used in Gujarat in use on the Swahili coast. For these sailors, this aesthetic similarity brought about a sense of being at home. Although the Swahili coast of Tanzania and Kenya is geographically distant from India, a practice of equivalence is possible, generating awareness among Africans and Indians of the Indian Ocean that they are members of the same cosmopolitan.

Chaudhuri's theory of locative equivalence and Stewart's theory of linguistic equivalence reveal how equivalence mediates the Shiʿi cosmopolitan and its myriad vernacular expressions. Although the Indic anxiety of widowhood and taboo against widow remarriage may be foreign to Lebanese Shiʿa, Fatimah Kubra's presence in the universal narrative of Karbala roots her in the Shiʿi cosmopolitan. In South Asia, the hero(in)es of Karbala are portrayed as idealized Indian Shiʿa, produced through the dual praxis of linguistic and locative equivalence, and when the cosmopolitan becomes rooted in disparate local contexts and is vernacularized, these sacred figures are transformed into saints whose behavior is culturally, morally, and religiously meaningful.

Localizing a Universal Story: The Indianization of the Hero(in)es of Karbala

Within decades of *Rowẓat al-shohadā*'s arrival in the Deccan in the mid- to late sixteenth century, the Qutb Shahi kings commissioned vernacular Deccani-Urdu translations, thereby effecting two transformations in the Karbala narrative. At the most basic level, translating *Rowẓat al-shohadā* from Persian into Deccani-Urdu made the text linguistically understandable to the average Indian of the Deccan, who most likely did not know any Persian. More specifically, the translation of *Rowẓat al-shohadā* translated Karbala and its hero(in)es to reflect an Indic worldview. In short, *Rowẓat al-shohadā* was vernacularized, constructing a memory of Karbala refracted through an Indian lens. The vernacular is often the site of the dynamic transformations and adaptations of Islam to remain relevant and meaningful for the average person. Thus, for a Hyderabadi Shiʿa, several degrees of vernacularization (making equivalence) are enacted to make Islamic theology and spiritual practice meaningful in its Indic context.

One of the most visible markers of this vernacularizing impulse in the Indian Deccan can be seen in the ritual commemoration of Qasem and Fatimah Kubra's wedding in the 7 Muharram *mehndī* mourning assembly. Fatimah Kubra's translation in the Deccani-Urdu hagiographical martyrdom literature exemplifies the process of vernacularizing Karbala through the practice of making equivalence. Kashefi's treatment of Fatimah Kubra's transformation from bride to widow is negligible in *Rowẓat al-shohadā*. Kashefi devotes approximately ten pages to his account of Qasem's martyrdom but concludes the chapter with a rather terse description of Fatimah Kubra's experience:

> The daughter of Imam Husain (peace be upon him) rubbed her hand in Qasem's blood and smeared it on her head and face, and she thus spoke, revealing her emotional state:
>
> Those bereft ones, whose beloved is killed,
> They have rouged their faces with the blood of their beloved.
>
> They are the new brides, who washed the murdered saint [*walī*],
> They dye themselves like this from head to foot.[41]

Although Fatimah Kubra laments her husband's untimely death, Kashefi does not focus on her transformation from bride to widow because in the context of sixteenth-century Iran, the taboo of widow remarriage was not socially meaningful. In the practice of making equivalence, however, Fatimah Kubra's role in the Deccani-Urdu Karbala cycle assumes a much more significant role.

This event resonates for the Shiʿa of South Asia for two reasons. First, 7 Muharram was the day that the army of Imam Husain's opponent, the ʿUmayyad *khalīfah*, Yazid, denied the members of the Imam's entourage access to the waters of the Euphrates River, causing them to suffer from extreme thirst. Second, in the Indic context, marriage is universal and is typically arranged, and the cultural taboo against widow remarriage makes the choice of spouse a particularly momentous life-cycle event. One poem recited in Hyderabad dramatically emphasizes the trauma and social stigma of widowhood:

> It is such an outrage that everyone calls her *raṅḍ*,
> "O Why did I not die? Alas, bridegroom Qasem."[42]

Raṅḍ, a particularly powerful Urdu word, connotes two negative feminine gendered states. A *raṅḍ* or *raṅḍī* is a common prostitute; the word also refers to a widow. A more polite, less emotionally charged way to refer to a widow in Urdu is with the chaste word *bevāh* (literally "without being in a state of marriage"). Particularly in the context of a young widow, *raṅḍ* conveys a deep social anxiety about the powerful sexuality that cannot be diffused through lawful intercourse with her husband.[43] The cultural dominance of the Indic taboo against remarriage prevents young widows from remarrying and enjoying socially and religiously licit sexual relationships. As this couplet implies, even saintly figures are not immune to the gossip and social anxieties that capture the everyday South Asian Shiʿi imagination.

This wedding introduced in *Rowẓat al-shohadā* assured the enduring popularity of this hagiographical text. As many Hyderabadi Shiʿa explained, the historical veracity of the wedding of Qasem and Fatimah Kubra is irrelevant. They believe in the wedding, Fatimah Kubra's sacrifice, and Qasem's martyrdom for the cause of religion. For them, it is a matter of the heart, not of the mind. They do not require empirical proof that the wedding happened. For the Shiʿa of Hyderabad, the *mehndī* mourning assembly helps them to remember the Battle of Karbala, and hero(in)es like Fatimah Kubra and Qasem offer reminders of family members and friends who suffer bad marriages, poverty, and widowhood. This vernacularized story transforms Qasem and Fatimah Kubra into idealized Hyderabadi Shiʿa and thus orients everyday Shiʿa's faith and allegiance to the holiness of the *ahl-e bait*. They can imagine and feel Karbala in a truly real and immediate fashion through the Deccani idiom and worldview, not the Arab milieu of an Iraqi Karbala.

But not all Shiʿa accept *Rowẓat al-shohadā*'s influential role in effecting the consolidation of Shiʿism in the Deccan. Since the mid-nineteenth century, Indian Shiʿa in the cities of Lucknow and Hyderabad have debated the religious permissibility of observing such obviously Hindu-influenced Muharram rituals as the *mehndī* mourning assembly. Hyderabadis, however, have largely resisted the devernacularizing pressures exerted by Iran over the past 150 years.

Debating the Mehndī Mourning Assembly in Hyderabad

In 2005, I spent several months working in the archives at the Salar Jung Museum in Hyderabad. One day, as I was transcribing a manuscript section about Qasem's wedding—a laborious process considering the fragile condition of the manuscript and poor lighting in the reading room—the manuscript preservationist sitting next to me asked me if I was working on Shiʿi manuscripts. I described my research to him, and he told me about the Jaʿfari Library located just around the corner. Although I had been in Hyderabad for several months, no one had mentioned this Shiʿi library in Darulshifa, where I spent several days each week conducting interviews and attending religious events. The preservationist told me that if I asked for Shajaʿat at the library, he would be more than willing to help me locate some of the texts for which I had been searching.

I had walked past the Jaʿfari Library on several occasions without realizing what it was. The library was located in a small building on the grounds of the Alava-ye Sartauq Mubarak *ʿāshūrkhāna*, dedicated to the fourth Imam, Zain al-ʿAbidin, and no signs indicated its presence. When I entered the small room, three or four men were sitting quietly and reading. Shajaʿat was a young, bespectacled man sitting at one end of the long table, his head bent over a text with great interest. I introduced myself, explained my research, and asked for his help in obtaining several books, especially Sayyid Mahdi Lakhnavi's proof text of Qasem's wedding, *ʿAbāʾir al-anwār* (Tears of Lights).[44] This is one of a significant series of mid-nineteenth-century texts responding to critiques of the historical veracity of *Rowẓat al-shohadā* and defending the permissibility of observing the *mehndī* mourning assembly as a ritual expression of Indic vernacular Shiʿism. Shajaʿat found Lakhnavi's work and offered a dissenting voice in the Hyderabadi Shiʿi community regarding the *mehndī* mourning assembly.

I returned to the Jaʿfari Library on several more occasions, and one afternoon, Shajaʿat mentioned that Zahra Academy, the women's wing of the Daneshgah-e Jaʿfariyya *madrasah*, was hosting its annual seminar and graduation ceremony at the end of the month. I told Shajaʿat that I would try to attend. I did not realize, however, that I was invited as the "chief guest" at the institutional center of the Iranianized Shiʿi community of Hyderabad. When I walked into the hall and saw approximately two hundred seated women wearing Iranian-style *ḥijāb*, I was taken aback. My clothing, a loose *shalwār-qamīẓ* and *dupaṭṭa*, which are typical modest dress for most of Hyderabad's Shiʿi women, felt inadequate. It seemed like I was again in Iran; there was even a mullah sitting on the stage in his robes and turban.

After the ceremony, I explained my research to several women. Sayyidah Maryam Naqvi's mother asked me why I studied a wedding that never happened. Kaneez Fatima, a social worker in the Old City, repeatedly impressed on me that the Naqvi women are learned and represent the true perspective on the matter, and that I should try to learn from them.

One of Sayyidah Maryam Naqvi's sisters was to be married the next month in a "perfectly authentic" manner, following the wedding that the Prophet provided for his daughter, Fatimah. The Naqvi wedding, I was told, would not be tainted by Indic rituals such as *mehndī*, *sāchaq* (henna ceremony and presentation of gifts at the bride's house the day before the wedding), *manjha* (turmeric-grinding ceremony), and *barāt* (procession of the groom to the bride's natal home on the day of the wedding). Only the signing of the wedding contract (*ʿaqd-e nikāḥ*) and the bride's departure ceremony (*rukhṣatī*) would be observed. The bride's mother proudly drew a parallel to the Sunnah of the Prophet Muhammad, whose daughter, Fatimah Zahra, received a simple dowry and rejected an excessive wedding feast. The removal of all Indic elements from the wedding ceremony further drew this small group of Hyderabadi Shiʿa into the ideological cosmopolitanism of Khomeini's idealized Islamic Republic.

Following the graduation ceremony, I joined Shajaʿat and his wife, Seema, for lunch at their house, located just down the street. Seema had just completed a course of study at Zahra Academy and was one of the graduates. She was employed as a social worker for the Imam-e Zamanah Mission, a charitable Shiʿi organization that serves the Old City, and I was looking forward to hearing her thoughts about Qasem's marriage and whether such vernacular Indian Shiʿi devotional practices as *mehndī* are positive expressions of devotion to the *ahl-e bait*. When I tried to ask her questions, however, she always deferred to Shajaʿat. Frustrated, I tried to discern her thoughts by watching her reactions as I spoke with her husband about Kashefi and *mehndī*.

After a lunch of chicken and rice, we discussed whether it is appropriate for Indian Shiʿa to use *mehndī* as a tool for remembering the sacrifices of Imam Husain and his family. Shajaʿat asked me whether I believed that the wedding happened, a question I was often asked and hesitated to answer, wondering whether what I thought was important and what stake I had in this question. Ultimately, I realized, I have both a stake and an important role in this debate as an interpreter of the ways in which everyday Shiʿa have integrated into their daily life the imitable model of sainthood embodied by such figures as Fatimah Kubra and Qasem.

I asked Shajaʿat whether he thought that I believed in the wedding and then told him, "It doesn't matter what I think. I am here to find out about what Hyderabadi Shiʿa think about the wedding." His response to the question of whether he believed that the wedding took place was a click of his tongue, the lifting of his chin, and the slight closing of his eyes—a nonverbal "No." Hyderabadis often use these gestures in response to comments, questions, or situations that are perceived as annoying or not worth asking. I had already known that Shajaʿat did not believe that the wedding took place, but my curiosity was piqued by his willingness to help me. He subsequently elaborated that a wedding between Qasem and Fatimah Kubra would have been impossible and inappropriate considering the circumstances.

This response surprised me. Shajaʿat asked me how many daughters Imam Husain had. When I said "Three," Shajaʿat responded that there were only two: Sakinah (known as Roqayya in Iran) and Sughra. According to Shajaʿat, Sughra was purported to have married Qasem, and Fatimah Kubra never existed. I had heard this explanation from others, and I countered that countless references exist to Sughra being ill and remaining behind in Medina. Shajaʿat said that information was not true. Our conversation continued in this vein for a few minutes.

When asked why he does not believe in the hagiographical authority of *Rowẓat al-shohadā*, Shajaʿat gave me the standard response that many other more authoritative (*ṣaḥīḥ*) martyrdom narratives exist, citing Ibn-e Tawus's *Luhūf* (Laments), Muhammad Baqir Majlisi's *Biḥār al-anwār* (Oceans of Lights), and al-Mufid's *Kitāb al-irshād*. I told Shajaʿat that I was familiar with all of these important Arabic texts and suggested including Muhammad ibn Jarir al-Tabari's *Tārīkh* (History) on this list, since this monumental Arabic-language history of the early Muslim community mentions the Battle of Karbala. Shajaʿat heartily agreed, confirming the work's authority. I then asked Shajaʿat what makes Kashefi's *Rowẓat al-shohadā* so unauthoritative.

Aside from reiterating Motahhari's argument that *Rowẓat al-shohadā* is based on weak or faulty *riwāyāt* (traditions, narratives) and includes events that never happened, Shajaʿat could not specify what was wrong with the text. After I pointed out that this text has been influential in the development of Muharram hagiography and ritual in Hyderabad. Shajaʿat lowered his voice and said that as people pass along accounts of the events at Karbala, bits and pieces are added to or deleted from the narrative, much like a childhood game of "telephone." How then, I asked, can we be so certain that the "authoritative" texts are the correct narratives. He seemed a bit nonplussed by this questioning, and our conversation drifted off into topics of a less theological nature.[45]

When I met Shajaʿat again for lunch in March 2006, he was carrying a notebook. Over the meal, we chatted, and he filled me in on news about his wife and what was happening at the Shiʿi library. We then went outside to sit, hoping to catch a cooling breeze on a hot Deccan summer day. Shajaʿat then reopened the subject of the battlefield wedding: "I have been thinking a lot about this Qasem marriage, and I have even been looking through some of the books about this. See, in this text I found a reference to the marriage, and in this other text, too. But, I still cannot believe that it happened." As a member of the minority Iranianized Shiʿi community that does not accept the historical possibility of Qasem's wedding, Shajaʿat had begun to search for an answer to the question of whether it is permissible to observe the *mehndī* mourning assembly. He had not reached any conclusions. Shajaʿat's act of sharing his own research with me not only brought into dramatic relief the influence of the ethnographer's presence but also made me understand the emotional and intellectual contours of how and why Hyderabadis debate the appropriateness of observing the *mehndī* mourning assembly as an expression of their Indian and Shiʿi identities. In the context of the *mehndī* mourning assembly and the debates that have been prominent for the past century and a half, the local or vernacular matters very much.

The expansion of Muslim networks in the past 150 years have connected minority Shiʿi Muslim communities but have also resulted in pressures to conform to the notion of a cosmopolitan Shiʿi community. Shajaʿat had encountered this cosmopolitan authority when he studied at seminaries in Qom. miriam cooke and Bruce Lawrence observe that "because Islam is not homogeneous, it is only through the prism of Muslim networks—whether they be academic or aesthetic, historical or commercial—that one can gain a perspective on how diverse groups of Muslims contest and rearticulate what it means to be Muslim."[46] Networks of pilgrimage and the movement of Shiʿi religious scholars between the Indian cities of Lucknow and Hyderabad and the spiritual centers of Iran (Qom) and Iraq (Najaf, Karbala) connect Shiʿi Muslims transregionally, yet these networks highlight the significance of the vernacular/local in defining Shiʿi religious practices and worldviews.

The Hyderabadi Shiʿi community has strongly resisted campaigns by the

Iranian and Iraqi religious elite to abandon vernacular Muharram ritual/devotional practices. Hyderabadi Shiʿa steadfastly observe the *mehndī* mourning assembly on 7 Muharram in defiance of pressure from the *ʿulamā* in Iran and Iraq to eliminate such "unauthentic" and "un-Islamic" (and anti-modern) practices. Participation in the *mehndī* mourning assembly, however, narrates a worldview connecting Hyderabad's Shiʿa to Karbala through the ecology, aesthetics, and values of the local Deccani culture.

In attempts to construct a cosmopolitan, homogenized Shiʿism, the religious elite of Iran and Iraq have targeted practices such as the *mehndī* mourning assembly as inauthentic. I first became aware of the debates about Qasem and Fatimah Kubra's wedding in August 2002, when I was studying Urdu in Lucknow. When I asked a prominent scholar of Urdu Karbala literature about Hindu influence on the ritual remembrance of Qasem and Kubra's wedding, he emphatically assured me far fewer Lucknowi Shiʿa now observe such superstitious practices as the *mehndī* of 7 Muharram. Likewise, he asserted, *mehndī* is un-Islamic, and the myriad wedding rituals are too expensive. "Instead," he stated, "we celebrate the sacrifice of Fiza. Did you know that she was black—from Ethiopia? This is more modern."[47] Yet Hyderabadi Muslims, unlike those in other parts of India, have resisted pressures to conform to what they perceive as an arbitrarily defined set of Muharram practices.

Hyderabadi Shiʿa defend the practice of *mehndī* with three arguments. First, if one believes that Qasem and Fatimah Kubra married at Karbala, then historically verifying the event should not be important. Second, although the wedding rituals observed in the *mehndī* mourning assembly derive from vernacular Indic culture, Hyderabadi Shiʿa have adopted these practices and values, making them equally Islamic. Third, Hyderabadi Shiʿa should determine what is acceptable Muharram practice and what is not.

Hyderabadi Shiʿa commonly explain the enduring popularity of the *mehndī* mourning rituals by saying that because they have faith that Qasem's wedding happened, it does not matter whether the wedding appears in history books. Sabiha Asghar, an educator and well-known reciter of *nauḥas*, reflected that two famous nineteenth-century composers of Karbala poetry, Mir Anis and Mirza Dabir, "wrote about the marriage of Hazrat Qasem and Bibi Kubra, and Muslims believe that their poetry was signed by Imam Husain. Therefore, whatever they wrote about Karbala in their *marṡiyas* is historically verifiable."[48]

The second argument situates the *mehndī* of 7 Muharram in the local Hyderabadi context. Maulana Reza Agha, Hyderabad's most senior Shiʿi religious scholar and the *majlis* orator at M. M. Taqui Khan's annual *mehndī* mourning assembly, explained that the Urdu word for wedding, *shādī* (literally "joy"), is not what happened at Karbala. According to Agha, only the *nikāḥ* (the signing of the Muslim marriage contract) could have been performed in such a situation: "There is a big difference between the joyful rituals of a wedding and the actual marriage."[49] Reza Agha pointed out that the semantic range of meaning associated with *shādī* must be borne in mind. The marriage act may have taken place, but without any of the attendant rituals. Hyderabadis observe the *mehndī* because it is a central aspect of Indian marriage, both Hindu and Muslim. Another informant explained that the clothing, jewelry, and customs of Indian Muslims are derived from Hindu practices, but these practices have been thoroughly Islamicized over time and are considered completely authentic and are not in tension with religious law (*sharīʿah*).

The third explanation reflects the desire to assert the necessity and spiritual significance of the vernacular Karbala in the lives of everyday Shiʿa. At a *manjha* ceremony in the Old City, a female graduate student at Osmania University asked her father to speak with me about the battlefield wedding, explaining that although he works in the Persian Gulf, her father "has lived in Iraq and he has very strong feelings about Hazrat Qasem and the *mehndī*." Many Hyderabadi Shiʿa who have emigrated to the Gulf, Canada, or the United States have renounced the 7 Muharram *mehndī* rituals as un-Islamic and rooted in superstition, and I expected that this man would also have done so. However, his point of view surprised me:

> The *mehndī kī majlis* is a way of expressing our love, affection, and gratitude for [the *ahl-e bait*]. All of the rituals associated with the recollection of the *ahl-e bait* are acceptable because they help the devotee to remember the Prophet's family and their sufferings. Living in South Asia, we have been influenced by our environment. One can choose personally if one observes the rituals or not. Either way it should be fine. What is religiously allowed or not can only be determined by Allah. It is not the prerogative of individual religious scholars. None of them have the right to say what is *ḥalāl* [permitted] or *ḥarām* [forbidden].[50]

Through the Mehndī kī Majlis, *We Remember Karbala*

Two men, one Iranian and the other Indian, were deeply influenced by a devernacularized, cosmopolitan Shiʿism learned in the religious seminaries (*howzeh*) of Qom. Yet Shajaʿat found that his belief that Qasem and Fatimah Kubra could have never married at Karbala was tested through his interactions with me. Had Shajaʿat imbibed too much of the ethos of the Qom seminaries and in the process ceded a bit of his Hyderabadi Shiʿi identity? He struggled between being a Shiʿa deeply embedded in the transregional homogenizing interpretation of Shiʿism espoused by the postrevolution Iranian government and being an Indian embodying the vernacular, hybrid Deccani identity of Hyderabad.

The Shiʿa of Hyderabad feel deeply connected to the Imams and use devotional texts and practices to keep the memory of Karbala constantly in the present. For the majority of Shiʿa living in the Deccan, whose mother tongue is either Urdu or Telugu, the Arabic language and the worldview espoused by the *ʿulamā* of Iran and Iraq render this vernacular devotional spirituality into something that is as foreign and arid as the desert of Karbala. The nature of this debate indicates the importance of local/vernacular contexts in shaping a Hyderabadi Shiʿi religious world. The *mehndī* mourning assembly is both a method for remembering Karbala and demonstrating one's love for Imam Husain and his family and a means of articulating what it means simultaneously to be a Muslim, a Shiʿa, and an Indian.

Glossary

ʿAdālah: Justice.

Āfāqī: "Foreigners" from Iran who came to seek their fortunes in the Shiʿi ʿAdil Shahi and Qutb Shahi kingdoms in the Deccan.

Agniparīkṣā: The trial by fire that Sita underwent to prove her fidelity to her husband, King Rama, while she was imprisoned by Ravana.

Ahl-e bait: "The People of the House," the members of the Prophet Muhammad's family descended through his daughter, Fatimah al-Zahra.

ʿAlam: Metal battle standard or flag. In Hyderabad, the *ʿalam* is a nonfigural representation of various members of Imam Husain's family, including ʿAbbas, Qasem, Imam Husain, and Fatimah al-Zahra.

ʿAqd: Contract.

ʿArsī muṣḥāf: Husband's viewing of his wife's reflection in a mirror for the first time following the marriage ceremony.

ʿArūsī: Marriage.

Ashrāf: The Muslim noble class.

ʿĀshūrā: The tenth day of Muharram, when Imam Husain was killed in battle.

ʿĀshūrkhāna: The "House of the Tenth"; special buildings containing *ʿalams* where the sufferings of Imam Husain and his family are ritually remembered.

Āstāna: The threshold that separates the sacred from the profane.

Ayyām-e ʿazā: The two months and eight days of mourning, between 1 Muharram until 8 Rabiʿ al-Awwal.

Bājā: Brass band that heralds the groom's movement to his bride's home.

Band: Stanza of a poem.

Baraka: The grace and spiritual power of a saint emanating from his/her tomb.

Barāt: The groom's horseback wedding procession to his bride's home.

Bāṭin: That which is concealed; in the context of Islamic mysticism (Sufi and Shiʿi), that which is esoteric and not readily apparent.

Bayʿah: An oath of allegiance formalized through the act of shaking or giving one's hand.

Bāzārī: The powerful class of merchants, dealers, and traders who have historically had a close relationship with Iran's clerical class.

Bevāh: Widow.

Bevāhpā: The state of widowhood.

Bhakta: Devotee of a god, goddess, or saint.

Chakkī: Grinding stone.
Chārdah maʿsūmīn: The "Fourteen Infallibles," including the Prophet Muhammad, Fatimah al-Zahra, and the twelve Imams.
Chuṛi (pl. chuṛiyāṅ): Bangles.

Dahej: Dowry given by the bride's family to the groom and his family.
Darbar: Court of a king or other ruler.
Dargāh: Shrine/tomb of a Sufi saint.
Dharma: One's duty or responsibility in accordance with one's caste and station in life.
Ḍhaṭṭī: Cloth that is presented to the *ʿalam* during Muharram.
Dīwān: Prime minister.
Dorūgh-gū: False speech, lies.
Dupaṭṭa: A long oblong cloth draped over a woman's shoulders to cover her breasts.

Fiqh: Jurisprudence or interpretation of Islamic law (*sharīʿah*).

Gham: Grief, sadness.
Ghāzī: Warrior.
Ghūṅgaṭ: A large veil worn to cover the head and the face.
Giryān: Weeping, crying.

Ḥadīth/Ḥadīs̤: Reports of the deeds and words of the Prophet Muhammad; in the Shiʿi tradition, also includes the traditions of the twelve Imams.
Haldī: Turmeric.
Howzeh: Religious seminary where Shiʿi religious scholars receive their training; the most famous *howzehs* are located in Qom, Iran.
Ḥujjat: "Proof."
Ḥusainiyyat: The religious and social ethic of Imam Husain and his family's sacrifice at the Battle of Karbala; referred to in this book as "*ḥusaini* ethics."

Ijmāʿ: Consensus of legal scholars on a matter.
Ijtiḥād: Self-exertion to attain knowledge of a matter; the practice of independent reasoning in jurisprudence; an important component of Shiʿi jurisprudence following the occultation of the twelfth Imam, al-Mahdi.
Imam: One of the twelve spiritual successors of the Prophet Muhammad whose authority is recognized by the Shiʿa.
ʿImāmah: Turban.
Imāmah: The institution of the Imamate, or the twelve spiritual successors to the Prophet Muhammad who guide the Shiʿi community.
Indic: The articulation of an essential South Asian identity, worldview, and ethos that is shared by Hindus, Muslims, Buddhists, Iranians, and Europeans who have lived on the Indian Subcontinent.

Jāʾiz: Permissible.
Jashn: Celebration, joyous occasion.
Jahez: Dowry given by the bride's family to the groom and his family.
Julūs: The funeral procession in which the *ʿalam* is taken out and paraded, usually accompanied by devotees performing *mātam* and chanting *nauḥa*.
Jūtā chhupāʾī: Ritual performed during the *mehndī* ceremony in which the bride's sisters steal the groom's shoes and refuse to return them until a ransom is paid.

Kafn: Burial shroud.
Karāmat: A saint's miraculous power to intercede in matters and grant devotees' wishes.
Khalīfah: Vice-regent; the political successor to the Prophet Muhammad.
Khātim al-awliyā: The seal or last in a lineage of sainthood.
Khatm al-nubūwwah: The seal or the last in the line of prophecy.
Khuṭbah: A sermon or oration on a specific religious topic.
Khwāhar (pl. Khwāharān): "Sister/s"; women who volunteer to maintain order and decorum at holy sites throughout the Shiʿi world.
Kunya: Title given to the mother or father of a child; the father is "Abu," followed by the child's name, and a mother is referred to as "Umm," followed by the child's name.

Laqab: Epithet.

Mahr: Bride price given by the groom to the bride as stipulated in the Islamic marriage contract.
Majlis-e ʿazā: Mourning assembly to commemorate the martyrdom of Imam Husain and his family and supporters at the Battle of Karbala.
Maṅgalsūtra: "Auspicious thread" that married women wear around their neck, typically made of jet beads and a gold pendant; widowed women are not permitted to wear the *maṅgalsūtra*.
Manjha: Prewedding turmeric-grinding ceremony in which the bride or groom's body is rubbed with turmeric.
Maqtal: Genre of Islamic literature focusing on the martyrdom of Imam Husain at the Battle of Karbala.
Marjaʿ al-taqlīd: Source of emulation.
Marṡiya: Narrative poem eulogizing Imam Husain's martyrdom at the Battle of Karbala.
Marṡiya-khwān: Trained or professional reciter of *marṡiya*.
Maṣāʾib: Ritualized narration of the troubles and suffering of Imam Husain and his family at Karbala; the climax of the oration given by the *ẕākir* during the mourning assembly.

Mātam: Ritualized self-flagellation in the form of beating the breast with the hands or razor blades, cutting the head, or using flails to strike the back.
Maulā: Lord or master. Often used in Shiʿism to refer to ʿAli, whom the Shiʿa believe was designated by the Prophet Muhammad to be his successor.
Mehndī: The prewedding henna ceremony at the groom's home, to which the bride's family brings trays of henna and gifts.
Mehndī kī majlis: Ritualized remembrance of the marriage of Qasem to Fatimah Kubra and the bridegroom's martyrdom on 7 Muharram.
Mehndī kī mannat: Making a vow by applying *mehndī* to the hand and requesting the intercession of Qasem during Muharram.
Mehndī lagānā: The decoration of the hands and feet with henna.
Miṣrī: Rock sugar that symbolizes sweetness and harmony in marriage, ground over the head of the bride and groom during the wedding ceremony.
Maḥabbat: Love, especially for God.
Muḥaddath: Recipient of God's supernatural speech.
Mujāḥid: One who strives or struggles; a warrior of the faith.
Mujtāḥid: One who struggles to attain knowledge of a matter; a Shiʿi religious scholar.
Muʿjizah: Miracle.

Nabī: Prophet.
Nāmeh: Chronicle.
Nārā: Cord tied around the right wrist to receive protection and care from a saint, god, or goddess.
Naṣṣ: Divinely inspired designation by God of who will be an Imam's successor.
Nath: A pin or ring worn in the nose, traditionally a symbol of a woman's married status.
Nāṭiq: The teacher of God's revelation.
Nauḥa: Short poem written in couplets, sung rhythmically to the percussive action of *mātam*.
Nauḥa-khwān: A skilled or professional reciter of *nauḥa* poems.
Naushāh: "New king"; Urdu word that refers to a bridegroom.
Neg: The ritualized request of the bride's sisters for gifts and money from the bridegroom.
Nikāḥ: "Sexual intercourse"; the contract entered into by a man and a woman to live together as husband and wife and therefore to enter into lawful sexual relations.
Nubūwwah: Prophecy.
Nūr: The divine light of God that radiates from holy people, especially from the Prophet Muhammad and his family.

Pān: Popular digestive in India in which a betel leaf is stuffed with areca nuts, spices, tobacco, and other substances.

Panjetan-e Pāk: "The Holy Five": the Prophet Muhammad, Fatimah, ʿAli, Hasan, and Husain.
Pativratā: A wife who is faithful to her marriage vows.
Pīr: Sufi spiritual master and teacher.
Purdah: Sexual segregation of men and women.

Qaṣīdah: Panegryic, epic poetry.

Ranḍ: A prostitute or widow.
Rasūl: Messenger; one chosen by God to reveal a new book of law to a community.
Rekhtī: Indic poetic form in which male poets assume the feminine voice.
Risālah: Messengership.
Rithā: Extolling the merits and honor of a deceased male relation.
Rowẓeh: Grief or sadness.
Rowẓeh-khwān: A professional narrator of chapters of Mullah Husain Vaʿez Kashefi's *Rowẓat al-shohadā*.
Rowẓeh-khwānī: The practice of reciting sections of *Rowẓat al-shohadā*.

Sāchaq: A prewedding ritual in which the groom's family prepares trays (*kishtī*) containing articles of clothing, jewelry, cosmetics, and sweets for the bride.
Salām: Short mourning poem composed in couplet form with a refrain.
Ṣalāḥ: Social virtue.
Ṣāliḥ: Ethical authority of the highest order, an essential quality of saints.
Ṣāmit: "A silent one" who is initiated into the esoteric meaning of the Qurʾan; an Imam.
Sayyid: Descendent of the Prophet Muhammad.
Sehrā: A floral garland that covers the face like a veil; often worn by the bride and groom in South Asian wedding ceremonies.
Sehrā bandhānā: The tying of the *sehrā* on the head.
Shādī: "Joy"; commonly used word in Urdu and Hindi for wedding.
Shahādat: Martyrdom.
Shahādat-nāmeh: A narrative account of martyrdom, especially that of Imam Husain and his family at the Battle of Karbala.
Shahīd: Martyr.
Śakti: Feminine power.
Shīʿat ʿAli: "The Partisans of ʿAli"; Arabic term for the supporters of ʿAli as the successor to the Prophet Muhammad.
Silsilah: Lineage in a Sufi order.
Soz: Grief; genre of brief Urdu mourning poetry that increases feelings of grief and sadness in *majlis* participants.
Suhāgan: A married woman whose husband is still alive.

Tabarruk: Food that is blessed by the holiness of Imam Husain's family and distributed to devotees at the end of a *majlis*.
Tafsīr: Explanation and interpretation of the Qurʾan.
Taḥrīf (pl. taḥrīfāt): Distortion of facts or reality.
Tapasyā: The power and heat generated by the performance of yoga and other austerities that produce control of the body.
Taqiyya: The practice of dissimulation by which a Shiʿa masks her/his identity in situations in which there is danger or persecution.
Taṣawwuf: Islamic mysticism, Sufism.
Tawḥīd: The unity or absolute uniqueness of God.
Taʾwīl: Allegorical and symbolic interpretation of the Qurʾan.
Taẕkirah: Biographical dictionary that typically focuses on a particular group of people (e.g., writers, saints, *majlis* orators).

ʿUmrah: Supplementary pilgrimage to Mecca and Medina that is performed outside of the prescribed days in the Muslim month of Dhu'l-Hijja.

Vāʿeẓ: Preacher.

Waḥy: Revelation.
Walāyah: Sainthood of a transcendent nature bestowed by God upon a chosen person; referred to in this book as "transcendent sainthood."
Walī: Lord, master, saint.
Walī Allah: "Friend of God"; saint.
Walīmah: Feast(s) hosted by the bride's family in the weeks following the wedding.
Waṣīy: Executor authorized to carry out the prophet's teachings; one of the Imams' roles.
Waṣīyat: Last will and testament.
Wilāyah: Socially recognized and sanctioned sainthood; referred in this book as "imitable sainthood."

Yatīm: Orphan.
Yawm-e ḥashr: The Day of Judgment.

Żāhir: That which is exoteric and readily visible or understandable.
Ẕākir (fem. ẕākirah): "One who remembers"; narrator of the events of the Battle of Karbala, especially the suffering of Imam Husain and his family.
Zanāna: Women's quarters.
Ziyārat: "Visitation"; pilgrimage to the tombs of holy people.
Żulm: Tyranny.

Notes

INTRODUCTION

1 Nakash, "Muharram Rituals," 117.
2 Ibid., 132.
3 Karar, "Uṭho Mere ʿAmmū," 43.
4 al-Tabari, *Between Civil Wars*, 187–88.
5 Shahidi, "Mātam hai āj dilbar Umm al-Banain kā," 35.
6 al-Tabari quoted in Jafri, *Origins*, 189.
7 Anwar Alam, " 'Scholarly Islam,' " 251.
8 Masuzawa, *Invention*, 25.
9 *ʿĀshūrkhāna* is a compound word derived from the words *ʿāshūrā* (ten) and *khāna* (house), meaning "the house of ten" or "the house of the tenth." The *ʿāshūrkhāna* is the ritually consecrated space in which the *ʿalams* and other commemorative objects dedicated to Imam Husain's family are kept and displayed.
10 Wilce, *Eloquence*.
11 Orsi, *Between Heaven and Earth*, 167.
12 Ibid., 151.
13 Khayyami, "Islam and Husainiat," 257; see also Hyder, *Reliving Karbala*, 137–59.
14 Khayyami, "Islam and Husainiat," 254, 257.
15 Hawley, "Introduction," xiii.
16 Dakake, *Charismatic Community*, 27.
17 Ibid., 25.
18 Corbin, "Meaning," 170.
19 Hodgson, *Classical Age*, 59.

CHAPTER 1

1 Ernst, *Following Muhammad*, 22–23.
2 Said, *Orientalism*, 92.
3 Sulami, *Early Sufi Women*, 48–49.
4 Ibid., 54, 58.
5 For a more in-depth analysis of the gendered dimension of sainthood, in particular with regard to the Roman Catholic tradition, see chapter 2.
6 Dakake, *Charismatic Community*, 25.
7 Mooney, "Voice, Gender, and the Portrayal of Sanctity," 13.
8 John Carlos Rowe, "Structure," 30–31.

9 The Latin word *sanctus* also conveys the meaning "holy."
10 Kitchen, *Saints' Lives*, 52.
11 Brown, *Cult*, 5, 88.
12 Ibid., 73.
13 Ibid., 21.
14 Ibid., 8.
15 Ibid., 63.
16 Delehaye, *Legends*, 63.
17 Hollywood, "Inside Out," 78, 90, 92.
18 Ibid., 78.
19 Cornell, *Realm*, 283. Cornell's seven typologies of sainthood are outlined on pp. 277–84.
20 Ibid., 102.
21 Ibid., 95.
22 Ibid., 94.
23 Suvorova, *Muslim Saints*, 200.
24 For a full analysis of the warrior saint, see Digby, *Sufis and Soldiers*.
25 Hassett, "Open *Samaʿ*," 43.
26 Khafi Khan, *Muntakhāb al-lubāb*, 346.
27 According to other traditions in circulation in Hyderabad, it was not a merchant but rather a mendicant (other stories identify the informer as a cobbler), Sayyid Miran Husaini Majdhub, who told Yusuf and Sharif the secret to entering Golconda fort. Sayyid Miran Husaini Majdhub's tomb is located near Dargah Husain Shah Wali in the Tolichowki neighborhood, not far from Golconda. I am grateful to Scott Kugle for information regarding this alternate though apocryphal figure who was instrumental in bringing about the defeat of the Qutb Shahi dynasty.
28 Muslims and Hindus have been making pilgrimage (*ziyārat*) to the tomb of Ghazi Miyan since the twelfth century, although not until at least 1250 C.E. did Sultan Nasiruddin Mahmud commission the construction of the formal tomb complex. For more information on Ghazi Miyan, see Suvorova, *Muslim Saints*, 155–61.
29 Ibid., 155.
30 Ibid., 158.
31 Nizami, "Ghazi Miyan," 1047.
32 For an overview of the history of the repeated destruction of the temple at Somnath, see Davis, *Lives*.
33 Thapar, *Somanatha*, 155.
34 Suvorova, *Muslim Saints*, 159.
35 Thapar, *Somanatha*, 156.
36 Visuvalingam and Chalier-Visuvalingam, "Between Mecca and Banaras," 28.
37 Wehr, *Arabic-English Dictionary*, 1100.

38 Other references to God as the friend of the believers can be found in 3:68, 42:9, and 42:28.
39 Corbin, "Meaning," 173.
40 al-Tirmidhi's *laqab* (epithet) was al-Ḥakīm, "the Wise One."
41 al-Tirmidhi, *Concept*, 15–16.
42 Ibid., 17.
43 Ibid., 24–29, 31–36.
44 Ibid., 101–2.
45 Ibid., 106.
46 Ibid., 109–10.
47 Ibid., 124.
48 Ibid., 111–12.
49 Austin, introduction, 17.
50 Chodkiewicz, *Seal*, 50.
51 Ibn al-ʿArabi, *Bezels*, 67.
52 Ibid., 67.
53 Ibid., 66.
54 Dakake, *Charismatic Community*, 17.
55 Ibn Ishaq, *Life*, 86.
56 Ibn al-ʿArabi, *Futūḥāt al-makkiyah*, in Chodkiewicz, *Seal*, 119.
57 Cornell, *Realm*, xix.
58 Madelung, "Ismāʿiliyya," 203.
59 Murata, *Tao*, 53.
60 Elias, "Female and Feminine," 216.
61 Amir-Moezzi, *Divine Guide*, 70.
62 Ibid., 30.
63 Momen, *Introduction*, 156.
64 Amir-Moezzi, *Divine Guide*, 71.
65 al-Saduq, *Shiite Creed*, 85.
66 Ibid., 94.
67 Nazmi, "Imam Husain," 13.
68 Quoted in Khayyami, "Islam and Husainiat," 257.
69 Sadiq Naqvi, interview.
70 Hussaini, *Sayyid Muhammad al-Husayni-i Gisudiraz*, 50.
71 Ibid., 51.
72 Khalidi, "Shiʿahs," 41.
73 Motahhari, *Wilayah*, 50–62.
74 "Shah Nawaz," "Hum ḥaidarī haiṅ sāre zamāne pechhāyenge," 20.
75 Quoted in Takim, *Heirs*, 2.
76 Massignon, *Salman Pak*, 10.
77 Ibn Abi al-Hadid, *Sharḥ nahj al-balāgha*, 18:36, 38.
78 Kashefi, *Rowẓat al-shohadā*, 289–93. See chapter 4 for a detailed discussion of

the remembrance and portrayal of Qasem and Fatimah Kubra in *Rowẓat al-shohadā* and in the Hyderabadi *mehndī* mourning assembly.

79 Sayyid Saeed Akhtar Rizvi, "Martyrs," 41.

80 "Zakir," *Tears and Tributes*, 38.

CHAPTER 2

1 Asghar, interview.

2 Ibid.

3 Ibid.

4 Ibid.

5 Kitchen, *Saints' Lives*, 105.

6 Elias, "Female and Feminine," 211.

7 Ibid., 211.

8 The daughters of the Mughal emperors were not allowed to marry to avoid creating a dangerous number of heirs to the throne.

9 Kohlberg, "Authoritative Scriptures," 303.

10 Fatimah and Zainab's role as exemplars of idealized Shiʿi womanhood is an important theme in the discourses of the Iranian intellectual ʿAli Shariʿati, whose writings provided the philosophical foundation for the 1979 revolution. To see how Fatimah al-Zahra was transformed into a revolutionary, political figure, please refer to Shariʿati's series of lectures "Fatimah Fatimah Ast [Fatimah Is Fatimah]," delivered at the Husainiyyah Irshad in Tehran in 1971; Shariʿati, *Fatimah*.

11 Shamsi, "Karbala," 248.

12 Flueckiger, "Wandering," 36.

13 Reddy, *With Respect*, 114.

14 Khayyami, "Islam and Husainiat," 254.

15 Schimmel, *Mystical Dimensions*, 39.

16 Ordoni, "Fatima the Gracious."

17 For a full transcript of Fatimah's speech (*khuṭbah*), see M. M. Taqui Khan, *Khutbat-un-Nissa*.

18 Khan, interview.

19 Ibid.

20 Lalljee, *Janab-e Zainab*, 3.

21 "Bashir" has the ironic meaning of a "bearer of good news," which establishes a profoundly ironic tone in this *nauḥa*.

22 ʿAṣr is one of the five daily prayers, taking place in the afternoon, before sunset.

23 The fourth Imam, ʿAli Zain al-ʿAbidin, was the only male to survive the Battle of Karbala; he was ill with fever and remained in the women's quarters.

24 "Baqir," "Luṭ gaye ḥaram, mar gaye ḥusain," 210.

25 Shariʿati quoted in Uberoi, *Religion*, 133.
26 Ibid.
27 Soufi, "Image," 12.
28 Ramanujan, "On Women Saints," 320.
29 This argument has been made with regard to the status of widows in Indian society, and Ramanujan corroborates the discomfort that the female renouncing saint creates in the Hindu context. For a provocative analysis of Hindu women's sexuality and the anxieties it engenders, see Gupta, *Sexuality*.
30 Abu ʿAli al-Fadl ibn al-Hasan ibn al-Fadl al-Tabarsi, *Beacons*, 237.
31 Kitchen, *Saints' Lives*, 105.
32 Ibid., 103.
33 Ibid., 104.
34 Kashefi, *Rowẓat al-shohadā*, 366.
35 Lalljee, *Janab-e Zainab*, 3. The *Lauḥ-e Maḥfūż* is the Preserved Tablet, which is placed with God in the heavens and is the source of the Qurʾan.
36 Ibn ʿAbd al-Wahhab, *ʿUyūn al-muʿjizāt*, 46, quoted in Veccia-Vaglieri, "Fatima," 2:847.
37 Ibn Shahrashub, *Manāqib Āl Abī Ṭālib*, 106, quoted in ibid.
38 Eliade, *Myth*, 6–11. Although Eliade's analysis focuses on celestial archetypes of cities and other places, his framework can be extended to include celestial-terrestrial models of human sanctity.
39 Nasr, "Shiʿism and Sufism," 104.

CHAPTER 3

1 Mohammed Mazher ʿAli Khan, "New ʿAshur Khanas," 64–66.
2 Moosvi and Fatima, *Ḥaidarābād kī ʿazādārī meiṅ khavātīn kā ḥiṣṣah*, 127.
3 Ibid., 128.
4 Agha, *majlis*.
5 Ibid.
6 Ibid.
7 Gupta, *Sexuality*, 302–3.
8 Sayyidah Maryam Naqvi, *majlis*.
9 Najmabadi, *Women with Mustaches*, 31.
10 Ibid., 30–31.
11 Warhol, *Gendered Interventions*, 32.
12 Lukács, *Theory*, 66.
13 Frye, *Secular Scripture*, 65–93.
14 Rao, "When Does Sita Cease to Be Sita?," 222.
15 Ibid.
16 In the sixteenth-century North Indian *Rāmāyaṇa* of Tulsidas, a variation on Sita's second trial by fire occurs in the *Lavakuśakāṇḍa* (The Chapter of Lava and

Kuśa). In Tulsidas's narrative, Sita, pregnant with her twin sons, Lava and Kusa, is banished to the forest. Rama commands his ever-loyal brother, Laksmana, to abandon the pregnant queen in the forest in the care of Valmiki, a hermit and the narrator of the epic.

17 Rao, "When Does Sita Cease to Be Sita?," 226.

18 For a description of the use of the word "transvestic" in Urdu *rekhtī* poetry, see Naim, "Transvestic Words?," 42–66.

19 Ibid., 45.

20 Shields, *Speaking*, 118.

21 Moosvi and Fatima, *Ḥaidarābād kī ʿazādārī meiṅ khavātīn kā ḥiṣṣah*, 49.

22 Najmabadi, *Women with Mustaches*, 30.

23 For a detailed analysis of the relationship of cosmopolitan and vernacular in the composition of Shiʿi religious life, see chapter 5.

24 Kashefi, *Rowẓat al-shohadā*, 366.

25 Clarke, "Some Examples," 16.

26 Mohtasham's *marśiya* is most popularly known as the *Dawāzdah-band* (Twelve Stanzas), although in my master's thesis, "'Verses Dripping Blood': A Study of the Religious Elements of Muhtasham Kashani's *Karbala-nāmeh*," I ascribe to the poem a title that is indicative of its function rather than its form. In Persian, the word *nāmeh* refers to a written chronicle or account of something. The name *Dawāzdah-band* refers to the poem's stanzaic structure and is a title bestowed by literary historians, whereas the alternate title, *Karbala-nāmeh*, indicates the poem's subject.

27 In the Persian language, the word *mātam* means lamentation and mourning. With the advent of Shiʿism in South Asia, the meaning of the word *mātam* became intensified to refer to the ritual practice of self-flagellation with one's hands, knives, or flails.

28 Schechner, *Performance Theory*, 170.

29 Rinehart, *One Lifetime*, 12.

30 Delehaye, *Legends*, 3.

31 Rinehart, *One Lifetime*, 8, 11–12.

32 The Arabic-language exclamation *Hażā Husain* punctuates Zainab's speech to her grandfather, which reminds *majlis* participants of her blood relationship to the Prophet Muhammad and her origins in Mecca and Medina, the Arab cities in which Islam was born.

33 This couplet begins with the phrase *īn māhī-ye fatādeh*, a play on the word *māhī*, which means both "fish" and "moon." The first line plays on the image of a fish that has fallen into the murky waters of a sea of blood, where it flops about with wounds more numerous than the stars in the heavens, a direct comparison to the countless wounds on the Imam's body.

34 Kashani, *Dīwān-e maulānā moḥtasham kāshānī*, 283–84.

35 Saiyid Athar Abbas Rizvi, *Socio-Intellectual History*, 1:248.

36 In the medieval Deccan, *āfāqī* referred to the foreigners who flocked to the courts of the ʿAdil Shahi, Bahmani, and later Qutb Shahi dynasties. The word most generally refers to the Iranians who assumed many positions of power and influence in the Deccani kingdoms.

37 Saiyid Athar Abbas Rizvi, *Socio-Intellectual History*, 1:311–12.

38 Naqvi, *Qutb Shahi Ashur Khanas*, 62.

39 Hyder, "Recasting Karbala."

40 Munis, "Riyaẕ al-ṭāhirīn."

41 Mir ʿAlam, "Dah majlis."

42 Moosvi, *Dakhan meiṅ marśiya aur ʿazādāri*, 87.

43 *Ibn-e Shabbar* refers to Qasem, the son of Imam Hasan, whose epithet (*laqab*) was Shabbar.

44 "This bloody shroud" refers to the red color of a traditional wedding *sāṛī*. In this case, the wedding is again being attached to its binary opposite, a funeral and death. We have already seen the wedding procession (*barāt*) transformed into its binary opposite of funeral procession (*julūs*) in Agha's *khuṭbah*.

45 Bano is the diminutive of Shahrbano, who was Imam Husain's first wife and the daughter of the last Sasanian shah, Yazdigird III (r. 632–51). Shahrbano was the mother of the fourth Imam, Zain al-ʿAbidin.

46 Khan, interview.

47 For a detailed discussion of Fatimah Kubra's gendering as a widow, see chapter 4.

CHAPTER 4

1 Moosvi and Fatima, *Ḥaidarābād kī ʿazādārī meiṅ khavātīn kā ḥiṣṣah*, 128.

2 Ibid.

3 Chelkowski, "Naḵl."

4 For an analysis of the form and symbolic meaning of the *ʿalam*, see Naqvi, *Qutb Shahi ʿAshurkhanas*, 10–12, 20–21. See also Diane D'Souza, "In the Presence."

5 For a complete description of the *manjha* and *mehndī* ceremonies in nineteenth-century South India, see Shurreef, *Qanoon-e Islam*, 64–69.

6 Sallie, *Kitab un-Nikah*, 124–25.

7 S. K. Husain, *Social Institutions*, 66.

8 Ibid., 66–67.

9 Kulsum, interview.

10 Foucault, "Technologies of the Self," 35. For a more detailed analysis and application of Foucault's technologies of the self, see Mahmood's study of the women's mosque movement in Cairo, *Politics*, 118–52.

11 Mahmood, *Politics*, 120.

12 Butler, *Gender Trouble*, 10, 24–25, 33.

13 Stewart and Ernst, "Syncretism," 586–88.

14 From a narratological perspective, as chapter 3 illustrates, the epic structure of the Karbala narratives is predicated on the female voice, and the male figures occupy static roles.
15 Salehah ʿAbid Husain, *Khavātīn-e karbalā*, 85.
16 Mir ʿAlam, "Dah majlis."
17 Butler, *Gender Trouble*, 39.
18 Ibid., 39.
19 Mahmood, *Politics*, 120.
20 Ibid., 131.
21 Sauda, *Intikhāb-e marāsī*, 7.
22 This is an indirect reference to the scene in *Rowẓat al-shohadā* in which Qasem gives Fatimah Kubra a piece from the sleeve of his robe and promises her that they will find each other on the Day of Resurrection with this piece of fabric.
23 Sauda, *Intikhāb-e marāsī*, 8.
24 Quoted in Rozehnal, *Islamic Sufism Unbound*, 158.
25 *Naushāh* literally means "new king" (of his home, wife, and future children), an allusion to the status of the groom on his wedding day.
26 Sauda, *Intikhāb-e marāsī*, 7.
27 al-Zaman, *Urdū marsiya kā irtiqā*, 259–60.
28 Either on the fourth day after the *sāchaq* or on the day after signing the marriage contract, the bride and groom visit her family. The family celebrates with a special meal, and then the bride and groom play with one another, beating each other with sticks covered with flowers. The hope is that whatever disagreements arise in the future will be solved softly and without rancor or violence.
29 al-Zaman, *Urdū marsiya kā irtiqā*, 259–60.
30 Naim, "How Bibi Ashraf Learned," 207–8.
31 Lawrence, *Shattering*, 118; Noever, "Women's Choices."
32 Quoted in Usmani, *Islamic Law*, 194–95.
33 "Rasheed," "Bazm-e shādī kī hai hotā hai ye kaisā mātam," 69.
34 Khan, 19 May 2005.
35 Connerton, *How Societies Remember*, 43.
36 Gross, *Lost Time*, 77.

CHAPTER 5

1 Momen, *Introduction*, 41.
2 "Mashhad, Iran."
3 The Paykan is the national car of Iran, noted for its boxy shape and 1970s style. Tehran has tens of thousands of Paykan taxis that pick up and drop off passengers along fixed routes (*savārī*) while belching noxious exhaust.
4 ʿAbbasi, interview.

5 Motahhari, *Majmūʿah-ye āsār*, 94–95.
6 ʿAbbasi, interview.
7 Motahhari, *Majmūʿah-ye āsār*, 94.
8 ʿAbbasi, interview.
9 Mottahedeh, *Mantle*, 71; for the full account of this class, see pp. 70–76.
10 Ibid., 74.
11 Fischer, *Iran*, 1.
12 Ibid., 2.
13 al-Shaybi, *Tashiyyuʿ wa taṣawwuf*, 324.
14 The Naqshbandi Sufi order was established by Bahaʾuddin Naqshbandi (d. 1390) and is characterized by its sobriety of practice and discipline. The Naqshbandiyya are found throughout Central Asia and the Indian Subcontinent.
15 al-Shaybi, *Tashiyyuʿ wa taṣawwuf*, 324.
16 Ibid., 324.
17 Subtelny, "Husayn Vaʿiz-i Kashifi," 466.
18 Ibid.
19 Ibid.
20 Ernst, *Shambhala Guide*, 138.
21 Pourjavady, interview.
22 Chishti, *Dīwān-e khwājah-e khwājagān gharīb nawāz muʿinuddīn ajmerī chishtī*, 196, cited in Hyder, *Reliving Karbala*, 105.
23 According to local traditions, after ʿAli was assassinated in 661 C.E., his supporters, fearing desecration of the Imam's body, disinterred it and placed it upon the back of a camel. This camel was set free to wander the earth until she collapsed. The camel wandered hundreds of miles, eventually collapsing and dying in the Balkh region of Afghanistan in what is now called Mazar-e Sharif. Imam ʿAli's body was removed from the camel and buried, according to tradition, forgotten for centuries. In 1136, a Seljuk sultan, Sanjar, commissioned the construction of a tomb, which was destroyed during the Mongol invasions in the thirteenth century. A Timurid shah, Husain Bayqara, had a dream in which he was informed of the location of Imam ʿAli's true grave, and he was instructed to rebuild the tomb. For an in-depth history of ʿAli's tomb at Mazar-e Sharif, see McChesney, *Waqf*.
24 Subtelny, "Husayn Vaʿiz-i Kashifi," 463.
25 Ibid., 465.
26 Motahhari, *Majmūʿah-ye āsār*, 71–72.
27 Ibid., 72.
28 Metcalf, *Islamic Revival*; Thanawi, *Bihishti Zewar*.
29 In 1925, Saʿudi authorities razed the graves of Fatimah al-Zahra, Imam Hasan, Imam Zain al-ʿAbidin, Imam Muhammad al-Baqir, and Imam Jaʿfar as-Sadiq at the Jannat al-Baqiʿ cemetery in Medina. Shiʿa who have gone on the *ʿumrah*

(supplementary) pilgrimage to Medina commonly recount being beaten by the religious police (*al-mutawīn*) with sticks if they exhibit any form of emotion when visiting the Prophet Muhammad's grave, which evaded demolition. Shiʿa in particular feel uncomfortable performing the *ḥajj* and *ʿumrah*. To view photographs of the Jannat al-Baqiʿ cemetery before and after the demolition of the graves of the Imams and *ahl-e bait*, see "Baqi Collection."

30 Motahhari, *Majmūʿah-ye āśār*, 75–76, 94.

31 Ibid., 95.

32 This issue is further amplified by the current geopolitical situation in Iraq. National Public Radio aired a story on 12 November 2006 about the reorientation of Shiʿi devotional poetry to reflect the current religiopolitical strife in post-Saddam Iraq. In "Revived Lament Tradition," Jaime Tarabay reported that "in Iraq, Shiite Muslims have publicly revived an ancient tradition long banned by the former regime of Saddam Hussein. Laments about the most beloved Shiite saint are now heard in mosques, on car stereos, and on the Internet. But the mournful chants that hark back to past grief are now making way for new pain and show how many Shiites still feel they face persecution at the hands of Iraq's Sunnis." One *nauḥa* poem compares the dangers of making pilgrimage to the holy cities of Najaf and Karbala to those encountered by Imam Husain and his entourage fourteen hundred years ago. This *nauḥa* mourns the death of Shiʿi pilgrims who are stopped en route to Najaf and Karbala and executed by Sunni militias.

33 According to Deeb, the Shiʿi community in the Beirut suburb of al-Dahiyya has stopped observing the martyrdom of Qasem because it has been deemed "inauthentic" (*Enchanted Modern*, 156–58).

34 "Situation."

35 White, "Historical Text," 397.

36 Tweed, "On Moving Across," 262.

37 Simpson and Kresse, "Introduction," 2–3.

38 Stewart, "In Search," 269.

39 Ibid., 276.

40 Simpson and Kresse, "Introduction," 20.

41 Kashefi, *Rowẓat al-shohadā*, 328.

42 "Bint-e shāh kehtī thī, hā'e qāsem bane," 45.

43 Gupta, *Sexuality*, 108–22.

44 Lakhnavi, *ʿAbā'ir al-anwār*. According to the author's son, who now lives in Karachi, Pakistan, two of the three volumes are extant, while the third has been lost.

45 Shajaʿat, interview; Seema, interview.

46 cooke and Lawrence, introduction, 1.

47 Rudaulvi, interview. Fiza was an Abyssinian princess who converted to Islam and was Fatimah al-Zahra's maidservant. According to tradition, after

Fatimah's death, Fiza remained loyal to the *ahl-e bait* and was present at the Battle of Karbala.

48 Asghar, interview.

49 Agha, interview.

50 Riaz, interview.

Bibliography

INTERVIEWS

ʿAbbasi, Ghulam. Mashhad, Iran, 23 October 2004.
ʿAbedi, Hasan. Hyderabad, India, 5 April 2005.
Agha, Maulana Reza. Hyderabad, India, 17 February, 31 May 2005.
ʿAli, Mir Shajaʿat. Hyderabad, India, 2005–6.
Asghar, Sabiha. Hyderabad, India, 8 February, 10, 24 May 2005.
Fatima, Riaz. Hyderabad, India, 16 August 2003; 2005.
Khan, M. M. Taqui. Hyderabad, India, 15 April, 31 May 2005.
Kulsum. Hyderabad, India, 17 February 2005.
Naqvi, Mrs. Hyderabad, India, 31 July 2005.
Naqvi, Sayyidah Maryam. Hyderabad, India, 7 February 2006.
Naqvi, Sadiq. Hyderabad, India, 16 August 2003, 30 March 2005.
Pourjavady, Nasrollah. Tehran, Iran, 19 October 2004.
Riaz, Dr. Hyderabad, India, 12 December 2005.
Rizvi, Salim. Hyderabad, India, 5 April 2005.
Rudaulvi, Sharib. Lucknow, India, August 2002.
Seema. Hyderabad, 31 July 2005.
Shajaʿat, Mir Ali. Hyderabad, 31 July 2005.
Shireen, Mashhad. Iran, 23 October 2004.
Sultana, Zakia. Hyderabad, India, 16 August 2003; 2005.

OTHER SOURCES

Abbas, Shameem Burney. "Sakineh, the Narrator of Karbala: An Ethnographic Description of a Women's *Majles* Ritual in Pakistan." In *The Women of Karbala: Ritual Performance and Symbolic Discourses in Modern Shiʿi Islam*, edited by Kamran Scot Aghaie, 141–60. Austin: University of Texas Press, 2005.

———. *The Female Voice in Sufi Ritual: Devotional Practices of Pakistan and India*. Austin: University of Texas Press, 2002.

Abu-Lughod, Lila. "Do Muslim Women Really Need Saving?: Anthropological Reflections on Cultural Relativism and Its Others." *American Anthropologist* 104:3 (September 2002): 783–90.

Aghaie, Kamran Scot. *The Martyrs of Karbala: Shiʿi Symbols and Rituals in Modern Iran*. Seattle: University of Washington Press, 2004.

———, ed. *The Women of Karbala: Ritual Performance and Symbolic Discourses in Modern Shiʿi Islam*. Austin: University of Texas Press, 2005.

Akhtar, Syed Waheed. *The Early Imamiyyah Shiʿite Thinkers*. New Delhi: Ashish, 1988.

Alam, Anwar. "'Scholarly Islam' and 'Everyday Islam': Reflections on the Debate over Integration of the Muslim Minority in India and Western Europe." *Journal of Muslim Minority Affairs* 27:2 (August 2007): 241–60.

ʿAli, Mrs. Meer Hassan. *Observations on the Mussulmauns of India*. 1832; Karachi: Oxford University Press, 1973.

ʿAli, Mir Ahmad, ed. *Karbalā-wāle*. Hyderabad: Salman Book Depot, 1425/2004.

Amanat, Abbas. "*Meadow of the Martyrs*: Kashifi's Persianization of the Shiʿi Martyrdom Narrative in Late Timurid Herat." In *Culture and Memory in Medieval Islam: Essays in Honour of Wilferd Madelung*, edited by Farhad Daftary and Josef W. Meri, 250–75. London: I. B. Tauris, 2003.

Amir-Moezzi, Mohammad ʿAli. *The Divine Guide in Early Shiʿism: The Sources of Esotericism in Islam*. Translated by David Streight. Albany: State University of New York Press, 1994.

Andringa, Els. "The Effects of 'Narrative Distance' on Readers' Emotional Involvement and Response." *Poetics* 23:6 (May 1996): 432–52.

Anis, Mir Babar ʿAli. *The Battle of Karbala: A Marsiya of Anis*. Translated by David Matthews. New Delhi: Rupa, 1994.

Arib, Asad. *Urdū marṡiye kī sarguzasht: Āghāz se zamāna-ye ḥāl tak*. Delhi: ʿAkif, 1990.

Arjomand, Said Amir. *The Shadow of God and the Hidden Imam: Religion, Political Order, and Societal Change in Shiʿite Iran from the Beginning to 1890*. Chicago: University of Chicago Press, 1984.

Asad, Majda. *Indian Muslim Festivals and Customs*. Translated by M. R. Sharma. New Delhi: Ministry of Information and Broadcasting, Government of India, 1988.

Austin, Ralph. Introduction to *The Bezels of Wisdom*, by Ibn al-ʿArabi, 1–44. Mahwah, N.J.: Paulist, 1980.

Ayoub, Mahmoud. *Redemptive Suffering in Islam: A Study of the Devotional Aspects of ʿAshuraʾ in Twelver Shiʿism*. The Hague: Mouton, 1978.

Bahadur, Mir ʿAlam. "Dah majlis" [Deccani-Urdu manuscript]. 1196/1781. Oriental Manuscripts Library and Research Institute, Hyderabad. Ta. 437.

Baig, Safdar ʿAli. "Impact on Sufis." In *Red Sand*, edited by Mehdi Nazmi, 226–42. New Delhi: Abu Talib, 1984.

Baqari, Mir Hadi Ali. "The Old ʿAshur Khanas of Hyderabad." In *Hyderabad ki Azadari*, edited by Sayyed Taqi Hasan Wafa, 50–61. Translated by Sayyed Muhammad Taher Bilgrami. Hyderabad: Idara-e Jaʿfaria, 2000.

"The Baqi Collection." ⟨http://www.al-islam.org/gallery/photos/image2nd.htm⟩. Accessed 8 January 2007.

"Baqir." Luṭ gaye ḥaram, mar gaye ḥusain." In *Mātam-e ḥusain*, 210. Hyderabad: Bazm-e Jan Nishan-e Shabbih-ye Paighambar, 1413/1993.

Bard, Amy C. "Desolate Victory: Shiʿi Women and the *Marsiyah* Texts of Lucknow." Ph.D. diss., Columbia University, 2002.

———. "Value and Vitality in a Literary Tradition: Female Poets and the Urdu *Marsiya*." *Annual of Urdu Studies* 15 (2000): 323–35.

"Bint-e shāh kehtī thī, hā'e qāsem bane." In *Mātam-e ḥusain*, 45. Hyderabad: Bazm-e Jan Nishan-e Shabbih-ye Paighambar, 1413/1993.
Bourdieu, Pierre. *Outline of a Theory of Practice*. Translated by Richard Nice. Palo Alto, Calif.: Stanford University Press, 1977.
Bowen, John R. "What Is 'Universal' and 'Local' in Islam?" *Ethos* 26:2 (June 1998): 258–61.
Bredi, Franco Coloi, and Bianca Maria Scarcia. "Shiʿism in the Deccan: Hypothesis for Research." *Annali di Ca'Fosscari Rivista della Facolta e Litterature Straniere dell' Universita di Venezia* 26 (1987): 279–88.
Brown, Peter. *The Cult of the Saints: Its Rise and Function in Latin Christianity*. Chicago: University of Chicago Press, 1981.
Browne, Edward G. *A Literary History of Persia*. 4 vols. Cambridge: Cambridge University Press, 1928.
Bruijn, J. T. P. de. "Safawids (Literature)." In *Encyclopaedia of Islam*, 8:774–77. Leiden: Brill, 1995.
———. "Muhtasham Kashani." In *Encyclopaedia of Islam*, 7:477–78. Leiden: Brill, 1993.
Butler, Judith. *Gender Trouble: Feminism and the Subversion of Identity*. New York: Routledge, 1990.
Calmard, Jean. "Ḥejla." In *Encyclopaedia Iranica Online*, 15 December 2003. ⟨http://www.iranica.com/articles/hejla⟩. Accessed 20 June 2010.
———. "Popular Literature under the Safavids." In *Society and Culture in the Early Modern Middle East: Studies in Iran in the Safavid Period*, edited by Andrew J. Newman, 315–40. Leiden: Brill, 2003.
Caton, Steven C. *"Peaks of Yemen I Summon": Poetry as Cultural Practice in a North Yemeni Tribe*. Berkeley: University of California Press, 1990.
Chelkowski, Peter J. "Naḵl." In *Encyclopaedia Iranica Online*, 8 April 2008. ⟨http://www.iranica.com/articles/nakl-object-in-the-mourning-rituals⟩. Accessed 20 June 2010.
———, ed. *Taʿziyeh: Ritual and Drama in Iran*. New York: New York University Press, 1979.
Chishti, Khwajah Muʿinuddin. *Dīwān-e khwājah-e khwājagān gharīb nawāz muʿinuddīn ajmerī chishtī*. Translated by ʿAbdul Qadir Chishti. Dhanbad: ʿAbdul Qadir Chishti, 1984.
Chodkiewicz, Michel. *Seal of the Saints: Prophethood and Sainthood in the Doctrine of Ibn ʿArabi*. Cambridge: Islamic Texts Society, 1993.
Chughtai, ʿIsmat. *Ek qaṭrah-ye khūn*. Delhi: Kitab-e Dunya, 2000.
Clarke, Lynda. "Some Examples of Elegy on the Imam Husayn." *Al-Serat* 12 (Spring and Autumn 1986): 13–28.
Clifford, James. *The Predicament of Culture: Twentieth-Century Ethnography, Literature, and Art*. Cambridge: Harvard University Press, 1988.
Cole, Juan. "Popular Shiʿism." In *India's Islamic Traditions, 711–1750*, edited by Richard M. Eaton, 311–39. New Delhi: Oxford University Press, 2003.

———. "Iranian Culture and South Asia, 1500–1900." In *Iran and the Surrounding World: Interactions in Culture and Cultural Politics*, edited by Nikki R. Keddie, 15–35. Seattle: University of Washington Press, 2002.

———. "Women and the Making of Shiʿism." In *Sacred Space and Holy War: The Politics, Culture and History of Shiʿite Islam*, 138–60. London: I. B. Tauris, 2002.

———. *Roots of North Indian Shiʿism in Iran and Iraq: Religion and State in Awadh, 1722–1859*. New Delhi: Oxford University Press, 1989.

Connerton, Paul. *How Societies Remember*. Cambridge: Cambridge University Press, 1989.

cooke, miriam, and Bruce B. Lawrence. Introduction to *Muslim Networks: From Hajj to Hip Hop*, edited by miriam cooke and Bruce B. Lawrence, 1–30. Chapel Hill: University of North Carolina Press, 2005.

Corbin, Henry. *The Man of Light in Iranian Sufism*. Translated by Nancy Pearson. 1978; New Lebanon, N.Y.: Omega, 1994.

———. "The Meaning of the Imam for Shiʿi Spirituality." In *Shiʿism: Doctrines, Thought, and Spirituality*, edited by Seyyed Hossein Nasr, Hamid Dabashi, and Seyyed Vali Reza Nasr, 167–87. Albany: State University of New York Press, 1988.

———. *Spiritual Body and Celestial Earth: From Mazdean Iran to Shiʿite Iran*. Translated by Nancy Pearson. Princeton: Princeton University Press, 1977.

Cornell, Vincent. *Realm of the Saint: Power and Authority in Moroccan Sufism*. Austin: University of Texas Press, 1998.

Dabashi, Hamid. *Authority in Islam: From the Rise of Muhammad to the Establishment of the Umayyads*. New Brunswick, N.J.: Transaction, 1989.

Dakake, Maria Massi. *The Charismatic Community: Shiʿite Identity in Early Islam*. Albany: State University of New York Press, 2007.

Dar, S. N. *Costumes of India and Pakistan: A Historical and Cultural Study*. Bombay: Taraporevala, 1969.

Das, Neeta. *The Architecture of the Imambaras*. Lucknow: Lucknow Mahotsav Patrika Samiti, 1991.

Davis, Richard H. *Lives of Indian Images*. Princeton: Princeton University Press, 1997.

Deeb, Lara. *An Enchanted Modern: Gender and Public Piety in Shiʿi Lebanon*. Princeton: Princeton University Press, 2006.

———. "Living Ashura in Lebanon: Mourning Transformed to Sacrifice." *Comparative Studies of South Asia, Africa, and the Middle East* 25:1 (2005): 122–37.

Delehaye, Hippolyte. *The Legends of the Saints*. Translated by Donald Atwater. New York: Fordham University Press, 1962.

Digby, Simon. *Sufis and Soldiers in Aurangzeb's Deccan*. New Delhi: Oxford University Press, 2001.

al-Din, Sayyid Muhammad Naʿim. *Sawāniḥ-ye karbalā*. Delhi: Rizvi Kitab Ghar, n.d.

D'Souza, Andreas. "'Zaynab I Am Coming!': The Transformative Power of Nawhah." *Bulletin of the Henry Martyn Institute of Islamic Studies* 16:3–4 (July–December 1997): 83–94.

———. "Love of the Prophet's Family: The Role of Marâthin in the Devotional Life of Hyderabadi Shiʿahs." *Bulletin of the Henry Martyn Institute of Islamic Studies* 12:3–4 (July–December 1993): 31–47.
———. "Jesus in Ibn ʿArabi's "*Fuṣūṣ al-Ḥikām*." *Islamochristiana* 8 (1982): 185–200.
D'Souza, Diane. "Devotional Practices among Shiʿa Women in South India." In *Lived Islam in South Asia: Adaptation, Accommodation and Conflict*, edited by Imtiaz Ahmad and Helmut Reifeld, 187–206. Delhi: Social Science Press, 2004.
———. "The Night of Mercy: Ritual and Gender in Indian Islam." *Journal of the Henry Martyn Institute* 23:1 (January–June 2004): 3–27.
———. "In the Presence of the Martyrs: The ʿ*Alam* in Popular Shiʿi Piety." *Muslim World* 88:1 (January 1998): 67–80.
Eaton, Richard M. *The New Cambridge History of India: The Social History of the Deccan*. Cambridge: Cambridge University Press, 2005.
———. *The Rise of Islam and the Bengal Frontier, 1204–1760*. Berkeley: University of California Press, 1993.
Eliade, Mircea. *The Myth of the Eternal Return; or, Cosmos and History*. Translated by Willard R. Trask. Princeton: Princeton University Press, 1954.
Elias, Jamal. "Female and Feminine in Islamic Mysticism." *Muslim World* 78:3–4 (October 1988): 209–24.
Elmore, Gerald T. *Islamic Sainthood in the Fullness of Time: Ibn al-ʿArabi's Book of the Fabulous Griffin*. Leiden: Brill, 1999.
Ende, Tonja van den. "In Search of the Body in the Cave: Luce Irigaray's Ethics of Embodiment." In *Belief, Bodies, and Being: Feminist Reflections on Embodiment*, edited by Deborah Orr, Linda López McAllister, Eileen Kahl, and Kathleen Earle, 141–50. Lanham, Md.: Rowman and Littlefield, 2006.
Ernst, Carl W. *Following Muhammad: Rethinking Islam in the Contemporary World*. Chapel Hill: University of North Carolina Press, 2003.
———. *The Shambhala Guide to Sufism*. Boston: Shambhala, 1997.
———. "From Hagiography to Martyrology: Conflicting Testimonies to a Sufi Martyr of the Delhi Sultanate." *History of Religions* 24:4 (May 1985): 308–27.
Fatima, Kulsum. "Hyderabadi Customs of Azadari during the First Ten Days of Muharram." In *Hyderabad ki Azadari*, edited by Sayyed Taqi Hasan Wafa, 105–7. Translated by Sayyed Muhammad Taher Bilgrami. Hyderabad: Idara-e Jaʿfaria, 2000.
Fatima, Riaz. "Ḥaidarābād meiṅ riṡā-ye shāʿirī." Ph.D. diss., Osmania University, 1995.
Fentress, James, and Chris Wickham. *Social Memory*. Oxford: Blackwell, 1992.
Fischer, Michael M. J. *Iran: From Religious Dispute to Revolution*. Cambridge: Harvard University Press, 1980.
Fischer, Michael M. J., and Mehdi Abedi. *Debating Muslims: Cultural Dialogues in Postmodernity and Tradition*. Madison: University of Wisconsin Press, 1990.
Flueckiger, Joyce Burkhalter. "Wandering from 'Hills to Valleys' with the Goddess:

Protection and Freedom in the *Matamma* Tradition of Andhra." In *Women's Lives, Women's Ritual in the Hindu Tradition*, edited by Tracy Pintchman, 35–55. New York: Oxford University Press, 2007.

———. *In Amma's Healing Room: Gender and Vernacular Islam in South India*. Bloomington: Indiana University Press, 2006.

Foucault, Michel. "Technologies of the Self." In *Technologies of the Self: A Seminar with Michel Foucault*, edited by Luther H. Martin, Huck Gutman, and Patrick H. Hutton, 16–49. Amherst: University of Massachusetts Press, 1988.

Frye, Northrop. *The Secular Scripture: A Study of the Structure of Romance*. Cambridge: Harvard University Press, 1976.

Garcin de Tassy, M. *Muslim Festivals in India and Other Essays*. Translated and edited by M. Waseem. New Delhi: Oxford University Press, 1995.

Gauhar, Samsam ʿAli. "Marsia Khani of Hyderabad." In *Hyderabad ki Azadari*, edited by Sayyed Taqi Hasan Wafa, 96–100. Translated by Sayyed Muhammad Taher Bilgrami. Hyderabad: Idara-e Jaʿfaria, 2000.

Geertz, Clifford. *Interpretation of Cultures*. New York: Basic Books, 1973.

Ghauri, Iftikhar. "Muslims in the Deccan in the Middle Ages: An Historical Survey." *Islamic Culture* 49:3 (July 1975): 151–64.

Gilmartin, David, and Bruce B. Lawrence, eds. *Beyond Turk and Hindu: Rethinking Religious Identities in Islamicate South Asia*. Gainesville: University of Florida Press, 2000.

Gonzalez, Michelle A. *Created in God's Image: An Introduction to Feminist Theological Anthropology*. Maryknoll, N.Y.: Orbis, 2007.

Green, Nile. "Shiism, Sufism and Sacred Space in the Deccan: Counter-Narratives of Saintly Identity in the Cult of Shah Nur." In *The Other Shiites: From the Mediterranean to Central Asia*, edited by Alessandro Monsutti, Silvia Naef, and Farian Sabahi, 195–218. Bern: Lang, 2007.

———. "Making a 'Muslim' Saint: Writing Customary Religion in an Indian Princely State." *Comparative Studies of South Asia, Africa, and the Middle East* 25:3 (November 2005): 617–33.

Gross, David. *Lost Time: On Remembering and Forgetting in Late Modern Culture*. Amherst: University of Massachusetts Press, 2000.

Gupta, Charu. *Sexuality, Obscenity, Community: Women, Muslims, and the Hindu Public in Colonial India*. New Delhi: Permanent Black, 2001.

al-Hadid, Ibn Abi. *Sharḥ nahj al-balāgha (Commentary on the Peaks of Eloquence)*. Edited by Muhammad Abu al-Fadl Ibrahim. Vol. 18. Cairo: ʿIsa al-Babi al-Halabi, 1959–64.

Haidar, Sayyid ʿAli. *Majāles-e khātūn*. Hyderabad: Matbaʿ Islah, 1364/1944.

Halsema, Annemie. "Reconsidering the Notion of the Body in Anti-Essentialism, with the Help of Luce Irigaray and Judith Butler." In *Belief, Bodies, and Being: Feminist Reflections on Embodiment*, edited by Deborah Orr, Linda López McAllister, Eileen Kahl, and Kathleen Earle, 152–61. Lanham, Md.: Rowman and Littlefield, 2006.

Hampsen, Daphne. "The Sacred, the Feminine, and French Feminist Theory." In *The Sacred and the Feminine: Imagination and Sexual Difference*, edited by Griselda Pollock and Victoria Turvey Sauron, 61–74. London: I. B. Tauris, 2007.
Hanaway, William L. "*Marthiya* (in Persian Literature)." In *Encyclopaedia of Islam*, 6:608–9. Leiden: Brill, 1991.
Hasan, Maha al-Din. *Dihlī kī begumātī zubān*. New Delhi: Na'i Awaz, 1982.
Hasan, Maulana Iftikhar. *Khāk-e karbalā*. Delhi: Adabi Duniya, 2005.
Hashmi, Nasir al-Din. *Dakhan meiṅ urdū*. 2nd ed. New Delhi: National Council Bureau for the Promotion of Urdu, 2002.
Hassett, Philip. "Open *Sama*ʿ: Public and Popular Qawwali at Yusufayn Dargah." *Bulletin of the Henry Martyn Institute of Islamic Studies* 14:3–4 (July–December 1995): 29–63.
Hawley, John Stratton. Introduction to *Saints and Virtues*, edited by John Stratton Hawley, xi–xxiv. Berkeley: University of California Press, 1987.
Hegland, Mary Elaine. "The Power Paradox in Muslim Women's *Majales*: North-West Pakistani Mourning Rituals as Sites of Contestation over Religious Politics, Ethnicity, and Gender." *Signs: Journal of Women and Culture and Society* 23:2 (Winter 1998): 391–428.
Hodgson, Marshall G. S. *The Classical Age of Islam*. Vol. 1 of *The Venture of Islam*. Chicago: University of Chicago Press, 1974.
Hollister, John Norman. *The Shiʿa of India*. 1953; New Delhi: Oriental Books Reprint Corporation, 1979.
Hollywood, Amy E. "Inside Out: Beatrice of Nazareth and Her Hagiographer." In *Gendered Voices: Medieval Saints and Their Interpreters*, edited by Catherine M. Mooney, 78–98. Philadelphia: University of Pennsylvania Press, 1999.
Howarth, Toby M. *The Twelver Shīʿa as a Muslim Minority in India: Pulpit of Tears*. London: Routledge, 2005.
———. "Pulpit of Tears: Shīʿī Muslim Preaching in India." Ph.D. diss., Free University, 2001.
Husain, S. K. *Social Institutions of Shia Muslims: An Anthropological Analysis*. New Delhi: Classical Publishing, 1998.
Husain, Salehah ʿAbid. *Khavātīn-e Karbalā: Kalām-e Anīs ke ā'ine meiṅ*. New Delhi: Maktabah-ye Jamiʿah, 1973.
Husain, Sayyid Morteza. *Āwāz-e karbalā*. Hyderabad: Anjuman-e Ahl-e Bait, 1415/1994.
Husain, Sheikh Abrar. *Marriage Customs among Muslims in India: A Sociological Study of the Shia Marriage Customs*. New Delhi: Sterling, 1976.
Husam, Hakim Shaykh Abu al-Qasem, ed. *Hilāl-e muḥarram*. Hyderabad: Kutbkhaneh-ye Haidari, 1995.
Hussaini, Syed Shah Khusro. *Sayyid Muhammad al-Husayni-i Gisudiraz (721/1321–825/1422): On Sufism*. Delhi: Idarah-i Adabiyat-i Delhi, 1983.
Hyder, Syed Akbar. *Reliving Karbala: Martyrdom in South Asian Memory*. New York: Oxford University Press, 2006.

———. "To Die and Yet Live: Karbala and Martyrdom in Urdu Discursive Landscapes." Ph.D. diss., Harvard University, 2000.

———. "Recasting Karbala in the Genre of Urdu *Marsiya*." *SAGAR: South Asia Graduate Research Journal* 2:1 (Spring 1995), ⟨http://www.asnic.utexas.edu/asnic/pages/spring.1995/akbar.hyder.art.html⟩. Accessed 10 June 2010.

Ibbatson, Sir Denzil. *Rites and Rituals of Hindus and Muslims*. Edited by K. V. Singh. New Delhi: Vista International, 2005.

Ibn ʿAbd al-Wahhab, Husain. *ʿUyūn al-Muʿjizāt*. Najaf: n.p., 1369/1950.

Ibn al-ʿArabi, Muhyi al-Din. *The Bezels of Wisdom* [*Fuṣūṣ al-Ḥikām*]. Translated by R. W. J. Austin. Mahwah, N.J.: Paulist, 1980.

Ibn Ishaq, Muhammad. *The Life of the Prophet Muhammad* (*Sīrat rasūl allāh*). Translated by Alfred Guillaume. London: Oxford University Press, 1955.

Ibn Shahrashub, Muhammad ibn ʿAli. *Manāqib Āl Abī Ṭālib*. Najaf: n.p., 1956.

Jaffri, Syed Husain ʿAli. "Muharram Ceremonies in India." In *Taʿziyeh: Ritual and Drama in Iran*, edited by Peter J. Chelkowski, 222–27. New York: New York University Press, 1979.

Jafri, S. Husain M. *Origins and Early Development of Shiʿa Islam*. Beirut: Librairie du Liban; London: Longman, 1979.

Jahan, Iqbal. "Dakhanī kalchur meiṅ adab ke ā'ine meiṅ." Ph.D. diss., Osmania University, 1994.

Jahanbegloo, Ramin, ed. *Iran: Between Tradition and Modernity*. Lanham, Md.: Lexington, 2004.

Jaunpuri, Amir ʿAli. *Taẕkirah-ye marṡiya nigārān-e urdū*. 2 vols. Lucknow: Sarfaraz, 1986.

Jilani, Sayyid Muhammad Madani Ashrafi. *Maḥabbat-e ahl-e bait-e rasūl*. Hyderabad: Maktabah Anwar al-Mustafa, 2004.

Kabir. *The Bījak of Kabir*. Translated by Linda Hess and Shukdev Singh. Delhi: Motilal Banarsidass, 1983.

Kamil, Hashmi. "Karbala and the People of India." In *Red Sand*, edited by Mehdi Nazmi, 157–65. New Delhi: Abu Talib, 1984.

Kashani, Mohtasham. *Dīwān-e maulānā moḥtasham kāshānī*. Edited by Maher ʿAli Gorgani. N.p.: Kitab Forushi-ye Mahmudi, 1344 SH./1965.

Kashefi, Husain Vaʿez. *Rowẓat al-shohadā*. Edited by Abu al-Hasan Shaʿrani. Tehran: Kitab Forushi-ye Islamiyya, 1979.

———. *The Royal Book of Spiritual Chivalry*. Translated by Jay R. Cook. Chicago: University of Chicago Press, 2000.

Khalidi, Omar. *A Guide to Architecture in Hyderabad, Deccan, India*. Cambridge: Agha Khan Program for Islamic Architecture and MIT Libraries, 2008.

———. "The Shīʿahs of the Deccan: An Introduction." *Hamdard Islamicus* 15:4 (Winter 1992): 31–52.

———. "Shiʿite Religious Literature in the Deccan." *Rivista degli Studi Orientali* 64:1–2 (1991): 17–35.

Khan, Khafi. *Muntakhāb al-lubāb*. Translated by Anees Jahan Syed. Bombay: Somaiya, 1977.
Khan, M. M. Taqui. *Khutbat-un-Nissa: The Contribution of the Ladies of Ahlbait to Islam*. Hyderabad: Moula Ali, 2003.
Khan, Masʿud Husain. *Qadīm urdū*. Part 2. Hyderabad: Osmania University, 1967.
Khan, Mirza Zulfikar ʿAli. *Ashk wa mātam*. Hyderabad: Anjuman-e Parvaneh-ye Qasem, 2004.
Khan, Muhammad Mazher ʿAli. "The New ʿAshur Khanas of Hyderabad." In *Hyderabad ki Azadari*, edited by Sayyed Taqi Hasan Wafa, 62–75. Translated by Sayyed Muhammad Taher Bilgrami. Hyderabad: Idara-e Jaʿfaria, 2000.
Khani, Sayyed Baqer Rizvi Amanat. "Azadari of Hyderabad—As I Have Seen It." In *Hyderabad ki Azadari*, edited by Sayyed Taqi Hasan Wafa, 78–89. Translated by Sayyed Muhammad Taher Bilgrami. Hyderabad: Idara-e Jaʿfaria, 2000.
Khayyami, Saghar. "Islam and Husainiat." In *Red Sand*, edited by Mehdi Nazmi, 251–57. New Delhi: Abu Talib, 1984.
Kitchen, John. *Saints' Lives and the Rhetoric of Gender: Male and Female in Merovingian Hagiography*. New York: Oxford University Press, 1998.
Knauft, Bruce M. *Genealogies for the Present in Cultural Anthropology*. New York: Routledge, 1996.
Kohlberg, Etan. "Authoritative Scriptures in Early Imami Shiʿism." In *Les retours aux écritures: Fondamentalismes présents et passés*, edited by Evelyne Patlagean and Allain le Boulluec, 295–312. Louvain: Peeters, 1993.
Korom, Frank J. *Hosay Trinidad: Muharram Performances in an Indo-Caribbean Diaspora*. Philadelphia: University of Pennsylvania Press, 2003.
Kulkarni, A. R., and M. A. Nayeem, eds. *History of the Modern Deccan, 1720/1724–1948*. Hyderabad: Abul Kalam Azad Oriental Research Institute, 2000.
Lakhnavi, Sayyid Mahdi. *ʿAbā'ir al-anwār*. 3 vols. Lucknow: Sarfaraz Qaumi, 1925.
Lalljee, Yousuf. *Janab-e Zainab A.S.: Grand-Daughter of the Holy Prophet*. Bombay: Lalljee, n.d.
Landolt, Herman. "Walāyah." In *Encyclopedia of Religion*, 15:316–23. New York: Macmillan, 1987.
Lawrence, Bruce B. *Shattering the Myth: Islam beyond Violence*. Princeton: Princeton University Press, 1998.
Litvak, Meir. *Shiʿi Scholars of Nineteenth-Century Iraq: The ʿUlama of Najaf and Karbala'*. Cambridge: Cambridge University Press, 1998.
Loewen, Arley. "Proper Conduct (*Adab*) Is Everything: The *Futūwwat-nāmeh-i Sulṭānī* of Husayn Vaʿiz-i Kashifi." *Iranian Studies* 36:4 (December 2003): 543–70.
Lukács, George. *The Theory of the Novel: A Historico-Philosophical Essay on the Forms of Great Epic Literature*. Translated by Anna Bostock. Cambridge: MIT Press, 1989.
Madelung, Wilferd. "Ismāʿiliyya." In *Encyclopaedia of Islam*, 4:203. Leiden: Brill, 1990.
Mahmood, Saba. *Politics of Piety: The Islamic Revival and the Feminist Subject*. Princeton: Princeton University Press, 2005.

"Mashhad, Iran." ⟨http://www.sacredsites.com/middle_east/iran/mashad.htm⟩. Accessed 16 October 2009.

Massignon, Louis. *Salman Pak and the Spiritual Beginnings of Iranian Islam*. Translated by Jamshedji Maneckji Unvala. Bombay: Bombay University Press, 1955.

Masʿud, Naiyer. *Marśiya-khwānī kā fann*. Lucknow: Uttar Pradesh Urdu Academy, 1990.

Masuzawa, Tomoko. *The Invention of World Religions; or, How European Universalism Was Preserved in the Language of Pluralism*. Chicago: University of Chicago Press, 2005.

Mātam-e ḥusain. Hyderabad: Bazm-e Jan Nishan-e Shabbih-ye Paighambar, 1413/1993.

Matthews, David J. "The Kulliyat of Muhammad Quli Qutb Shah: Problems and Prospects." In *Urdu and Muslim South Asia: Essays in Honour of Ralph Russell*, edited by Christopher Shackle, 39–48. London: School of Oriental and African Studies, 1989.

McChesney, Robert D. "Editor's Preface." *Iranian Studies* 36:4 (December 2003): 461–62.

———. *Waqf in Central Asia: Four Hundred Years in the History of a Muslim Shrine, 1480–1889*. Princeton: Princeton University Press, 1991.

Mehdi, Sayyed Akbar. "Azadari of Hyderabad and Its Background." In *Hyderabad ki Azadari*, edited by Sayyed Taqi Hasan Wafa, 5–25. Translated by Sayyed Muhammad Taher Bilgrami. Hyderabad: Idara-e Jaʿfaria, 2000.

Metcalf, Barbara Daly. *Islamic Revival in British India, 1860–1900*. 1982; New Delhi: Oxford University Press, 2002.

Michell, George, ed. *Islamic Heritage of the Deccan*. Bombay: Marg, 1986.

Momen, Moojan. *An Introduction to Shiʿi Islam: The History and Doctrines of Twelver Shiʿism*. New Haven: Yale University Press, 1985.

Mooney, Catherine. "Voice, Gender, and the Portrayal of Sanctity." In *Gendered Voices: Medieval Saints and Their Interpreters*, edited by Catherine Mooney, 7–13. Philadelphia: University of Pennsylvania Press, 1999.

Moosvi, Rasheed. *Dakhan meiṅ marśiya aur ʿazādārī, 1857–1957*. New Delhi: Taraqqi Urdu Bureau, 1970.

Moosvi, Rasheed, and Riaz Fatima. *Ḥaidarābād kī ʿazādārī meiṅ khavātīn kā ḥiṣṣah*. Hyderabad: n.p., 2003.

Motahhari, Mortaza. *Majmūʿah-ye āśār: Ḥamāsat-e ḥusainī*. Tehran: Intisharat-e Sadra, 1368 SH./1991.

———. *Wilayah: The Station of the Master*. Translated by Yahya Cooper. Tehran: World Organization for Islamic Services, 2001.

Mottahedeh, Roy. *The Mantle of the Prophet: Religion and Politics in Iran*. New York: Pantheon, 1985.

al-Mufid, Shaykh. *Kitab al-Irshad: The Book of Guidance into the Lives of the Twelve Imams*. Translated by I. K. A. Howard. London: Muhammadi Trust, 1981.

Munis, Mir Vali Khan. "Riyāẓ al-ṭāhirīn" [Urdu manuscript]. 1138/1725. Salar Jung Museum, Hyderabad. Ta. 42.

Murata, Sachiko. *The Tao of Islam: A Sourcebook on Gender Relations in Islamic Thought.* Albany: State University of New York Press, 1992.
Naim, C. M. "How Bibi Ashraf Learned to Read and Write." In *Urdu Texts and Contexts: The Selected Essays of C. M. Naim*, 202–24. New Delhi: Permanent Black, 2004.
———. "Transvestic Words?: The Rekhti in Urdu." *Annual of Urdu Studies* 16 (2001): 42–66.
———. "Poet-Audience Interaction at Urdu *Mushaʿiras*." In *Urdu and Muslim South Asia: Essays in Honour of Ralph Russell*, edited by Christopher Shackle, 167–74. London: School of Oriental and African Studies, 1989.
———. "The Art of the Urdu *Marsiya*." In *Islamic Society and Culture: Essays in Honour of Professor Aziz Ahmad*, edited by Milton Israel and N. K. Wagle, 101–16. Delhi: Manohar, 1983.
Najmabadi, Afsaneh. *Women with Mustaches and Men without Beards: Gender and Sexual Anxieties of Iranian Modernity*. Berkeley: University of California Press, 2005.
Nakash, Yitzhak. "The Muharram Rituals and the Cult of the Saints among Iraqi Shiites." In *The Other Shiites: From the Mediterranean to Central Asia*, edited by Alessandro Monsutti, Silvia Naef, and Farian Sabahi, 115–36. Bern: Lang, 2007.
———. *The Shiʿis of Iraq*. Princeton: Princeton University Press, 1994.
Naqvi, Sadiq. *Essays in Islam*. Hyderabad: Bab ul-ʿIlm Society, 1999.
———. *The Iran-Deccan Relations*. Hyderabad: Bab ul-ʿIlm Society, 1994.
———. *Muslim Religious Institutions and Their Role under the Qutb Shahs*. Hyderabad: Bab ul-ʿIlm Society, 1993.
———. *Qutb Shahi ʿAshurkhanas of Hyderabad City*. Hyderabad: Bab ul-ʿIlm Society, 1982.
Naqvi, Sadiq, and V. Kishan Rao, eds. *The Muharram Ceremonies among the Non-Muslims of Andhra Pradesh*. Hyderabad: Bab-ul-ʿIlm Society, 2004.
Nasim, Wahidah. *ʿAurat aur urdū zubān*. Karachi: Ghazanfar Academy, 1989.
Nasr, Seyyed Hossein. "Shiʿism and Sufism." In *Shiʿism: Doctrines, Thought, and Spirituality*, edited by Seyyed Hossein Nasr, Hamid Dabashi, and Seyyed Vali Reza Nasr, 100–108. Albany: State University of New York Press, 1988.
Nazmi, Lallan. "Imam Husain: The Benefactor of Mankind." In *Red Sand*, edited by Mehdi Nazmi, 11–15. New Delhi: Abu Talib, 1984.
Nigam, M. L. "Indian Ashur Khanas: A Critical Appraisal." In *Red Sand*, edited by Mehdi Nazmi, 115–23. New Delhi: Abu Talib, 1984.
Nisar, Habib. *Dakhanī kī makhṣūṣ shāʿirī-ye inṣāf, aur dūsre maẓāmīn*. Hyderabad: Urdu Research Center, 1995.
Nizami, K. A. "Ghazi Miyan." In *Encyclopaedia of Islam*, 2:1047–48. Leiden: Brill, 1991.
Noever, Ixy. "Women's Choices: Norms, Legal Pluralism, and Social Control among the Ayt Hdiddu of Central Morocco." In *Shattering Tradition: Custom, Law, and the Individual in the Muslim Mediterranean*, edited by Walter Dostal and Wolfgang Kraus, 189–207. New York: I. B. Tauris, 2005.

Ordoni, Abu Muhammad. "Fatima the Gracious." ⟨http://www.al-islam.org/gracious/41.htm⟩. Accessed 31 May 2010.

Orsi, Robert A. *Between Heaven and Earth: The Religious Worlds People Make and the Scholars Who Study Them*. Princeton: Princeton University Press, 2005.

Pellat, Charles. "*Marthiya* (in Arabic Literature)." In *Encyclopaedia of Islam*, 6:602–8. Leiden: Brill, 1991.

Petievich, Carla. *When Men Speak as Women: Vocal Masquerade in Indo-Muslim Poetry*. New Delhi: Oxford University Press, 2007.

Pinault, David. *Horse of Karbala: Muslim Devotional Life in India*. New York: Palgrave, 2001.

———. "Zaynab bint ʿAli and the Place of the Women of the Household of the First Imams in Shiʿite Devotional Literature." In *Women in the Medieval Islamic World: Power, Patronage, and Piety*, edited by Gavin R. G. Hambly, 69–98. New York: St. Martin's, 1998.

———. *The Shiites: Ritual and Popular Piety in a Muslim Community*. New York: St. Martin's, 1992.

Platts, John T. *A Dictionary of Urdu, Classical Hindi, and English*. New Delhi: Munshiram Manoharlal, 1997.

Pollock, Sheldon. "Cosmopolitan and Vernacular in History." *Public Culture* 12:3 (Fall 2000): 591–625.

Prabhudass, D. S. "An Empirical Study of Telugu Lyrics Used during the Observance of Muharram in Warangal." Master's thesis, Gurukul Lutheran Theological Seminary, 1999.

Prasad, Dharmendra. *Social and Cultural Geography of Hyderabad City*. Delhi: Inter-India, 1986.

Qommi, Shaykh ʿAbbas. *Dar karbalā che guzasht?* Qom: Intisharat-e Masjid-e Muqaddis Jamkaran, 1378 SH./2000.

Qureshi, Regula Burkhardt. "Islamic Music in an Indian Environment: The Shiʿa *Majlis*." *Ethnomusicology* 25:1 (January 1981): 41–71.

Qutb Shah, Muhammad Quli. *Kulliyyāt-e muḥammad qulī quṭb shāh*. Edited by Sayyidah Jaʿfar. New Delhi: National Council Bureau for the Promotion of the Urdu Language, 1985.

Ramanujan, A. K. "On Women Saints." In *The Divine Consort*, edited by John S. Hawley and Donna M. Wulff, 316–24. Berkeley: University of California Press, 1982.

Rao, Velcheru Narayana. "When Does Sita Cease to Be Sita?: Notes toward a Cultural Grammar of Indian Narratives." In *The Rāmāyaṇa Revisited*, edited by Mandakranta Bose, 219–41. New York: Oxford University Press, 2004.

"Rasheed." "Bazm-e shādī kī hai hotā hai ye kaisā mātam." In *Ashk wa mātam*, edited by Mirza Zulfikar ʿAli Khan, 69. Hyderabad: Anjuman-e Parvaneh-ye Qasem, 2004.

Reddy, Gayatri. *With Respect to Sex: Negotiating Hijra Identity in South India*. Chicago: University of Chicago Press, 2005.

Reynolds, Dwight D. *Heroic Poets, Poetic Heroes: The Ethnography of Performance in an Arabic Epic Oral Tradition*. Ithaca: Cornell University Press, 1995.
Reynolds, Frank E., and Donald Capps, eds. *The Biographical Process: Studies in the History and Psychology of Religion*. The Hague: Mouton, 1976.
Rinehart, Robin. *One Lifetime, Many Lives: The Experience of Modern Hindu Hagiography*. Atlanta: Scholars Press, 1999.
Rizvi, Saiyid Athar Abbas. *A Socio-Intellectual History of the Isna ʿAshari Shiʿis in India*. 2 vols. Delhi: Munshiram Manoharlal, 1986.
Rizvi, Sayyid Muhammad. *Shiʿism: Imamate and Wilayat*. Qom: Ansariyan, 2000.
Rizvi, Sayyid Saeed Akhtar. "The Martyrs of Karbala." In *Imam Husayn: The Savior of Islam*, edited by Sayyid Muhammad Rizvi, n.p. Richmond, Canada: Sayyid Muhammad Rizvi, 1984.
Rizvi, Syed Zamin Hussain, ed. *Ṣadā-ye mātam*. Hyderabad: Anjuman-e Haidariyya al-Hind, n.d.
Rowe, John Carlos. "Structure." In *Critical Terms for Literary Studies*, edited by Frank Lentricchia and Thomas McLaughlin, 23–38. Chicago: University of Chicago Press, 1990.
Rowe, Ruth E. "Lady of the Women of the Worlds: Exploring Shiʿi Piety and Identity through a Consideration of Fatima al-Zahra." Master's thesis, University of Arizona, 2008.
Rozehnal, Robert. *Islamic Sufism Unbound: Politics and Piety in Twenty-first Century Pakistan*. New York: Palgrave Macmillan, 2007.
Rudaulvi, Sharib, ed. *Urdū marṡiya*. Delhi: Urdu Academy, 1991.
Ruffle, Karen G. "May Fatimah Gather Our Tears: The Mystical and Intercessory Powers of Fatimah Zahra in Indo-Persian, Shiʿi Devotional Literature and Performance." *Comparative Studies of South Asia, Africa, and the Middle East* 30:3 (November 2010): 386–97.
———. "Karbala in the Indo-Persian Imaginaire: The Indianizing of the Wedding of Qāsim and Fāṭima Kubrā." In *Islam in the Indo-Iranian World during the Modern Epoch*, edited by Denis Hermann and Fabrizio Speziale, 181–200. Berlin: Klaus Schwarz Verlag, 2010.
———. "Who Could Marry at a Time Like This?: Debating the *Mehndi ki Majlis* in Hyderabad." *Comparative Studies of South Asia, Africa, and the Middle East* 29:3 (November 2009): 502–14.
———. "Writing Muharram: The Influence of Mullah Husain Vaʿez Kashefi and Mohtasham Kashani on the Development of Shiʿi Devotionalism in the Medieval Deccan." In *A Thousand Laurels: Dr. Sadiq Naqvi (Studies on Medieval India with Special Reference to Deccan)*, edited by V. Kishan Rao and A. Satyanarayana, 334–45. Hyderabad: Osmania University, 2005.
———. "'Verses Dripping Blood': A Study of the Religious Elements of Muhtasham Kashani's *Karbala-Nameh*." Master's thesis, University of North Carolina at Chapel Hill, 2001.

Rypka, Jan. "History of Persian Literature Up to the Beginning of the 20th Century." In *The History of Iranian Literature*, edited by Karl Jahn, 69–352. Dordecht, Holland: Reidel, 1968.

Sadiq, Muhammad. *A History of Urdu Literature*. Delhi: Oxford University Press, 1984.

al-Saduq, Shaykh. *A Shiite Creed*. Translated by Asaf A. A. Fyzee. Tehran: World Organization for Islamic Services, 1999.

Said, Edward. *Orientalism*. New York: Vintage, 1978.

Saiyid, A. R. "Ideal and Reality in the Observance of Muharram: A Behavioural Interpretation." In *Ritual and Religion among Muslims in India*, edited by Imtiaz Ahmad, 113–42. New Delhi: Manohar, 1984.

Sallie, Sheikh Abdurraghiem. *Kitab un-Nikah: The Book of Muslim Marriage*. New Delhi: Islamic Book Service, 2001.

Sauda, Mir Muhammad Rafiʿ. *Intikhāb-e marāsī*. Lucknow: Uttar Pradesh Urdu Academy, 2003.

Schechner, Richard. *Performance Theory*. Revised ed. New York: Routledge, 1988.

Scherwin, Kerrin Graefin V. "Saint Worship in Indian Islam: The Legend of the Martyr Salar Masud Ghazi." In *Ritual and Religion among Muslims in India*, edited by Imtiaz Ahmad, 143–61. New Delhi: Manohar, 1984.

Schimmel, Annemarie. *A Two-Colored Brocade: The Imagery of Persian Poetry*. Chapel Hill: University of North Carolina Press, 1992.

———. "Karbala and the Imam Husayn in Persian and Indo-Muslim Culture." *Al-Serat* 12 (Spring and Autumn 1986): 29–39.

———. *Mystical Dimensions of Islam*. Chapel Hill: University of North Carolina Press, 1975.

Schubel, Vernon J. *Religious Performance in Contemporary Islam: Shiʿi Devotional Rituals in South Asia*. Columbia: University of South Carolina Press, 1993.

Shahidi, Rashid. "Mātam hai āj dilbar-e umm al-banain kā." In *Karbalā-wāle*, edited by Mir Ahmad ʿAli, 34–35. Hyderabad: Salman Book Depot, 1425/2004.

"Shah Nawaz." Hum ḥaidarī haiṅ sāre zamāne pechhāyenge." In *Ṣadā-ye mātam*, edited by Syed Zamin Hussain Rizvi, 20. Hyderabad: Anjuman-e Haidariyya al-Hind, n.d.

Shamsi, Shamsul Hasan. "Karbala and Mass-Media." In *Red Sand*, edited by Mehdi Nazmi, 243–50. New Delhi: Abu Talib, 1984.

Sharar, ʿAbdul Halim. *Lucknow: The Last Phase of an Oriental Culture*. Edited and translated by E. S. Harcourt and Fakhir Hussain. New Delhi: Oxford University Press, 1989.

Shariʿati, ʿAli. *Fatimah Is Fatimah*. Translated by Laleh Bakhtiar. Tehran: Shariʿati Foundation, 1980.

———. *Shahādat (Martyrdom)*. Translated by Laleh Bakhtiar and Husain Salih. Tehran: Abu Dharr Foundation, 1972.

Sharif, Tayba Hassan al-Khalifa. "Sacred Narratives Linking Iraqi Shiite Women across Time and Space." In *Muslim Networks: From Hajj to Hip Hop*, edited by

miriam cooke and Bruce B. Lawrence, 132–54. Chapel Hill: University of North Carolina Press, 2005.
al-Shaybi, Kamal Mostafa. *Tashiyyuʿ wa taṣawwuf: Tā āghāz sadeh-ye dawāzdahom hijrī*. Tehran: Intisharat-e Amir Kabir, 1359 SH./1981.
Sherwani, H. K., and P. M. Joshi. *History of Medieval Deccan (1295–1724)*. 2 vols. Hyderabad: Government of Andhra Pradesh, 1973.
Shields, Stephanie A. *Speaking from the Heart: Gender and the Social Meaning of Emotion*. Cambridge: Cambridge University Press, 2002.
Shurreef, Jaffur. *Qanoon-e Islam; or, The Customs of the Mussalmans of India*. Translated by G. A. Herklots. 2nd ed. New Delhi: Asian Educational Services, 1991.
Simpson, Edward, and Kai Kresse. "Introduction: Cosmopolitanism Contested: Anthropology and History in the Western Indian Ocean." In *Struggling with History: Islam and Cosmopolitanism in the Western Indian Ocean*, edited by Edward Simpson and Kai Kresse 1–42. London: Hurst, 2007.
"The Situation in Bombay vis-à-vis Sister Tahera Jaʿfer." ⟨http://www.shiachat.com/forum/index.php?/topic/50781-situation-in-bombay-vis-a-vis-sister-tahera-jafer/page_st_100⟩, 25 February 2005. Accessed 1 June 2005.
Soufi, Denise. "The Image of Fatima in Classical Muslim Thought." Ph.D. diss., Princeton University, 1997.
Steingass, F. *A Comprehensive Persian-English Dictionary*. New Delhi: Munshiram Manoharlal, 1996.
Stewart, Tony K. "In Search of Equivalence: Conceiving Muslim-Hindu Encounter through Translation Theory." *History of Religions* 40:3 (February 2001): 260–87.
Stewart, Tony K., and Carl W. Ernst. "Syncretism." In *South Asian Folklore: An Encyclopedia*, edited by Peter J. Claus and Margaret A. Mills, 586–88. New York: Routledge, 2003.
Subtelny, Maria E. "Husayn Vaʿiz-i Kashifi: Polymath, Popularizer, and Preserver." *Iranian Studies* 36:4 (December 2003): 463–67.
———. "A Late Medieval Persian Summa on Ethics: Kashifi's *Akhlāq-e Moḥṣinī*." *Iranian Studies* 36:4 (December 2003): 601–14.
Sulami, Muḥammad ibn al-Ḥusayn. *Early Sufi Women*. Edited and Translated by Rkia Cornell. Louisville, Ky.: Fons Vitae, 1999.
Suvorova, Anna. *Muslim Saints of South Asia, the Eleventh to Fifteenth Centuries*. Translated by M. Osama Faruqi. 1999; London: Routledge Curzon, 2004.
al-Tabari, Abu Jaʿfar Muhammad b. Jarir. *Between Civil Wars: The Caliphate of Muʿawiyah, A.D. 661–680/A.H. 40–60*. Vol. 18 of *The History of al-Tabari*. Translated by Michael G. Morony. Albany: State University of New York Press, 1987.
al-Tabarsi, Abu ʿAli al-Fadl ibn al-Hasan ibn al-Fadl. *Beacons of Light*. Translated by Lynda C. Clarke and Mahmoud Ayoub. Tehran: World Islamic Services, 1986.
al-Tabarsi, Shaykh Hajji al-Nuri. *Lūʾlūʾ wa marjān*. Qom: Payam-e Mahdi, 1381 SH./2003.
Tabataba'i, Allamah. "The Imams and the Imamate." In *Shiʿism: Doctrines, Thought,*

and Spirituality, edited by Seyyed Hossein Nasr, Hamid Dabashi, and Seyyed Vali Reza Nasr, 156–67. Albany: State University of New York Press, 1988.

Takim, Liyakat. *The Heirs of the Prophet: Charisma and Religious Authority in Shiʿite Islam*. Albany: State University of New York Press, 2006.

Tarabay, Jaime. "Revived Lament Tradition Makes Way for New Grief." 12 November 2006. ⟨http://www.npr.org⟩. Accessed 8 January 2007.

Thackston, Wheeler. *A Millennium of Classical Persian Poetry: A Guide to the Reading and Understanding of Persian Poetry from the Tenth to the Twentieth Century*. Bethesda, Md.: Iranbooks, 1994.

Thanawi, Maulana Ashraf ʿAli. *Bihishti Zewar (Heavenly Ornaments): Perfecting Women*. Translated and edited by Barbara D. Metcalf. New Delhi: Oxford University Press, 1992.

Thapar, Romila. *Somanatha: The Many Voices of a History*. New Delhi: Penguin India, 2004.

al-Tirmidhi, al-Hakim. *The Concept of Sainthood in Early Islamic Mysticism: Two Works by al-Hakim al-Tirmidhi*. Translated by Bernd Radtke and John O'Kane. London: Curzon, 1996.

Turner, Victor. *The Ritual Process: Structure and Anti-Structure*. Ithaca: Cornell University Press, 1977.

Tweed, Thomas A. "On Moving Across: Translocative Religion and the Interpreter's Position." *Journal of the American Academy of Religion* 70:2 (June 2002): 253–77.

Uberoi, J. P. S. *Religion, Civil Society, and the State: A Study of Sikhism*. New Delhi: Oxford University Press, 1999.

Usmani, Fuzail al-Raham Hilal. *The Islamic Law: Marriage, Divorce, Inheritance*. Malerkotla: Darus Salam Islamic Centre, 2000.

Veccia-Vaglieri, L. "Fatima." In *Encyclopaedia of Islam*, 2:841–50. Leiden: Brill, 1991.

———. "al-Husayn b. ʿAli b. Abi Talib." In *Encyclopaedia of Islam*, 3:607–15. Leiden: Brill, 1986.

Vellori, Vali. "Rowẓat al-shohadā" [Deccani-Urdu manuscript]. 1130/1717. Oriental Manuscripts Library and Research Institute, Hyderabad. Ta. 1401.

———. "Rowẓat al-shohadā" [Deccani-Urdu manuscript]. 1130/1717. Oriental Manuscripts Library and Research Institute, Hyderabad. Ta. 2514.

Visuvalingam, Sunthar, and Elizabeth Chalier-Visuvalingam. "Between Mecca and Banaras: Towards an Acculturation-Model of Muslim-Hindu Relations." *Islam and the Modern Age* 24:1 (February 1993): 20–69.

Warhol, Robyn R. *Gendered Interventions: Narrative Discourse in the Victorian Novel*. New Brunswick, N.J.: Rutgers University Press, 1989.

Wehr, Hans. *Arabic-English Dictionary*. 4th ed. Edited by J. M. Cowan. 1979; Ithaca, N.Y.: Spoken Language Services, 1994.

White, Hayden. "The Historical Text as Literary Artifact." In *Critical Theory since 1965*, edited by Hazard Adams and Leroy Searle, 395–409. Tallahassee: Florida State University Press, 1986.

Wilce, James M. *Eloquence in Trouble: The Poetics and Politics of Complaint in Rural Bangladesh*. New York: Oxford University Press, 1998.
Zaidi, Sayyed Zahoor Hyder. "Azadari of Mir Osman Ali Khan—The Seventh Nizam." In *Hyderabad ki Azadari*, edited by Sayyed Taqi Hasan Wafa, 26–33. Translated by Sayyed Muhammad Taher Bilgrami. Hyderabad: Idara-e Jaʿfaria, 2000.
"Zakir." *Tears and Tributes*. Qom: Ansariyan, 2001.
al-Zaman, Masih. *Urdū marsiye kā irtiqā: ibtadā se anīs tak*. Lucknow: Uttar Pradesh Urdu Academy, 1983.

Index

ʿAli Asghar: thirst of, 4; commemoration in Hyderabad, 10; martyrdom of, 10; embodiment of *ḥusaini* ethics, 51
ʿAli ibn Abi Talib, 83, 146, 152, 185 (n. 23); as Imam, 7; as member of *ahl-e bait*, 30; as Muhammad's successor, 38, 49; transcendent sainthood, 38, 39, 82; esoteric role as Imam, 48; executor (*waṣīy*) of Muhammad's teaching, 48; member of *ahl-e kisāʾ*, 53; member of *panjetan-e pāk*, 53; Ḥaidar, 54; blood descent through, 56; relationship with Salman al-Farsi, 56; marriage to Fatimah, 73–74
ʿAli Khan, Asaf Jah II (Nizam), 107
Amtul Zahra Begum, 85
ʿAqd-e nikāḥ, 62, 113, 115, 124, 126, 165
Arabic, 54, 102, 105, 157, 170, 182 (n. 32); textual authority, 54, 166
Ardhanarisvara, 67
ʿArsī muṣḥāf, 113
Asaf Jahi dynasty, 85, 107; patronage of Shiʿi institutions, 107, 110; patronage of Shiʿi hagiography, 108, 110
Asghar, Sabiha, 11, 59–63; everyday Shiʿism of, 12; career of, 59, 60, 63; idealized femininity of, 61; attitude toward widowhood, 61; cultivation of idealized self, 61; veneration of Fatimah Kubra and Qasem, 62, 168; marriage of, 62–63
ʿĀshūrā, 9, 69–70
ʿĀshūrkhāna, 3, 10, 13, 60, 85, 86, 89, 106, 107, 121, 122, 128, 152, 164, 177 (n. 9)
Astan-e Qods, 15, 146
Astarabadi, Mir Muʾmin, 106
ʿAun (son of Zainab), 8, 58
Aurangzeb (Mughal emperor), 35–36, 107
Ayodhya, 36, 96, 97
Ayyām-e ʿazā, 13, 24, 122
ʿAzakhane-ye Zahra, 85

Bahadur, Mir ʿAlam, 21, 108, 110, 117, 134; strategies of narrative engagement, 110, 119; transvestic voice of, 110; strategies of narrative distancing, 116, 117, 119
Bahmani dynasty, 106, 183 (n. 36)
Bahraich, 36, 37, 38
Bait al-Qaʾem, 89
Bakhtin, Mikhail, 94
Baraka, 89
Barāt, 86–87, 123, 165, 183 (n. 44)
Bargah-e ʿAbbas, 69
Bayʿah (oath of allegiance), 6, 100, 151–52
Bayqara, Husain (Timurid sultan): commissioning of *Rowẓat al-Shohadā*, 150; commissioning of ʿAli's tomb, 152, 185 (n. 23)
Beliefs of the Imamis, 49
Bevāh, 89, 118, 163. *See also* Widowhood
Bezels of Wisdom. See *Fuṣūṣ al-ḥikām*
Bhakti, 67, 72
Bibi Ashraf, 140–41
Bībī kā ʿalam, 10, 69; submersion in Musi River, 70
Bibi ka Alava, 13
Bidʿah (innovation), 156
Bihar, 158
Biḥār al-Anwār, 73, 166
Bihishtī Zewār, 155
Bijapur, 106, 107
Blood: intercessory power of, 14; and *wilāyah*, 18
Bonalu, 68, 70
Bourdieu, Pierre, 33
Brown, Peter, 32, 33
Butler, Judith, 132–35

Cairo, 131
Caitanya, Krishna, 67
Canada, 169
Castro, Fidel, 159
Chakkī, 73, 75
Chārdah maṣūmīn, 53, 76
Charisma, 5, 14, 18, 19, 32, 56, 72
Chaudhuri, K. N., 161
Chishti, Shaykh ʿAbdur Rahman, 37
Chishtiyya, 35, 36, 152
Clarke, Lynda, 102
Colonialism, 154, 155
Complementary pairing, 20, 45, 51, 66; binary theory, 29; feminine-masculine, 46, 66
Consanguinity: and *ḥusainiyyat/ḥusaini* ethics, 19; and Shiʿi sainthood, 30, 45, 51, 53, 56; and Sufi sainthood, 45; Salman al-Farsi and fictive consanguinity to *ahl-e bait*, 56
cooke, miriam, 167
Corbin, Henry, 20
Cornell, Rkia, 27–28
Cornell, Vincent, 34, 46, 178 (n. 19)
Cosmopolitan: Shiʿi, 21, 99, 141, 142, 154, 156, 157, 158, 161, 165, 167, 170, 182 (n. 23); linguistic, 54, 159; Karbala as, 158, 159; locative, 159, 161; sacred, 160

Dabirpura, 8
Dahej. *See* Dowry
Dah majlis, 21, 108, 110; portrayal of Qasem in, 110–19 passim, 134; portrayal of Fatimah Kubra in, 110–19 passim, 134–35
Dakake, Maria Massi, 18, 28
Damascus, 10, 78, 86, 88, 98, 99, 100
Daneshgah-e Jaʿfariyya, 164
Darulshifa, 8, 85, 164
Dawāzdah-band, 182 (n. 26)
David, 41
Day of Judgment, 42, 76, 82, 112, 159
Day of Resurrection (*qiyāmat*), 79, 87, 105, 185 (n. 22)
Deccan, 21, 36, 108; enculturation of Shiʿism, 22, 106, 107, 170, 183 (n. 36); vernacular religious traditions, 70, 99; Shiʿism in, 93, 107, 168
Deccani-Urdu, 21, 106, 107; Karbala hagiography, 27, 88, 108, 132, 136, 162; translation of texts into, 106, 107, 161
Deeb, Lara, 186 (n. 33)
Delehaye, Hippolyte, 103
Delhi, 35
Deoband, 154, 155
Dilgir, 138–40
Dowry, 2, 125, 126, 127; culturally compulsory, 126; Muslim critiques of, 126, 165
Dreams, 14, 76; al-Tirmidhi and theory of sainthood, 40, 42; Ibn al-ʿArabi and theory of sainthood, 42
Durga, 68

Egypt, 154
Eliade, Mircea, 82, 181 (n. 38)
Emotion: and femininity, 20, 21, 94, 102; and masculinity, 20, 94, 95, 98; in the *majlis*, 25; and female voice, 92, 94, 102; and epic narrative, 97–98, 102; in remembering Karbala, 102
Epic: hero in Indo-Muslim literature, 19, 94, 95; Indic-Karbala tradition, 20, 21, 94–95, 112, 115, 116; female voice and emotion, 92; characterization in, 93, 94, 100; hero, 97, 119; experiential dimension of, 103; gendered dimensions of, 108; heroine, 119

Femininity: authentication by *ahl-e bait*, 60, 63; South Asian idealized, 60–61; potency, 68
Feminism, 11, 24, 134
Fischer, Michael M. J., 149
Fiza, 168, 186–87 (n. 47)
Foucault, Michel, 131, 133; positive ethics, 131, 183 (n. 10)
Frye, Northrop, 94
Fuṣūṣ al-ḥikām, 40, 42; theory of *walāyah* in, 42
Futūwwat-nāmeh-ye sulṭānī, 153

Gabriel (angel), 49
Gangamma, 68
Gaudiya Vaisnavism, 67
Gender: in hagiography, 11, 110; Fatimah Kubra and gender roles, 21, 110, 132, 134, 135, 141–42, 163; and messengership and masculinity, 47; and women's organization of wedding rituals, 115; inversion of, 130; performativity of, 132–33; and cultivation of idealized states, 133; women's gendered states, 133; binaries, 134, 136; and vernacular practice in South Asia, 155
Ghawth, 34
Ghāzī, 31, 34, 35, 36
Ghazi Miyan, 36–38, 57, 178 (n. 28); as bridegroom/warrior, 36; as *naushāh*, 36, 37; comparison to Qasem, 36–38; as friend of the Hindu, 37; marriage to Zahra Bibi, 37; *ʿurs* and wedding rituals performed, 38
Ghaznavi, Mullah Muhammad, 37
God, 43–44, 48, 51, 179 (n. 38); as *al-Walī*, 39; masculine and feminine qualities of, 47; ninety-nine names of, 47; uniqueness of (*tawḥīd*), 68
Goddess tradition, 68; as *ammā*, 68
Golconda, 35, 36, 106, 107, 178 (n. 27)
Gregory of Tours, 81
Gupta, Charu, 88

Habitus, 33
Ḥadīth, 34, 38, 39, 54, 80; and Shiʿi sainthood, 40, 48; as God's supernatural speech, 44
Hagiography, 1, 15, 17; as form of moral communication, 2, 15, 101, 103, 105, 108, 119; as form of sacred biography, 2, 103; function of, 2, 103, 133, 136; social role of, 3; as religious literature, 3, 103; as performative genre, 15; cultural adaptability of, 25; of Ghazi Miyan, 36–38; Sufi, emphasis on asceticism, 71; didactic function of, 102–3; experiential dimension of, 102–3; as interactive genre, 103; as collective autobiography, 142
—Roman Catholic, 33; emphasis on asceticism, 71
—Shiʿi, 107; defining gendered action in *majlis*, 2; as integrative genre, 3, 4; in Iraqi Shiʿism, 3, 131; women's role in, 5, 25, 61; and the everyday, 11, 12; engaging the subjective realm, 15, 133, 136; and *ḥusaini* ethics-imitable sainthood, 46, 72; and love for *ahl-e bait*, 54; and the body, 65; portrayal of women, 65, 69, 72, 80, 90–91; use of feminine voices and emotions, 66–67, 109; Fatimah's poverty in, 73–75; use of Zainab's voice, 77–78, 93; focus on kinship, 79; and the vernacular, 91; as source of authority, 147–49; *Rowẓat al-Shohadā* as form of, 148–49
Ḥaidarī, 54
Ḥajj. *See* Pilgrimage
Al-Hallaj, Mansur, 151
Hanuman, 96

Hasan ibn ʿAli, Imam, 1, 6, 79, 86, 111, 112, 182 (n. 32), 185 (n. 29); as member of *ahl-e kisāʾ*, 53; as member of *panjetan-e pāk*, 53
Henna. See *Mehndī*
Herat, Afghanistan, 150, 151, 152
Hijṛa, 68; identification as Muslim, 69; ritual role of, 69
Hinduism, 155, 160, 163
Hodgson, Marshall G. S., 21
Howzeh, 170; and employment of disputational methodology in, 148–49
Husain, ibn ʿAli, Imam, 1, 9, 36, 77–78, 79, 80, 86, 100, 159, 182 (n. 32), 183 (n. 45); embodiment of *ḥusaini* ethics-imitable sainthood, 5, 19, 30, 45, 57, 60, 79, 101, 105; and *ṣalāt al-khawf*, 9; martyrdom of, 9, 49, 78, 100, 103, 104; static epic figure of, 19; and Imamate-transcendent sainthood, 19, 20, 30, 51, 79; portrayal of emotion, 20; as theophanic form, 20; as model man, 50; as role model for Shiʿa, 50; as member of *ahl-e kisāʾ*, 53; as member of *panjetan-e pāk*, 53; Shiʿi love for and veneration of, 54, 158; as King of the Martyrs, 104; in *Dah majlis*, 111, 112; as father-like figure to Qasem, 112
Husain, S. K., 126
Ḥusaini ethics, 5, 11, 15, 24, 49, 57, 131; women's embodiment of, 5, 58, 109; doctrine of, 18; Imam Husain's family and, 25, 28, 50, 54, 101, 143; and idealized selfhood, 45, 51, 63, 118, 142; and justice, 50; and martyrdom, 52; and sacrifice, 72, 143. See also *Ḥusainiyyat*
—/imitable sainthood, 17, 18, 20, 21, 38, 46–52, 86, 105; and complementary pairing, 18, 26, 29, 45; mimetic qualities of, 19; of the *ahl-e bait*, 22, 54, 143; as socially grounded, 29; socioethical and religious qualities, 31; four indexical features of, 45; central role of women, 45, 93; and cultural specificity, 50; and vernacular values, 50; *ʿalam* as symbol of, 60; Zainab's embodiment of, 77
Ḥusainiyyat, 5, 18, 25, 28; moral and ethical qualities of, 19. See also *Ḥusaini* ethics
Ḥusainiyyat-wilāyah. See *Ḥusaini* ethics—/imitable sainthood
Hyderabad, 16, 35, 85, 86, 158, 164; Old City, 1, 6, 9, 11, 13, 23, 59, 69, 85, 124, 165, 169; hagiographical traditions in, 4, 12, 50, 59, 80, 141, 168; Shiʿi ritual calendar, 6, 8, 10, 122, 158; religious processions, 10, 70; social ideals and values, 14, 60, 73, 120; and the vernacular, 21, 168, 170; Shiʿi population of, 23; women's social engagement in, 61; veneration of women of *ahl-e bait* in, 67, 69; Shiʿi religious practice, 76, 162, 163; archives, 107; wedding rituals, 113, 123, 130; Iranianized community, 164, 167

Ibn ʿAbd al-Wahhab, Muhammad, 155
Ibn al-ʿArabi, Muhyi al-Din, 38, 40; dreams and theory of sainthood, 42; theory of sainthood, 42–45
Ibn ʿAqil, Muslim, 6, 7
Ibn ʿAwf, ʿAbd al-Rahman, 80
Ibn Babawayh al-Qummi, Muhammad, 49
Ibn Dhu'l-Jawshan, Shimr, 8, 10
Ibn Ishaq, Muhammad, 44
Ibn Saʿd, ʿUmar, 8, 9
Ibn Shahrashub, Muhammad ibn ʿAli, 83
Ibn ʿUrwa, Hani, 7
Ibn Zaman, Muhammad ʿAli, 92

152, 156; drama of, 98; tomb of Imam Husain, 146; as site of Shiʿi cosmopolitan, 159
—Battle of, 1, 2, 5, 6, 20, 23, 25, 49, 52, 57, 66, 69, 83, 85, 98, 100, 102, 103, 106, 132, 148, 187 (n. 47); and battlefield wedding of Fatimah Kubra and Qasem, 1, 88, 168, 169; hero(in)es of, 1, 130; Shiʿi memory of, 16, 58, 66, 77, 83, 91, 101, 102, 105, 153, 154, 163, 170; women's survival of, 93, 101; historical record of, 93, 148, 157; universal narrative of, 157, 158
—epic tradition of, 21, 93–95, 106; female characters in, 99
Karbalā-nāmeh, 93, 99–100, 102, 105, 106, 182 (n. 26); didactic function of, 102–3; vernacularization in Deccan of, 106–7; and *Rowẓat al-Shohadā*, 157
Kashani, Mohtasham, 93, 99, 102–3, 105, 106, 107, 182 (n. 26)
Kashefi, Mullah Husain Vaʿez, 16, 27, 81, 100, 106, 107, 108, 147, 148, 152, 153, 157, 162, 166, 185 (n. 22); education of, 150; patronage of, 150; Sufi credentials of, 150, 151; religious identity of, 150–52
Khan, Khafi, 35
Khan, Kulsum, 86, 123, 124, 127, 128
Khan, M. M. Taqui, 76, 118, 126, 127, 142; as *ẕākir*, 23, 24, 27, 122; *majlis* discourse of, 24, 27; focus on Fatimah Kubra, 24, 119; daughters of, 25, 122–23, 124, 142; Fatimah's appearance in dreams of, 76; men's *mehndī* mourning assembly sponsored by, 86, 89, 121, 124, 137, 169; women's *mehndī* mourning assembly sponsored by, 89
Khātūn-e jannat, 83
Khaybar, Battle of, 75
Khayyami, Saghar, 18
Khoja Twelver Shiʿas, 158
Khomeini, Ayatollah Ruhollah, 90, 165
Khudī, 18
Khwāharān, 145, 146
Kitāb al-irshād, 148, 157, 166
Kitchen, John, 81
Kresse, Kai, 159, 161
Krishna, 37, 67, 72
Kubra, Najm al-Din, 47
Kubrawiyyah, 47
Kufah, 50; invitation to Imam Husain, 6; Imam Husain prevented from entering, 7; loyalty of, 7
Kuśa, 182 (n. 16)

Lahore, Pakistan, 158
Lakhnavi, Sayyid Mahdi, 164, 186 (n. 44)
Laksmana, 96, 182 (n. 16)
Lauḥ-e maḥfūż, 82
Lava, 182 (n. 16)
Lavakuśakāṇḍa, 181–82 (n. 16)
Law, Islamic. See *Sharīʿah*
Lawrence, Bruce B., 167
Lebanon, 154, 157, 158
Life-cycle events, 11, 16, 21, 62, 132, 163
Lizzie, 127–28
Love: God's, for saints (*maḥabba*), 42; for *ahl-e bait* (*maḥabbat*), 54; Imam Husain's, for God, 152
Lucknow, India, 163, 167, 168
Lukács, George, 94, 95, 97
Lūʾlūʾ wa marjān, 153–54
Luqman, 56

Madaʾin, Iraq, 57
Madras (Chennai), India, 85, 158
Madrasah Jada Buzurg, 149
Maḥabba. *See* Love
Mahābhārata, 94, 95, 109

Mahankali, 68, 70
Mahmood, Saba, 131, 183 (n. 10)
Mahmud of Ghazna (Ghaznavid sultan), 37
Mahr, 116, 126
Majlis-e ʿazā. *See* Mourning assembly
Majlisi, Muhammad Baqir, 166
Majlis orators, 1, 5, 23, 50, 122; women as, 16, 89; and performance, 24, 92; and transvestic voice, 98; etiquette for, 154
Maʿmun (ʿAbbasid *khalīfah*), 146
Manjha, 73, 124, 165, 169
Mannat, 60, 128
Mantle of the Prophet, 148–49
Maqtal, 27, 66
Mariyamman, 68
Marriage: in Hinduism, 2; as Islamic imperative, 2, 13, 37, 80, 127, 128, 141, 162; arranged in South Asia, 2, 14, 62, 91, 124, 128, 130, 162; as charged life-cycle event, 2, 162; Hyderabadi attitudes toward, 13, 23, 127, 165; good marriage alliances, 24, 60, 127, 128; Indic anxieties about, 38, 87, 91; Muslim women's legal rights in, 62; and divorce, 62–63; South Asian Muslim rituals for, 73, 90, 110–19 passim, 123, 126, 129, 131, 136–42; of Fatimah al-Zahra to ʿAli, 73, 165; Muhammad's Sunnah on, 141, 165; "authenticated" rituals, 165. See also *ʿArsī muṣḥāf*; *Barāt*; *Jūtā chhupaʾī*; *Mahr*; *Manjha*; *Mehndī*; *Neg*; *Rukhṣatī*; *Sāchaq*; *Sehrā bandhānā*; *Walīmah*
Marriage contract. See *ʿAqd-e nikāḥ*
Marsiya, 1, 23, 66, 89, 90, 121, 169; of Mohtasham Kashani, 93, 99, 102–5; Arabic origins of, 101, 102; as women's genre, 101, 102, 105; didactic function of, 102–3; as moral communication, 105; of Sauda, 136–38, 141; of Dilgir, 138–39
Martyrdom. See *Shahādat*
Martyrium, 31
Martyr saint: typology of, 30, 31, 32; Roman Catholic, 31; Shiʿi, 31, 32, 45, 58; social involvement of, 32; Jesus Christ as model for, 33
Marv, Turkmenistan, 146
Maṣāʾib, 9, 101; and hagiography, 24; in the mourning assembly, 87, 91; and narrative engagement, 92
Mashhad, Iran, 14, 145, 146, 147, 148, 150, 152
Mātam, 10, 78, 89, 102, 182 (n. 27); bloody, 14, 69–70; as performance of masculinity, 69–70
Mātamī gurūhān, 10, 69
Maulā, 38, 48
Mazar-e Sharif, Afghanistan, 152, 185 (n. 23)
Mecca, 7, 35, 56, 155, 182 (n. 32)
Medina, 56, 155, 182 (n. 32), 185–86 (n. 29)
Mehndī, 14, 24, 89, 126, 168; *lagānā*, 14, 127, 128; and memory, 90, 160; trays, 123, 125, 127; wedding ritual, 124, 126, 129, 157; as un-Islamic, 168–69; defense of practice, 168–70
—mourning assembly, 21, 85, 87, 111, 163; permissibility of observing, 17, 163, 165, 167; and vernacular, 22, 162, 167; debates about, 23, 163; popularity in Hyderabad, 23, 163; ritual activities of, 59; of ʿAbbas Sahib, 85; women's, 89, 95; men's, 89, 122, 128; and ideology, 90; gendered aspects, 90, 95; Khan family preparations for, 121–24, 126–27
Memorial of Female Sufi Devotees, 27
Memory, 20; of Karbala, 77; role of feminine voice and emotion, 66;

Shiʿi collective, 66, 87, 101, 130, 158; gendered, 91, 101
Messengership. See *Risālah*
Miami, Florida, 159
Mirabai (Rajput princess), 72
Miracle (*muʿjizah*), 13, 34, 36, 128
Mir ʿAli, Shajaʿat, 164–67, 170
Mir Anis, 168
Mirʾāt-e maṣʿūdī, 37
Mirza Dabir, 168
Mombasa, Kenya, 158
Mooney, Catherine, 28
Moral communication, 2, 15, 101, 105, 108, 119
Moses, 41
Motaheddeh, Roy, 148–49
Motahhari, Morteza, 90, 147, 154, 166
Mourning assembly, 1, 5, 13, 17, 23, 99, 131; and ritual performance, 1, 2, 135; hagiographical recitation in, 2, 20; as site for teaching Islamic law and theology, 5; performance of emotion, 25, 99; collective memory, 66, 91; Fatimah's presence in, 76; women's, 89
Al-Mufid, Shaykh, 148, 157, 166
Muḥaddath, 42
Muhammad, Prophet, 13, 32, 41, 52, 66, 72, 74, 76, 78, 79, 82, 83, 99, 102, 103, 127, 152, 155, 185–86 (n. 29); *ahl-e bait*, sainthood, and blood descent through, 18, 29, 45, 53, 55, 56, 72, 137, 182 (n. 32); as *insān al-kāmil*, 30; as transcendent model, 30; as messenger, 30, 39; as prophet, 30, 39; as imitable model, 30, 165; and *walāyah*, 38; appointed ʿAli Imam, 38, 49; laying keystone of Kaʿba, 44; as teacher (*nāṭiq*) of revelation, 48; as member of *ahl-e kisāʾ*, 53; as member of *panjetan-e pāk*, 53; one of Fourteen Infallibles (*chārdah maʿsumīn*), 53; closeness to Zainab, 76; and marriage imperative, 80
Muhammad (son of Zainab), 8, 58
Muhammad II (Bahmani king), 106
Muhammad al-Baqir, Imam, 185 (n. 29)
Muhammad Quli Qutb Shah (Qutb Shahi king), 106, 107
Muharram, 6, 154, 163; Hyderabad *sabīl* tents, 6; religious processions (*julūs*), 70; vernacular practice and reform of, 168
Muʿin al-Din Chishti, Shaykh, 151, 152
Mujāḥid, 31, 34
Mullah Abdollah, 149
Mulla Sadra (Sadr al-Din Shirazi), 18
Mumbai, India, 158
Munis, Mir Vali Khan, 108
Muntakhāb al-lubāb, 35
Muṣḥaf fāṭimah, 66
Musi River, 70, 85, 121
Muslim networks, 167

Naim, C. M., 98, 140
Najaf, Iraq, 146, 154, 156, 167, 186 (n. 32)
Najmabadi, Afsaneh, 92, 99
Nakash, Yitzhak, 3, 4
Naqshbandiyya, 36, 150, 151, 152, 185 (n. 14)
Naqvi, Sadiq, 50–51
Naqvi, Sayyidah Maryam, 165; historical authenticity, 90; *majlis* discourse of, 90–91; portrayal of Fatimah Kubra, 91; and narrative distancing, 95, 98; transvestic discourse of, 98
Narayan, Kirin, 137
Narrative distancing, 95, 98, 115, 119
Narrative ellipsis, 87
Narrative engagement, 20, 77, 92, 99, 109, 110, 139; in *Karbalā-nāmeh*, 93, 99, 103; in *Rāmāyaṇa*, 97; in *Dah majlis*, 110, 112, 118, 119

Narrative metalepsis, 111
Nasr, Seyyed Hossein, 83
National Public Radio, 186 (n. 32)
Nauḥa, 14, 66, 77–78, 101, 121, 141, 186 (n. 32)
Naushāh, 36, 115, 147, 156, 184 (n. 25)
Nawaz, Jenab Shah, 54
Nazmi, Lallan, 50
Neg, 117, 129
Ninety-nine names of God, 39, 47
Nishapur, Iran, 150
Nizams. *See* Asaf Jahi dynasty
Nubūwwah, 19; and exoteric revelation, 19, 42; subordinate to *walāyah*, 43; symbolized as earthen brick, 43; Fatimah as mother of, 79
Nūr, 43, 82; existing before Creation, 48
Al-Nuri, Shaykh Hajji, 153–54, 156–57
Nūr muḥammadī, 82, 83; apportioning of, 83

Orientalism, 12, 26, 27
Orsi, Robert, 15, 17
Osman ʿAli Khan, Asaf Jah VII (Nizam), 85
Osmania University, 23, 50, 122, 124, 169
Osmania University Shiʿi students' association, 23, 24

Panjetan-e Pāk, 53, 111
Pativratā, 92, 94, 120
Patriarchy, 12, 133; Islamic textual traditions and, 12; hagiography and, 31; control of female bodies, 64, 77, 78, 133, 134, 139; and marriage, 79, 90, 135, 136, 139, 143; and family, 80; and Imamate, 82; subversion of, 94; and authority, 98
Persian Gulf, 169
Persian language, 21, 54, 100, 102, 106, 148, 153, 157, 182 (n. 27)
Pilgrimage: concurrent with *ḥajj* (*ʿumrat al-tammatu*), 7; to Mecca (*ḥajj*), 35; to saints' shrine/tombs (*ziyārat*), 55, 57, 66, 145, 146; to *ʿalams*, 122; networks, 167; supplementary (*ʿumrah*), 185–86 (n. 29)
Prophecy. See *Nubūwwah*
Prophets, 48, 51
Purani Haveli, 8, 13, 89
Purdah, 27, 63, 65; imagery in Sufism and *bhakti*, 67; and Muharram ritual, 69–70, 86, 89, 122, 123

Qasem, 1, 11, 13, 80, 86, 87, 95, 127, 128, 166; sainthood of, 3, 15, 19, 166; Hyderabadi commemoration of martyrdom of, 8, 23; martyrdom of, 10, 90, 99, 110, 111, 116, 118, 119, 132, 138, 139, 163, 186 (n. 33); in *majlis*, 11; blood of, 14; as bridegroom/warrior, 24, 57, 67, 111, 113, 129, 132; embodiment of *ḥusaini* ethics-imitable sainthood, 24, 59, 111; comparison to Ghazi Miyan, 36; comparison to Wahab, 57–58; *ʿalam*, 60, 85–86; popularity of, 86; as orphan (*yatīm*), 86, 111–12; role in hagiographical narrative, 88, 139; wedding to Fatimah Kubra, 90, 95, 111–19 passim, 126, 130, 139, 157, 164; in *Dah majlis*, 110–19 passim; idealized qualities of, 111; dressed in burial shroud, 128, 138
Qiyāmat. *See* Day of Resurrection
Qom, Iran, 56, 66, 145, 148–49, 156, 167
Qurʾan, 9, 34, 36, 38, 39, 44, 46, 48, 61, 65, 72, 75, 126, 127, 155; *walī*, 39, 179 (n. 38); and Shiʿi sainthood, 40; and interpretation (*tafsīr*), 54
Quraysh, 44
Quṭb, 34

dered status of, 65; feminine power, 69; role of kinship in, 71–72
Sainthood, Sufi, 25, 40; Islamic studies focus on, 28; *walāyah*, 28; *wilāyah*, 28; typologies of, 30, 34, 35, 38; generative authority, 34; warrior model of, 34, 35; imitable model of, 34, 38; as socioethically exemplary, 34, 38; vernacularization of, 38; al-Tirmidhi's theory of, 40–42; Ibn al-ʿArabi's theory of, 42–45; consanguinity not required for, 45
—female, 28, 69, 79; inferiority of, 28, 64; hagiographical transvestism of, 28, 64–65; gendered aspects of, 31; and control of female sexed body, 64; emphasis on celibacy in, 65, 71
Saints, 26, 45, 68; as lived example, 3; as "living" beings, 15; as "real" people, 17; miracles of, 26; Christocentric meaning of, 29; Christian definition of, 31; as *walī Allah*, 39; difference from prophets and messengers, 42
Śaiva, 107
Sakinah, 25, 55, 65, 66, 83, 117, 129, 130, 142, 166; thirst of, 4, 9; sainthood of, 20; as socioethical exemplar, 20; popularity of, 86; voice of, in "*ghar chalo bhāʾī*," 131
Śakti, 68, 70, 92
Ṣalāḥ, 34, 36
Salām, 1, 23, 66, 89, 90, 101, 117, 131
Salar Jung Museum, 164
Salar Masʿud. *See* Ghazi Miyan
Ṣāliḥ, 34
Salman Pak (Salman al-Farsi), 19, 57; fictive blood relationship to Muhammad, 56
Sanjar (sultan), 185 (n. 23)
Sarah, 15; devotion to *ahl-e bait*, 13; miracles witnessed, 13; unmarried state of, 13, 14, 128
Sauda Mir Muhammad Rafiʿ, 136–38, 141
Saudi Arabia, 155–56, 185–86 (n. 29); site of Sunni cosmopolitan ideology, 155
Sayyidat nisāʾ al-ʿalamain, 76
Seal of Muhammadan sainthood, 43
Seal of prophecy (*khatm al-nubūwwah*), 41, 44, 79; Muhammad as, 42, 48
Seal of the prophets (*khātim al-nabiyyīn*), 42
Seal of the saints (*khātim al-awliyā*), 40–45; social institution of, 42; Ibn al-ʿArabi's account of, 42–45; as pinnacle of sainthood, 43; preeternality of, 43; as embodiment of *ḥusaini* ethics, 44; as ethical authority, 44; initiatic knowledge of, 44; symbolized as silver and gold brick, 44; *walāyah*, 44; *wilāyah*, 44; Arab and Hashemite, 45
Seema, 165
Sehrā bandhānā, 113
Selfhood, idealized Shiʿi, 2, 5, 14, 15, 17, 27, 45, 50, 51, 63, 64, 132, 135, 142, 143
Seljuk dynasty, 185 (n. 23)
7 Muharram: in Hyderabad, 59–60, 124, 158, 162, 168–69; votive requests (*mannat*), 60, 128
Sex segregation. See *Purdah*
Shādī, 87; "wedding," 87, 109, 130, 141, 169; "joyfulness," 130
Shafath, 124, 126
Shah ʿAbul ʿAzim, 56
Shahādat: at Karbala, 9; in Shiʿi sainthood, 31; without sainthood in Shiʿism, 53
Shahādat-nāmeh, 27

Vellori, Vali, 108
Vernacular, 154, 167, 169, 182 (n. 23); wedding of Qasem and Fatimah Kubra, 22, 111–19 passim; social ideals and values, 23, 25, 50, 52, 135; gender ideals, 60–61, 132, 141; sainthood, 68; South Asian religious traditions, 68, 70, 170; hagiographical tradition, 90–91, 102, 109, 111, 135, 153, 161; social context in Deccan, 99, 142; practice, 155–56, 159, 160, 169
Vernacularization, 45, 108, 157, 158, 162
Vishnu, 68

Wahab, 56, 132; as bridegroom/warrior, 57; comparison to Ghazi Miyan, 57; lacking *ḥusaini* ethics, 57; martyrdom of, 57; comparison to Qasem, 57–58
Waḥdat al-wujūd, 44
Wahhabi movement, 155; destruction of Jannat al-Baqiʿ cemetery, 155, 185–86 (n. 29); antagonism toward vernacular practice, 156; attitude toward Shiʿism, 156
Waḥy, 42
Walāyah, 18, 38, 43; in Shiʿi theology, 19, 39; and Imamate, 28, 29, 38, 39; and Fatimah al-Zahra, 29, 30; and Prophet Muhammad, 29, 38; and ʿAli, 38; and transcendence, 38; relationship to prophecy and messengership, 40; al-Tirmidhi's theory of, 40; and Day of Judgment, 42; inimitability of, 42; esoteric (*bāṭin*) qualities of, 44, 49; as complement to *wilāyah*, 46; otherworldly model of, 51
Walāyat-e fāṭimiyyah, 30, 82, 83
Walī, 38
Walī Allah, 38, 39
Walīmah, 73, 165, 184 (n. 28)
Warhol, Robyn, 92
Warrior saint, 31; interreligious appeal of, in South Asia, 34; Sufi, 34, 35
Weber, Max, 56
Wedding of Fatimah Kubra and Qasem: popularity in Hyderabad, 2, 23, 163; on battlefield, 17, 22, 88, 111–19 passim, 136, 138, 149, 163, 168, 184 (n. 22); in Hyderabadi rituals, 21, 88, 138, 143; unconsummated, 24; in Hyderabadi discourse, 90, 110
Widowhood, 61, 89, 119; and Indic taboo on remarriage, 1, 22, 37, 80, 88, 91, 127, 131, 140, 162, 163, 181 (n. 29); Indic anxieties about, 38, 88, 98, 110, 115, 140, 161, 163, 181 (n. 29); and caste/social status, 88, 140, 141; and sexuality, 88, 163; Fatimah Kubra's gendered performance of, 137–42, 162–63. See also *Bevāh*; *Ranḍ*
Wilāyah, 18, 38; and blood relationship to Muhammad and Fatimah, 18; and charisma, 18; in Shiʿi theology, 19; socially constructed, 19, 28, 49; Imam Husain's family as possessors of, 25; and immanence, 38; exoteric (*ẓāhir*) qualities of, 44; and socio-ethical authority, 45, 49; as complement to *walāyah*, 46; al-Simnani's theory of, 51

Yadgar Husaini, 13, 128
Yaqutpura, 8, 24, 85, 121
Yashoda, 37
Yazdigird III (Sasanian shah), 183 (n. 45)
Yazid (ʿUmayyad *khalīfah*), 6, 7, 18, 50, 52, 77, 78, 80, 89, 116, 162; army of, 6, 8; demanding *baʿyah*, 6, 151, 100; court of, 10, 81, 88–89, 100, 101

Karen G. Ruffle, *Gender, Sainthood, and Everyday Practice in South Asian Shiʿism* (2011).

Jonah Steinberg, *Ismaʿili Modern: Globalization and Identity in a Muslim Community* (2011).

Iftikhar Dadi, *Modernism and the Art of Muslim South Asia* (2010).

Gary R. Bunt, *iMuslims: Rewiring the House of Islam* (2009).

Fatemeh Keshavarz, *Jasmine and Stars: Reading More than "Lolita" in Tehran* (2007).

Scott A. Kugle, *Sufis and Saints' Bodies: Mysticism, Corporeality, and Sacred Power in Islam* (2007).

Roxani Eleni Margariti, *Aden and the Indian Ocean Trade: 150 Years in the Life of a Medieval Arabian Port* (2007).

Sufia M. Uddin, *Constructing Bangladesh: Religion, Ethnicity, and Language in an Islamic Nation* (2006).

Omid Safi, *The Politics of Knowledge in Premodern Islam: Negotiating Ideology and Religious Inquiry* (2006).

Ebrahim Moosa, *Ghazālī and the Poetics of Imagination* (2005).

miriam cooke and Bruce B. Lawrence, eds., *Muslim Networks from Hajj to Hip Hop* (2005).

Carl W. Ernst, *Following Muhammad: Rethinking Islam in the Contemporary World* (2003).